The 1975 Referendum on Europe

Volume 2

The 1975 Referendum on Europe

Volume 2
Current Analysis and Lessons for the Future

Mark Baimbridge, Philip Whyman
& Andrew Mullen

imprint-academic.com

Copyright © M. Baimbridge, P. Whyman & A. Mullen 2006

The moral rights of the authors have been asserted.
No part of any contribution may be reproduced in any form
without permission, except for the quotation of brief passages
in criticism and discussion.

Published in the UK by
Imprint Academic, PO Box 200, Exeter EX5 5YX, UK

Published in the USA by
Imprint Academic, Philosophy Documentation Center
PO Box 7147, Charlottesville, VA 22906-7147, USA

ISBN 184540 0356
ISBN-13 9781845400354

A CIP catalogue record for this book is available from the
British Library and US Library of Congress

Contents

	Acknowledgements	7
1.	From Membership to Referendum	9
2.	The Role of Referendums in British Politics	31
3.	The Labour Party and Europe	49
4.	The Conservative Party and Europe	75
5.	Trade Unions and Europe	99
6.	Public Opinion and Europe	121
7.	Economic Issues of Membership	147
8.	Political and Sovereignty Issues of Membership	167
9.	Implications of the Referendum for Britain and Europe	189
	Bibliography	211
	Index	220

Also by Mark Baimbridge

From Rome to Maastricht:
  A Reappraisal of Britain's Membership of the EC (Co-Author)
There is an Alternative:
  Britain and its Relationship with the EU (Co-Author)
The Impact of the Euro: Debating Britain's Future (Co-Editor)
Economic and Monetary Union in Europe:
  Theory, Evidence and Practice (Co-Editor)
Fiscal Federalism and European Economic Integration (Co-Editor)
Current Economic Issues in EU Integration (Co-Author)
Britain and the European Union: Alternative Futures (Co-Author)
Implications of the Euro: A Critical Perspective from The Left (Co-Editor)
The 1975 Referendum on Europe, I: Reflections of the Participants
Britain, The Euro And Beyond (Co-Author)

Also by Philip Whyman

There is an Alternative:
  Britain and its Relationship With the EU (Co-Author)
The Impact of the Euro: Debating Britain's Future (Co-Editor)
Economic and Monetary Union in Europe:
  Theory, Evidence and Practice (Co-Editor)
Fiscal Federalism and European Economic Integration (Co-Editor)
Sweden and the 'Third Way': A Macroeconomic Evaluation
An Analysis of the Economic Democracy Reforms in Sweden
Britain and the European Union: Alternative Futures (Co-Author)
Implications of the Euro: A Critical Perspective from The Left (Co-Editor)
'third Way' Economics: An Evaluation
Britain, The Euro And Beyond (Co-Author)

Also by Andrew Mullen

The British Left's 'Great Debate' on Europe
The Battle for British Hearts and Minds on Europe

Acknowledgements

There are many people to thank for their input into making this book possible. Firstly, Anthony Freeman of Imprint Academic for his immediate support for this project and patience over the duration of its development. Secondly, this book could not have been completed without the many and varied contributions. Seeking to undertake a project focusing upon an event that occurred some 30 years ago has posed inevitable difficulties as the march of time has severely depleted the number of participants still able to provide their first-hand account of the Referendum. Thirdly, colleagues in the Bradford Centre for International Development, Centre for European Studies at the University of Bradford, the Lancashire Business School at the University of Central Lancashire and the Politics Division at Northumbria University for their support for our research on European integration and the work of the multidisciplinary European Economies Research Unit (EERU) of which this is a prime example of the intersection between political science and economics. Finally, we owe a deep sense of gratitude to our families for their support and forbearance during the preparation of this book. It is to them that this book is dedicated: MB: Mary, Ken and Beibei, PW: Barbara, Boyd and Claire.

Any remaining errors and omissions we gladly attribute to each other.

Haworth, Heaton Norris and Gateshead
June 2006

One

From Membership to Referendum

Introduction

The Referendum of June 1975 was the first, and to-date only, post-legislative referendum to involve the whole of the UK. Theoretically, the issue was relatively simple, namely whether to accept the renegotiated terms of UK membership and remain within the European Economic Community (EEC). However, as with so many political events its apparent simplicity conceals hidden depths that were to plunge the then Labour administration of Harold Wilson and every successive British government into the quagmire that Britain's relationship with 'Europe' would become. This chapter firstly reviews the early development of the European Union (EU) from the initial post-war integrationalist trends which were largely driven by the growing reality of the Cold War to the renewed sense of dynamism generated by the 1969 Hague Summit which led to the first enlargement, thus bringing the EU-UK into focus. Secondly, it summarises Britain's 'road to membership' which was accelerated by various economic and political forces, both internal and external, that combined inexorably to suggest that EEC membership would provide a shield from the growing gales of globalisation and match the geopolitical reality of the UK in the post-war era. This section also includes a brief description of the countdown to the Referendum that was triggered several years before within the Shadow Cabinet of Harold Wilson in the interests of maintaining Party unity. Hence, following Labour's return to power in 1974 an inevitable series of events were placed into motion that led through a renegotiation process to the Referendum itself in June 1975. Finally, the chapter concludes with an overview of the book's principal themes.

Although the number of books analysing contemporary European economic integration have multiplied over recent years a number of weaknesses remain. Firstly, many texts seek to maximise their marketability by attempting to cover the entire spectrum of EU related topics, but ultimately only do so at a superficial level. Whilst certain areas may lend themselves to a brief examination presented in a single chapter, many others are too complex to summarise in such a manner and require a more sophisticated approach if all the principal issues are to be analysed. Clearly, even the most cursory discussion of the 1975 Referendum should seek to encompass the considerable underpinnings of this area in terms of its economic and political debate, review its historical background and consider how the Referendum features within the present discussion of Britain's membership of the EU.

Given the significance of the occurrence in terms of the British constitution, cabinet collective responsibility, party cohesion, let alone the possibility that Britain might leave the EEC a mere 203 days after gaining entry, it is surprising how little has been written on this topic with only Butler and Kitzinger (1976), Goodhart (1976) and King (1977) analysing the event itself in its immediate aftermath. Prior to the unfulfilled expectation of a referendum regarding Britain's entry into the single currency, a number of studies were made, *inter alia*, Baimbridge *et al.* (2000), Dyson (2000), Temperton (2001), El-Agraa (2002), Baimbridge and Whyman (2003). However, a more recent book by O'Hara (2006), *The referendum roundabout*, seeks to review the role of the referendum in modern British politics through a detailed analysis of the 1975 vote on Europe. Moreover the phenomenon of the referendum itself as a feature within the British political landscape has likewise received relatively scant attention with the works of Butler and Ranney (1980 & 1994), Bogdanor (1981), Gallagher and Uleri (1996), Hug (2002) and Qvortrup (2002) illustrating the fractured discourse on this topic.

Although numerous politicians and Whitehall insiders have frequently covered this topic in biographies, these are inevitably from a single perspective thereby offering a unique, yet ultimately limited analysis. Therefore, given the relative paucity of credible literature on this topic it was decided to divide the analysis of the Referendum across two separate, yet complementary, texts. Hence, the companion text: *The 1975 referendum on Europe: reflections of the participants* (Baimbridge, 2006) adopts a more informal approach through combining the analysis of selected themes with the personal recollections of figures such as David Owen, Tony Benn, John Edmonds,

Tam Dalyell, Teddy Taylor, Richard Body, Ernest Wistrich and Uwe Kitzinger.

A second problem for those seeking a greater understanding of European integration is that many books adopt a far from neutral stance when explaining the relevant arguments. It is, of course, natural that academics, politicians, trade unionists and general commentators who have self-selected European integration as their speciality, are likely to posses strong opinions towards this subject. Indeed, this is the case with the authors of this book. However, we have striven to ensure that this book succeeds in portraying the concept of the 1975 Referendum in a balanced light.

Thirdly, the fast-moving events of European integration can result in books becoming out dated soon after, or even before, their publication! Indeed, part of our initial strategy regarding this book was not only the advent of the 30th anniversary of the 1975 Referendum, but that the referendum issue would again become a central contemporary British political theme in relation to possible EMU membership, albeit at an unspecified date, and the European Constitutional Treaty which was pencilled-in for early 2006. However, the latter was derailed by the French and Dutch 'no' votes in mid-2005 resulting in a 'period of reflection' by the EU. Consequently, the immediate prospect of nationwide referendums on these EU-related questions is now diminished. However, the 1975 Referendum still represents the unique comparator for any future referendums, which have gathered considerable pace across the EU in the past 20 years with the noticeable exception of Britain.

This book seeks to both review aspects of the Referendum and look ahead to the prospect of two further referendums concerning the UK's relationship with the EU. Firstly, there is the longstanding commitment of the current Labour government to consult the people once the Treasury tests of October 1997 are satisfied regarding UK entry into Economic and Monetary Union (EMU). Although a recent speech by Tony Blair (2006) seems to suggest that 'the economics had to be got right and the politics follow', reversing the original position. Secondly, a key EU process has been the process started following the Laeken declaration in December 2001, when the European Convention was established to produce a draft of the Constitution, headed by former French President Valery Giscard d'Estaing. However, the failure of the French and Dutch electorate to support the proposed Treaty establishing a Constitution for Europe in May and June 2005 halted its progress. Whilst neither of these issues are currently at the forefront of political debate, they are nevertheless still on the long-term agenda of the EU and would involve nationwide referendums not previously witnessed since the 1975 Referendum. Hence, a method of resolving significant political and economic issues that had lain dormant at a national level for more than 30 years would potentially be activated twice in a matter of years.

Indeed, in many ways the situation then can be held as a mirror to possible future events. However, commentators such as Worcester (2000) indicate that the situation is more difficult than it was in 1975 for the pro-EU side, but important lessons can be gleaned by looking at both the similarities and differences, together with how far the key factors in 1975 will be replicated next time.

Firstly, in terms of the status quo, a key strength of the pro-Marketeers in 1975 was that they were asking the British public to affirm the status quo of continued membership on renegotiated terms. Essentially, the current situation is the opposite in so far as it is the pro-euro side which will be advocating a change.

Secondly, the near unanimity of 'establishment' opinion is unlikely to be repeated. In 1975 every major national newspaper and virtually the whole of the business community was pro-Market. However, the position of the press is now reversed such that it is likely to be predominantly against, at least in terms of circulation. Consequently, pro Europeans will have to try to bypass national newspapers and rely on the less ideological broadcast media, as well as local and regional newspapers. As far as business is concerned their opinions are by no means as monolithic as in the earlier campaign. Organisations such as *Business for Sterling* and the *No Campaign* are substantially better resourced than comparable groups in 1975, such that it will be difficult to persuade the public that business takes a united view.

Thirdly, the unanimity in 1975 of the Conservative and Liberal parties, who were overwhelmingly pro-Market, was regarded as a key persuasive factor. Only the Labour Party was seriously split as demonstrated with the party conference and Labour MPs against, compared to the Cabinet in favour. In contrast, presently it is the Labour and Liberal leaderships which are likely to be overwhelmingly in favour, with the Tories split, but predominantly against.

Fourthly, in 1975 it was notable that the leading figures on the pro-side (Roy Jenkins, Ted Heath, Jeremy Thorpe, Shirley Williams, Harold Wilson and Jim Callaghan) were more popular than their opponents (Tony Benn, Michael Foot and Ian Paisley) although some (Enoch Powell and Peter Shore) showed marginal positive public approval. Following Labour's 1997 and 2001 General Election victories, the commonly held opinion was that the antis may well suffer from the same disadvantage with Conservative politicians regarded less favourably than their Labour counterparts. However, the growing disillusionment with the Premiership of Tony Blair and the ascendancy of the new Tory leader, David Cameron, has potentially shifted this balance in the credibility of leaders.

Fifthly, a key lesson from the 1975 campaign is the advantage which the government had in choosing the timing of the Referendum. As indicated above, this is inevitably inter-twined with the standing of parties and their leaders in the opinion polls and is therefore likely to be a decisive factor in future referendums. The pro-Labour honeymoon periods following the 1997 and 2001 elections have now dissipated to the point where it is increasingly unlikely that a reversal of the negative opinion polls could reasonably be expected to be overcome. Consequently the failure by the Labour government to carry a referendum vote would potentially inflict a terminal blow to its credibility which is currently at rock bottom levels.

Sixthly, the turnout in the 1975 Referendum was 65%, only some 7 percentage points less than in the previous General Election, which it has been suggested, contributed to the scale of the pro- Marketeers' success. However, a threat to future pro-integrationalist causes would be indifference to the outcome, leading to a low turnout, which could enable the antis to more effectively mobilise their support while the majority of voters stay at home. Indeed, the turnout at the 1999 (24%) and 2004 (39%) European Parliamentary elections were down by 47.5 and 20.5 percentage points respectively compared to the previous 1997 and 2001 General Elections. Hence, the public appetite for focused European issues appears questionable, apart from those with strong beliefs, such that it is possible to speculate that any future European referendum may be characterised by a derisory turnout.

Although the above points suggest that the difference between any future referendum and that of 1975 have significantly narrowed, Worcester (2000) indicates that it may be more finely balanced than initially indicated. Firstly, public opinion is highly volatile on European issues whilst being far from one of the main issues to concern voters, hence as 1975 demonstrated, on complicated issues which are not wholly salient, the public is often willing to be led by people whose opinion they respect. Though less deferential than in 1975 most people admit to being ill-informed about EU developments and are therefore open to persuasion, such that the public's perceptions of the competence of the 'yes' and 'no' sides could be more important than the detail of any arguments they make.

Secondly, in 1975 renegotiation allowed Wilson to side-step the existing debate concerning the costs and benefits of membership by creating a different status quo regarding the revised membership terms. Similarly, Tony Blair and Gordon Brown will no doubt seek to use the Treasury's five economic tests to persuade the public that the goalposts have moved and that joining the euro is a different proposition from when the currency was originally established. Whilst the 'pause for reflection' following the defeat of the European Constitution in 2005 would also permit sympathetic politicians to re-brand any reconfigured version as a better deal for Britain.

Thirdly, the pro-integrationalist argument possesses one significant advantage in that 'Europe' is no longer an alien concept as it was to many in the early 1970s, but something that has influenced British values, lifestyles and politics. However, although people remain to be convinced that the EU is other than inefficient or meddling, the theoretical argument regarding the pooling of sovereignty has been generally accepted. But the pro-Europeans have not shifted the argument enough to take account of this and risk losing their way by relying on a traditional case regarding the economic and political benefits of European integration rather than building connections with ordinary voters. In particular, since people rate the Government's handling of the economy they are less likely to believe scare stories about Britain's economic fragility if further integration was to be spurned.

The Early History of the EU

This section seeks to provide a brief overview of the development of the EU from its immediate post-World War II origins, through its subsequent foundation and initial phase of growth to its first enlargement in 1973 of Denmark, Ireland and of course the UK, thereby bringing us to the starting point of our story. Whilst those familiar with these matters will undoubtedly be acquainted with this path of developments, it nevertheless demonstrates that the stop-start nature of European integration can be dated back to the early years of the 20th century in a form that we would recognise today. Thus the momentum of the 1920s was destroyed by the economic and political turmoil leading to the Second World War, such that it was not until its aftermath that further impetus was given to this idea. However, the continued economic hostility between France and (West) Germany over control of raw materials, such as coal and steel, almost halted cooperation. Subsequently, the EU has frequently lurched from crisis to crisis, with issues such as agriculture, budgetary contributions/receipts, voting rights, exchange rate mechanisms, the democratic deficit and external relations all remaining too familiar. However, key milestones have also been achieved, not least of which was the founding Treaty of Rome, together with the momentum following the 1969 Hague Summit which led to the initial enlargement in 1973. The latter, in the case of Britain led to the focus of this book examining the 1975 Referendum concerning the renegotiated terms of membership. Hence, this section is divided into historical phases that reflect various key time periods of the EU's development. Subsequently, the major events within each period are summarised to give a general introduction to the themes and trends at work surrounding the embryonic EU. To omit the story, albeit briefly discussed, of the evolution of this unique supranational body that has come to dominate not just the events of 1975, but much of British economic policy and politics for the post-war period would be a case of Hamlet without the Prince.

Origins of the EU (1945–58)

The immediate post-war priorities were a mixture of the urgent need for the bare essentials, such as coal and steel, the revival of economic activity, the promotion of trade and the modernisation of production, either via monetary agreements or by means of regional measures for dismantling customs barriers. However, the establishment of Communist regimes in Central and Eastern Europe, with the presence of Soviet troops, fomented a feeling of apprehension in Western Europe. Consequently, the initial aspect of European integration was the signing of the Brussels Treaty (1948) setting up the Western European Union (WEU), marking the start of European military cooperation. A little over a year later this was followed by the creation of the North Atlantic Treaty Organisation (NATO) on 4 April 1949 as a further step towards military cooperation between Europe and the United States.

In this context, a divided European continent could only prosper through establishing effective, common institutions, if necessary with American financial, technical and military support. Hence, it was at this point that pro-European movements and supporters of federalism began to promote the idea of European unification and established an International Committee for the Coordination of Movements for European Unity in 1947, which preceded the Hague Congress, from which emerged the European Movement also in 1948.

Consequently, these developments provided the impetus to an ideal of European unity, already popularised by certain elite circles during the inter-war period, which then spread rapidly after the Second World War. In 1946, various supporters of European federal unity founded the Union of European Federalists, bringing together some 50 federalist movements. With regard to the form and procedures for European unification, ideas often diverged according to political and ideological affiliation ranging from a federation led by a federal authority, or even a European government, to an association of sovereign States. At a more practical level within national parliaments, particularly those of the Netherlands, Belgium, France and Italy, the number of supporters of federalism was progressively increasing. In 1947, Richard Coudenhove-Kalergi, founder of the Paneuropean Union in the early 1920s, united these Members of Parliament in the European Parliamentary Union (EPU) to bring pressure to bear on national governments.

At the 1948 Hague Congress, the Federalists called for the rapid creation of a structure for political cooperation. The US, already giving financial backing to the free countries of Europe, also promoted the idea of political cooperation amongst the democracies of Western Europe. In August 1948 the Joint International Committee for the Coordination of the Movements for European Unity, submitted to the governments of the 16 member countries of the fledgling Organisation for European Economic Cooperation (OEEC) a project for a European Assembly that would be the linchpin of a future EU. However, although France and Benelux proposed the creation of an independent assembly and the transfer of a share of national sovereignty to a higher decision-making body, the UK and the Scandinavian countries preferred the idea of close intergovernmental cooperation. A compromise was finally reached between British and Continental interests with the governments of the European states appointing an advisory assembly and a committee of ministers, which would make decisions unanimously and would have the final say. Thus in London on 5 May 1949, ten states (Belgium, Denmark, France, Ireland,

Italy, Luxembourg, Norway, the Netherlands, the UK and Sweden) signed the Statute of the Council of Europe. It was the very first international parliamentary assembly with representatives appointed either by their national parliaments or governments.

However, the pioneering period with its ambitious plans for European integration fell victim to events and the inertia of governments. Consequently, it was left to individual countries to develop more concrete achievements through consensus and intergovernmental measures. Of particular significance, however, was the Schuman Plan where the EEC took its first steps and began to acquire organisational shape. Germany and France were at the heart of the plans to establish a new equilibrium in Europe, aware of the fact that Britain would not take the leading role. The issue of the mining regions of the Saarland and the Ruhr was, however, damaging relations given that the two regions in 1949 had been placed under the control of the International Authority for the Ruhr that controlled the production, export and distribution of the coal, coke and steel.

To resolve this problem the French Foreign Minister, Robert Schuman, proposed to put the two countries' joint production of coal and steel within the framework of a supranational structure as a means of avoiding a steel surplus in Western Europe. Hence, this sectoral economic integration plan created shared interests that automatically linked the two countries. Consequently, the Schuman Plan led to the signing of the Paris Treaty (1950) establishing the European Coal and Steel Community (ECSC).

The success of the Schuman Plan inspired a number of similar projects, particularly in the fields of chemicals, electricity, fisheries, aeronautical construction, transport, public health and agriculture. However, all failed for a variety of reasons from technical problems to the divergent political and economic interests prevailing in the various countries. Moreover, these projects, although often modelled on the coal and steel, seemed less urgent and numerous reservations were voiced by the professionals concerned. A supranational approach no longer seemed appropriate for these proposals, which were inspired more by economic than political considerations. However, two of these projects, agriculture and political union, can be seen as forerunners of the Common Agricultural Policy (CAP) and the EU itself.

Furthermore, following the rejection of the European Defence Community (EDC) by the French parliament in 1954, some European movements, together with some Benelux leaders, set about reviving a Community plan that provided solutions to the specific problems of economic integration where the success of the reconstruction of national economies made the development of external trade an even greater priority. Subsequently, two different initiatives were to combine during 1955 to revive the Community ideal: one of them concerned making atomic energy and the other aimed to stimulate international trade by the opening up of frontiers.

In addition to these immediate economic considerations, the international climate also helped to provide the necessary impetus for a relaunch. The declaration of the nationalisation of the Suez Canal in July 1956 and Soviet intervention in Hungary in November 1956 were forceful reminders that the lone ECSC did not carry much weight when faced with threats arising from international events.

Consequently, in response to the energy crisis caused by the 1956 Suez Crisis, the Common Assembly proposed extending the powers of the ECSC to other sources of energy such as gas, electricity and atomic energy. The OEEC concluded that there was a need for the countries of Europe to join together in creating a nuclear industry capable of taking up the challenge and filling the energy deficit facing Europe because of the exhaustion of its coal deposits and of its dependence on oil producers. However, rather than a mere Atomic Energy Community, Germany and the three Benelux countries advocated the development of a wider common market. This idea almost floundered on the strong protectionist tradition of the French businesses and even Monnet felt that such a community would be too large and too difficult to manage. However, ultimately, in order to reconcile these divergent interests, Monnet proposed the establishment of both Communities.

Hence, the preamble of the Treaty of Rome (1958) states that its main aim was to preserve peace and liberty and to lay the foundations of an ever closer union among the peoples of Europe. With a view to forging closer ties between member states (initially Belgium, France, Italy, Luxembourg, the Netherlands and West Germany), the objective was for balanced economic growth through the combination of a customs union, together with a Common External Tariff (CET), a common policy for agriculture, transport and trade and enlargement of the EEC to include other European states.

Crises and Revival (1958–)

However, by the mid–1960s, the EEC was shaken by a number of crises. One such cause was de Gaulle's policy whereby he sought to shift France's position within the EEC by keeping the latter's supranational powers to a minimum and pursuing intergovernmental cooperation among member states as an alternative. The failure in 1962 of the Fouchet Plan for a 'Union of States' and France's refusal of the British application to join increased tensions with the other five members. Even the Franco-German rapprochement embodied in the Élysée Treaty (1963) was insufficient to defuse the crisis within the Community which reached its peak in the 'empty chair' crisis of 1965, when French delegates no longer participated in Community activities, effectively bringing the Community's institutions to a standstill. Subsequently, the crisis was resolved with the 'Luxembourg compromise' of 1966, which allowed any member state to oppose a Community decision adopted by the majority if it considered its national interests to be seriously threatened.

Thus by the end of the 1960s there was evidently a need to end the political and institutional stalemate that had existed since 1967 when de Gaulle vetoed Britain's second application for membership. The fresh impetus that integration required came from the new President of the French Republic, Georges Pompidou, who suggested a meeting of the Six to discuss the urgent problems faced by the Community, summarising the EEC's new priorities in the phrase: 'Completion, deepening, enlargement'. The Hague Summit of December 1969 examined a threefold policy based on completion, deepening and enlargement. In particular, the latter resulted in the opening of negotiations between the Community and the four applicant countries (Denmark, Ireland, Norway and the UK).

Furthermore, as part of the package of decisions taken at the Hague Summit, the Six agreed on a system which, from 1975, would profoundly change the EEC's budgetary resources. The aim was to develop genuine fiscal powers and confer definitive financial independence from the member states and their parliaments. These new resources were also designed to enable the EEC to implement the common policies with the new financial resources consisting of agricultural levies, customs duties on imported goods and value added tax (VAT) limited to 1% of the total collected by the member states. However, most of the new resources of the EEC went towards financing the CAP whereby the Commission soon found itself having to consider how it might limit expenditure from its financial instrument, the European Agricultural Guidance and Guarantee Fund (EAGGF).

A second aspect of deepening is the idea of a common monetary policy which was initially referred to in the Treaty of Rome (Articles 103–108) and to the free movement of payments and capital (Articles 67–73). Indeed, since the end of the Second World War, the notion of a European monetary system had been a recurring theme of several European federalist movements. However, the idea met with strong reservations such that the founding Treaty's provisions covering monetary issues were therefore rather cautious, and neither the Commission nor the Council had any binding powers in the area of monetary coordination. Moreover, monetary cooperation was not an urgent matter, given that the Six had balance of payments surpluses and the international monetary situation was stable. Indeed, it appeared unrealistic to create an independent monetary system which did not include the US dollar or the pound sterling in light of the prevailing Bretton Woods system.

However, in 1962 the European Commission proposed a pathway for an EEC monetary policy through the introduction, after the transitional period, of fixed exchange rates for the currencies of the Six. The Commission also recommended the creation of a Committee of central bank governors, eventually set up in 1964, as well as a procedure for prior consultation on internal monetary policy. The first tangible attempt in this direction was made in 1969 in the wake of the 1968 currency crisis which affected both the French franc and the German mark. Furthermore, the growing indebtedness of the United States was increasingly eroding the dollar's international credibility and, consequently, that of the system of fixed exchange rates laid down under the Bretton Woods Agreements. Subsequently, the 1969 Hague Summit agreed to draw up a step-by-step plan with a view to creating a European economic and monetary union. However, it became clear that the international monetary climate was no longer conducive to such plans, with its going through a succession of crises, ranging from a series of speculative attacks on the dollar to the suspension of the dollar's convertibility into gold, which was the mainstay of the Bretton Woods system. However, this climate of monetary instability eventually forced the European authorities to set up the EEC's monetary system in March 1972 when the Six created the European currency snake, designed to guarantee a certain amount of stability by narrowing the fluctuation limits for the exchange rates between European currencies.

Although this exchange-rate agreement managed to alleviate the 1972 European currency crisis, the relative weakness of the British pound and the Italian lira was such that they could not remain for long within the system. Furthermore, a new devaluation of the dollar resulted in currencies being floated in 1973 and the first oil crisis caused a rapid imbalance in the external payments of the nine member states. Rather than leading to closer policy coordination and cooperation the EEC reacted in an uncoordinated fashion with each country struggling to protect its own national economy, thereby demonstrating all the more clearly the wide disparities between them.

In terms of institutional/democratic reform, since the 1950s, members of the ECSC's Common Assembly had regularly been calling for its successor, the European Parliament, to be elected under Article 138 of the Treaty of Rome, which provided for the election of Members of the European Parliament by direct universal suffrage. However, during the 1960s, the European Parliament itself sought to increase its democratic legitimacy, but the continued objection of France stymied this through its belief that the Council of Ministers was the only authorised legislative body in the EEC. In 1972 it was recommended to gradually increase of the European Parliament's legislative powers with a view to its eventually securing genuine powers of codecision and that the President of the Commission should be invested by Parliament before the other Commissioners were appointed. Subsequently, in 1974 the French President Giscard d'Estaing accepted the idea of direct elections to Parliament which he associated with the establishment of a European Council instructed to create a genuine European government.

Britain's Road to Membership

During the first accession negotiations in 1961, the Conservative-led British Government had laid down a number of conditions, since it wanted to preserve Britain's privileged economic and monetary relations with the Commonwealth countries (see Chapter 4). Similarly many Labour politicians were equally concerned at the prospect of throwing away the achievements of the Commonwealth for a Europe that was, in their view, largely capitalist (see Chapter 3). There was also a fear that they would see the price of Commonwealth imports soar because of the disappearance of the imperial preference system (see Chapter 7). Hence, senior British politicians were also careful to reassure their partners in the Dominions, who were worried that they would find themselves henceforth relegated to the second rank of British concerns.

However, by the late 1960s, links between Britain and the Commonwealth had considerably diluted. Whilst the Commonwealth countries still provided 48% of British imports and took 49% of its exports in 1954, by 1972 Britain was importing a mere 19% of its goods from the Commonwealth, which was taking no more than 20% of British exports. Simultaneously, the EEC was replacing the Commonwealth's share of UK outward investment. Additionally, political and strategic links between Britain and the countries of its former British Empire, despite a traditional sentimental attachment, had declined during the 1960s.

Accordingly, British negotiators adopted a more flexible line with fewer conditions to be met by their future European partners. The decision to accede was taken on both economic and political grounds. In terms of the latter, the British were well aware that, having virtually abandoned the imperial dimension of their foreign policy, it could no longer stand isolated from the Community which was, in contrast, becoming more assertive on the international scene (see Chapter 8). It was also increasingly difficult to reconcile the UK's privileged relationship with the United States with its closer involvement in European affairs. Simultaneously, the constant economic growth of the Six made the EEC more attractive. For its part, France, which had previously twice resisted UK membership, was now more favourable to British accession since it was seeking to balance German power in Europe by relying on British support.

Negotiations with Britain resumed officially on 30 June 1970 in the wake of the Hague Summit, which had associated the strengthening of the Community with its enlargement. Parallel diplomatic discussions were conducted with Denmark, Ireland and Norway, whose economies remained closely connected to the British market, particularly under the European Free Trade Association (EFTA). The negotiations took place in conditions very different from those of 1961 and 1967. Since then, the Community had consolidated its position, developed common policies and the establishment of the common market had entered its final phase. The entire body of Community legislation, which would have to be accepted by the applicant countries, was therefore much more extensive than it had been in 1961. in particular, the Treaty establishing the EEC laid down two conditions for potential new member states: (a) the applicant country must be a European country; (b) the unanimous agreement of the existing Member States of the EEC is required. Furthermore, the eligibility of an applicant country was also conditional on some implicit criteria: (a) the democratic and pluralist character of its political institutions; (b) its capacity to take over the entire body of legislation adopted by the Community (the acquis communautaire); (c) its acceptance of the fundamental objectives of the basic treaties establishing the Community.

It was therefore upon these seemingly innocuous grounds that negotiations commenced in 1970 between the Conservative government of Edward Heath and the European Commission with a view to Britain being in the first wave of enlargement.

The most contentious economic issues were Britain's financial contribution to Community resources and its participation in the CAP. However, these problems, which were closely linked, were never properly clarified. In contrast, a definitive solution was found for the other stumbling blocks, namely West Indian sugar and New Zealand butter.

Consequently, during the summer of 1971, Edward Heath's Government pursued an intensive campaign in Britain in favour of accession. On 7 July 1971, the Government published *The United Kingdom and the European Communities*, a White Paper which reviewed the advantages of British accession to the EEC on a point-by-point basis.

Although the House of Commons approved entry into the EEC on 28 October 1971 and the UK signed the Accession Treaty on 22 January 1972, British public opinion was, however, divided on the merits of joining the EEC. This uncertainty was evident in the behaviour of Members of Parliament at the time of the vote. The political make-up of the group of MPs who approved the Treaty was just as mixed as that of the group which opposed it. In addition to the majority of the Conservative Party, there were 69 Labour MPs among the 356 supporters of British involvement in European integration whilst among the 244 opponents of British membership of the EEC were the majority of Labour MPs, together with 39 Conservatives. Moreover, the number of supporters of British involvement declined further when national legislation was adapted to EEC legislation, although the House of Commons once again declared itself in favour of membership on 13 July 1972, whilst the House of Lords did the same on 20 September 1972. Subsequently, the UK's entry into the EEC came into effect on 1 January 1973, together with that of Denmark and Ireland.

Following the UK's accession a growing realisation had begun to develop in the minds of both politicians and the public of the enormity of this decision. Indeed, the luxury of hindsight has illuminated the innate feeling that many had at the time of Britain's accession to the EEC. Thus, accession proved to be the relatively straightforward aspect of EEC membership albeit with a number of problems evident from the outset. These included Britain's financial contribution, the operation of the CAP, the international role of sterling and Commonwealth relations.

The problem of Britain's financial contribution continued to prove to be problematic. Following the arrangements adopted by the Six in terms of the EEC's own resources, there was a danger that the cost to Britain would be extremely large and disproportionate. Furthermore, France called on Britain to pay its entire contribution of almost one-fifth of the entire budget upon accession. The particular difficulty arose given that according to EEC rules, Britain had to pay substantial sums in agricultural levies since it imported most of its food products from non-EEC countries at lower prices; hence the high levies. Simultaneously, as its agricultural sector was becoming less important to the national economy, the financial return from the European Agriculture Guidance and Guarantee Fund (EAGGF) would be small. Moreover, depending on the region involved, British agriculture was either extremely efficient and productive at very competitive prices, or very weak and in need of support by direct subsidy in the form of deficiency payments. However, such a system was now specifically prohibited by the CAP, which preferred a system of levies and refunds. Although the UK did its utmost to secure a reduction in its contribution, the Six were only prepared to offer a longer transitional period, such that Britain finally accepted the system of community agricultural preferences as well as a British contribution that would eventually account for 19% of the total community budget.

A further significant point of discord was the international role of sterling which the Commission had made a point of drawing the attention of the negotiators to, with France calling on Britain to abolish the pound sterling as an international reserve currency in the medium-term. Secondly, the Six had no desire to make an indefinite commitment to support the pound, which had been weakened over a long period by chronic British balance of payments deficits. These were a result of an ongoing imbalance between British revenue and expenditure, as well as Britain's large foreign debt. By increasing their holdings in dollars and their balances with the IMF, the countries of the EEC were in effect financing a major part of the financial aid which Britain was receiving from foreign central banks and the IMF. However, in 1971, a compromise was ultimately reached on the role of the pound and on the level and evolution of the British contribution, although the text adopted included certain ambiguities. These would allow the British to return to the subject of their budgetary contribution in the 1980s and again more recently following the 2004 accession of 10 new member states comprised largely of Central and Eastern European countries (CEECs) of the Warsaw Pact.

As previously outlined exports of sugar from the West Indies and butter from New Zealand were significant stumbling blocks during the negotiations between Britain and the EEC. As regards the former, Britain was satisfied with a commitment, to be formalised in agreements between the Community and the countries of the Commonwealth, which would agree to sign up to the second Yaoundé Convention that entered into force in 1971. Also that year, a compromise was also reached on imports of New Zealand butter for who the UK was an essential market. Eventually, the EEC granted Britain a special regime and a suitable transitional period to help the country conform to Community rules.

Book Outline

Chapter 2 seeks to illustrate that, firstly, the arguments both for and against referendums share at least one important characteristic in that they are compounds of preferences for certain values and empirical causal statements. Secondly, many of the arguments advanced against the referendum are problematic such that whilst the referendum remains an instrument of veto and not of initiative, the dangers of demagogy and extremism are likely to be remote. Nor need the referendum necessarily increase the power of government or permit the manipulation of public opinion. Moreover, it can be used without involving the upheaval of a written constitution or a judicial-type tribunal of interpretation. Thirdly, to the extent that the referendum is an entrenching device, it acts as a deterrent to government in terms of being a disincentive to legislate in the particular area that it protects. Consequently, in most of the democracies that employ the referendum, as typified by EU member states, it is used sparingly rather than frequently. Indeed, the pragmatic use of the referendum device is much more in accordance with the British approach to constitutional matters than a new constitutional settlement would be. Finally, the introduction of referendums into the European integration process was a belated development triggered by the initial enlargement process to both permit its occurrence and by candidate countries. However, Britain's referendum followed post-membership based on the renegotiated terms and was thus rooted on a significantly different basis in terms of confirming membership supported by all mainstream political parties, the majority of businesses and the media.

Chapter 3 argues that it is possible to identify a number of important features between the 1975 Referendum and the current state of affairs. The most obvious similarities are that Labour is in power and that the party is still divided on the question of European integration, whilst as in 1975, pro-EU forces enjoy the backing of the government and the considerable power resources of the British State. However, there are now three important differences: (i) during the 1975 Referendum, pro-EU forces were defending the status quo of continued membership, (ii) the business sector, the media, political parties and the trade union movement are more evenly divided on the question of further European integration and (iii) anti-EU forces have access to substantial financial resources. Consequently, conflict within the Labour Party regarding further European integration looks set to escalate, with the balance of power likely to shift from anti- to pro-EU forces. As the EU aggrandises more power over the potential for clashes between Brussels and Westminster increases, this begs the question as to whether a future Labour government would accept rulings from the EU that effectively undermined its programme? Secondly, if the EU continues in a neo-liberal direction it is likely that left-wing and trade union opposition to the EU will grow. Thirdly, the party faces the question of what is the ultimate objective of the European integration process?

Chapter 4 indicates that contrasting the state of affairs during the 1975 Referendum and the current situation is instructive in terms of assessing the present balance of power within the party. In 1975, the Conservatives were in favour of European integration and the party dominated the Yes campaign, whilst its current policy is to oppose further European integration, although it remains committed to continued membership. Hence, in terms of the future configuration of forces, the contours of Conservative European policy remain unclear. In the current quest for the 'centre ground' of British politics, it may seek to curb the party's scepticism and attempt to re-establish itself as the 'party of Europe'. However, defeating the anti-EU forces unleashed by Thatcher may prove problematic. Much depends on the future direction of the EU itself. If the European Constitution is revived and the process of deeper European integration continues, then the Conservatives may maintain their current opposition. If, however, the EU economy is further reformed in a neo-liberal direction and the EU continues to expand, necessitating a multi-speed and multi-level institutional framework, then the Conservatives may, once again seek to champion the cause of European integration.

Chapter 5 suggests that the contemporary trade union perspective has evolved significantly from its position in 1975. Opposition to membership has been relegated to a minority position, whilst the major current debates concern the future direction of the EU itself in terms of its development as a market-dominated or 'social model' form of society. Although fundamental disagreements still persist concerning whether or not the UK should join EMU and whether the EU should have a formal constitution. Indeed, such strategic differences hamper the development of trade union strategy towards issues like the development of a European labour market and the precise activities of the trade union movement within this new institutional creation.

From the polling evidence presented in Chapter 6 it is evident that public opinion on European integration, in both historical and contemporary terms, has been volatile. It is suggested that such variability is, in large part, a consequence of repeated interventions by anti- and pro-EU forces and their deployment of propaganda campaigns in an attempt to influence public opinion. Moreover, these campaigns were deployed at critical junctures in the relationship between Britain and the EU, with evidence suggesting that there is a positive correlation between the timing and duration of these campaigns and the changes in public opinion. Historically, there was a considerable imbalance between these opposing forces whereby until the 1990s, pro-EU forces enjoyed substantial financial and other resources, plus the backing of successive governments. However, the situation changed significantly in the late 1990s, as anti-EU forces increased their financial resources and their organisational capacity. Furthermore, business organisations, political parties (Chapters 3 and 4) and trade unions (Chapter 5) have become more evenly divided over further European integration, specifically whether to adopt the euro and whether to ratify the European Constitution. These developments have important consequences for the future configuration of forces, and balance of power, should Britain hold a referendum on euro entry or on a new Constitutional treaty.

Chapter 7 highlights the development of the economic element of the wider debate concerning the future relationship between the UK and the EU. Shifting from a referendum specifically concerning whether the UK should continue as a member or pursue an independent model of development, critics of further integration have tended to oppose piecemeal new initiatives rather than concentrate upon the advocacy of withdrawal. Likewise, whilst certain of the issues may remain as relevant today as they did thirty years ago, others have been considerably relegated in importance. Thus, whilst the cost of food and the inflationary impact of membership were major issues concerning the electorate in 1975, these are now treated as mostly peripheral issues to the main debate. In their place, the potential damage caused by participating in one or other of the EU's fixed exchange rate initiatives, whether ERM or EMU, has become one of the main economic features regarding opposition to further integration.

Chapter 8, firstly, examines the historical background to the relationship between Britain and the EU and disaggregates this into several discrete stages of shifting ideas and aspirations. This section provides a unique in-depth analysis of various manoeuvres by the British political establishment which wavered from enthusiasm to apathy through the late 1940s and 1950s until the initial membership applications in the 1960s. It then provides an insight into the road to accession in the early 1970s. Secondly, the chapter outlines the principal issues of debate regarding the political aspects of membership: defence and foreign policy, sovereignty, democracy, identity and federalism. In particular it reviews the changing pattern of importance of these factors. Finally, it briefly considers the latest major political development concerning the EU, the signed, but not ratified, Constitutional Treaty.

Chapter 9 concludes this book by examining a number of issues relating to the post-1975 repercussions of Britain's only nationwide referendum. Firstly, we demonstrate that the referendum result did little to change the fundamental differences between the UK and its European partners. Indeed, the issue of 'Europe' has come to be a dominant feature of British politics and to a lesser extent economic policy. Thus the 1975 Referendum failed to decisively settle the question of membership with the current level of interest and debate probably being at its highest since membership was first raised. However, in terms of the conduct of referendums significant progress has been made which alters the balance of power away from the incumbent government who were able to set the referendum's rules. Hence, the Political Parties, Elections and Referendums Act (2000) now formalises the procedures regarding the timescale, expenditure, designated originations, the question, publicity and vote counting. Consequently, it can be expected that the operation of future referendums will be more balanced particularly in terms of the campaign's financing. Finally, the chapter analyses the record of referendums relating to EU integration, in particular concerning accession and ratification of treaties. It indicates that there has been a dramatic decline in the approval rate of the latter. The collapse in successful ratification rates to 29% in the current decade potentially explains why 15 member states ignored the referendum option when seeking to ratify the EU's Constitutional Treaty. However, if public opinion is increasingly opposed to integrationalist trends then merely bypassing direct-democracy through parliamentary affirmation could still fail if electorates subsequently remove pro-integrationalist parties.

Two

The Role of Referendums in British Politics

Introduction

This chapter reviews the theoretical arguments regarding referendums. Firstly, we discuss their classification and the general arguments surrounding their advantages and disadvantages. These are largely based on the question of whether referendums enhance or diminish democracy through either increasing the degree of legitimacy through representing the direct will of the people or that they are subversive to representative democracy. Secondly, the British experience of referendums is examined in terms of its historical context. In particular, the issues of regarding referendums as a weapon of entrenchment, their usage, compatibility with the British constitution and pre-1975 experience. The chapter then concludes with a brief discussion of the origins of EU integration related referendums that commenced as a consequence of its first enlargement in the early 1970s. A brief overview of the issues, timescale and result of the UK's 1975 Referendum are outlined.

Classification and Legitimacy of Referendums

Numerous classifications regarding referendums are available focusing upon the specific features of the institutional provisions and legal system (see Smith, 1976; Butler and Ranney, 1980, 1994; Magleby, 1984; Cronin, 1989; Suksi, 1993; Hug, 2002). These can, for example, be divided into four general classifications in terms of the degree to which they remove control over the making of laws from elected representatives and transfer it to ordinary voters:

- Government-controlled referendums — where a majority of the legislature has the sole power to decide whether a referendum will be held, the subject matter and wording of the proposition to be voted on, the proportion of yes votes needed for the proposition to win, and whether the outcome will be binding on or merely advisory to the government.
- Constitutionally required referendums — these require that certain kinds of measures adopted by the government be approved before they can take effect. The government has exclusive power to decide whether to propose each amendment and to determine its wording, but the mandatory referendum determines whether it becomes part of the constitution.
- Referendums by popular petitions — where voters are authorised to file a petition demanding that a certain measure adopted by the government be referred to the voters.
- Popular initiatives — where voters are authorised to file a petition demanding that a certain measure which the government has not adopted be referred to the voters.

However, a more recent system of classification is largely centred on the twin issues of the triggering mechanism and the agenda-setting (Hug, 2002). Firstly, *required* referendums for constitutional issues or territorial changes, secondly, *nonrequired* or *active* referendums on either *government* or (thirdly) *opposition* proposals and finally, *nonrequired* or *passive* referendums permitting governments to submit proposals for the approval of the people.

The main argument for referendums consists of the propositions that all political decisions should be as legitimate as possible and that the highest degree of legitimacy is achieved by decisions made by the direct, unmediated vote of the people. Consequently, the most widely accepted case for referendums concludes that decisions by referendums are the most legitimate of all, whereby a decision in which all have opportunity to participate is more legitimate than one in which people have not participated. Indeed, increased participation is likely to be achieved through the use of referendums when people can vote directly on policy issues compared to the usual restriction of selecting candidates (Butler and Ranney, 1994).

Moreover, decisions in which popular participation is direct and unmediated by others, as in referendums, produce more accurate expressions of will than do decisions in which citizens participate only by electing others who make the decisions for them. Accordingly, whilst many feel that most political decisions should be made by those in public office there is agreement that the most fundamental decisions should at least be ratified by referendums. This explains why governments sometimes find it prudent to hold referendums even when they are not required to, such as regarding continued EEC membership in 1975.

Hence, the case for referendums has predominately centred on two main concepts concerning both the achievement and supplementation of democracy. In relation to the former, two main schools of thought (participationist and representationalist) developed regarding the institutions necessary to attain the principles of democracy. Firstly, the participationist or direct-democracy school argues that full and direct participation of all citizens is the only truly democratic form of public policy decision-making. Thus referendums are supported in all circumstances because they establish the essentials of the most democratic of all forms of government, namely direct rule by face-to-face assemblies of all the citizens. This, in turn, rests upon two central beliefs concerning the unorganised, free individual and hostility to intermediary organisations. Thus, any organisation that seeks to interpose itself between the people and their government is bound to subvert democracy and the public interest to some degree. Given such faith in the free individual and their hostility to intermediary organisations, the participationist school was confident that the referendum would give the citizens the best possible weapons for overpowering grasping corporations, greedy special interest groups, boss-ridden political machines, together with weak and corrupt legislatures (Butler and Ranney, 1978).

The latter fundamental concept views referendums as supplementary to representative democracy rather than an alternative. Whilst this approach broadly agrees with the representationalist school in relation to the primacy of representative government, however, it emphasises the potential for its enhancement through direct-democracy. Thus, referendums lead to greater legitimacy, mandate certainty and promote public interest over special interests.

In reality, most countries have only referendums when governments have chosen to hold them, and then only infrequently for reasons of political convenience, as was the case in 1975, rather than in response to overarching general theories about how laws should be made and unmade. Hence, it would appear uncontroversial to conclude that in most modern democratic nations referendums are held either rarely and in unusual circumstances or not at all. This suggests that the case against any general use of referendums has had substantially gained more acceptance and influence than the direct-democracy pro-referendum case (Bogdanor, 1981; Butler and Ranney, 1994). Thus, the most frequently encountered arguments against the general use of referendums are:

- that they threaten the control over the political system of the elected and other established authorities. Indeed, in a free society, the outcome of a referendum cannot be guaranteed as the governments of France and the Netherlands discovered in 2005.

- that a referendum may leave the government open to further demands for referendums, which could include subjects where the verdict of the people would run counter to the consensus of public office holders. Hence, the government-controlled referendum minimises such risks, leading to the observation that governments should use it only in circumstances in which its short-run advantages clearly outweigh the long-run dangers it poses.

- that in a modern nation-state it is impossible for all citizens to focus all their time on politics let alone meet to discuss and resolve issues. Indeed, the problems facing governments are numerous, complex, and demanding, such that only those who spend time thinking/debating them can understand them well enough to cast 'intelligent' votes. Hence, the essence of democracy is the more efficient location of power in all citizens through the election of accountable representatives[1].

- the problem of majority tyranny and the abridgement of minority rights and interests, particularly when referendums are based on popular initiatives rather than measures emanating from elected bodies. However, it is difficult to identify a successful referendum that has resulted in majority tyranny.

- that referendums are subversive of representative democracy in that they permit the rejection of decisions by elected representatives and/or the enactment of laws without their participation. Hence, they diminish the authority and prestige of elected bodies and permit the evasion of decision-making by representatives.

- in a referendum every vote counts equal, even though most votes in favour of an issue may represent only unenthusiastic

---

[1] Evidence, however, suggests that referendum voters appear better informed and more sophisticated than their counterparts in candidate elections (Magleby, 1984; Cronin, 1989).

marginal preference, while most votes against represent passionate opposition. But elected representatives can and do assess not only how many of their constituents approve or oppose a measure, but also how intensely.

- the ultimate goal of democratic decision processes is not a vote which identifies how many citizens support each of two irreconcilable alternatives, rather it is consensus in terms of a general agreement that a particular course of action is the best way of promoting the interests of all citizens. This cannot happen in a referendum where discussion is always adversarial.
- that the referendum process does not necessarily imply wiser or more prudent decision-making
- although advocates of referendums portray them as supplementary aids to representative democracy, legislatures lose power and popular respect, thus potentially weakening representative government.

The British Experience of Referendums

The idea of a referendum as a solution to particular problems had been raised, usually by Conservatives, who saw it as a brake on change. Indeed, A.V. Dicey, its first major sponsor, argued in the 1890s that by putting Irish Home Rule to a vote it could be blocked; indeed, he regularly used the phrase 'the national veto' to describe a referendum. However, the idea was more seriously considered in 1910 when the House of Lords rejected first the Lloyd George budget and then the notion of Lords reform. Ultimately, the Parliament Act of 1911 decided the question against advocates of the referendum such that it ceased to be a major issue until the 1970s although it was proposed on a number of occasions in the intervening years in an attempt to paper over political differences (Bogdanor, 1981). For example, during the controversy over women's suffrage, the anti-suffragists seriously considered whether they ought to call for a referendum on the issue. Whilst the Conservatives under Balfour committed themselves to establishing referendums as a means of resolving disputes between the House of Commons and a reformed House of Lords. Similarly, the referendum was kept alive as an issue through the home rule crisis (1912–1914), Churchill's suggestion in the 1920s regarding the equalisation of men's and women's franchise and the Baldwin-Beaverbrook agreement of 1930 concerning food taxes. Whilst in 1945 Churchill raised the idea of a referendum to authorise an extension of the life of Parliament. However, none of these proposals progressed into draft legislation. In contrast, the Labour Party was always more cautious, fearing the referendum as an extra line of defence against the changes in society that they sought and consequently never advocated a referendum until the 1970s. Hence, this section briefly reviews the notion of the referendum as a weapon of entrenchment, their appropriate use and whether it is compatible with the British constitution.

The Referendum as a Weapon of Entrenchment

The referendum is generally seen as an instrument of popular sovereignty whereby political authority derives from the people. Yet, as the history of the debate in Britain illustrates, the move towards popular participation or self-government has not played an important part in its advocacy. In contrast, since being proposed by Dicey, the referendum has been suggested as a means of either checking disagreeable legislation, or solving intra-party disputes as in the case of the EEC. It has been, in the words of Beaverbrook, 'not a spear but a shield', an adjunct to representative government and not a replacement for it (Bogdanor, 1981). In particular, as advocated and employed in Britain, the referendum has primarily been regarded as an instrument whereby the electorate can check the work of government. Thus, although Parliament remains the source of political authority, it becomes subject to public restraint.

Hence, Bogdanor (1981) argues that the referendum as used in Britain is a conservative device, providing an extra check against government, in addition to the protection given by Parliament. Hence, if the popular verdict approves of what Parliament has done, then the measure in question can be put into effect, whilst if the electors reject the work of Parliament, then the measure must be dropped. Consequently, the role of the electorate is essentially negative, such that the referendum is therefore an instrument of protection and not of change.

Moreover, Bogdanor (1981) suggests that insofar as the referendum is confined to a vote on a measure which has passed through Parliament, some of the fears regarding its use are unfounded. For example, that the actuality of referendums increase the likelihood of future referendums on subjects where the electorate would reach illiberal and unjust decisions. Indeed, such referendums would only be possible if Parliament had already agreed to pass the necessary legislation.

Thus, the use of the referendum as a checking device might seem appropriate for Britain which lacks a constitution imposing limits upon the power of government. Hence, the referendum could potentially offer a form of security, which is otherwise provided through a written constitution, against such changes. It achieves this by entrenching particular parts of the constitution against parliamentary majorities. Subsequently, a government can use the referendum to entrench parts of the Constitution against changes proposed by its opponents. However, the humiliation incurred by a government attempting to deprive the electorate of its right to be appealed to would make it hesitate before resorting to such a drastic act. The referendum, therefore, is a method of securing entrenchment, and may be the only means, in a country such as Britain without a rigid constitution, through which entrenchment is possible.

Use of the Referendum

As indicated above, difficulties arise when seeking to translate the referendum into a practical instrument of government given the UK's lack of a written constitution and hence a definitive source prescribing rules for their use. The question therefore becomes, firstly, one of how to distinguish between those laws which should be submitted to the electorate to receive validation and those which are not to be so submitted, and secondly, what is to be the mechanism by which the referendum is to be put into effect?

As described in this book and its accompanying volume, *The 1975 referendum on Europe: reflections of the participants*, the Labour Government avoided this problem by arguing that the EEC referendum was a unique occasion. However, following the devolution referendums of the late 1970s initiated by the same Labour administration it was clear that the problem cannot be evaded in this way.

Thus, if the referendum is to be restricted to certain types of issues, then it seems natural to suggest that it be restricted to 'constitutional' issues (Bogdanor, 1981). Indeed, attempts have been made to define which issues count as constitutional. As previously described the Conservatives in 1911 defined as 'constitutional' and therefore requiring a referendum any bill affecting:

- the existence of the Crown or the Protestant succession,
- the creation of a national legislature or Parliament within the UK,
- the constitution or powers of one of the Houses of Parliament, or their relations with each other.

However, this approach may include issues that are not of major importance, while excluding more fundamental issues whereby constitutional issues can easily arise out of seemingly non-constitutional legislation. Moreover, not only is there legitimate disagreement about such matters, but that disagreement will naturally mirror existing political differences. Consequently, it is difficult to see how a comprehensive list of 'constitutional' issues can be developed that would gain support from across the political spectrum. Moreover, even if it were possible to develop an agreed list of 'constitutional' issues, this would still require the introduction of some authority to decide whether or not a given piece of legislation in fact lay within the class of constitutional legislation (Bogdanor, 1981).

The closest to such an organisation is the relatively recently formed Electoral Commission, founded via the Political Parties, Elections and Referendums Act 2000, although its brief in relation to referendums is to:

- comment on the intelligibility of the question,
- register campaign organisations as permitted participants,
- designate (appoint) lead campaign organisations on both sides of the referendum question,
- monitor referendum expenditure limits and donations,
- provide the Chief Counting Officer at a referendum, who will be its Chairman, or a designated appointee.

Additionally, the European Union Bill, introduced in January 2005 to provide for a referendum to be held on whether or not to approve the European Constitution, gave the Electoral Commission the following additional responsibilities:

- encourage voting at the referendum,
- manage the administration of claims for fees and charges by Counting Officers.

Hence, it was not given the type of powers that Bogdanor (1981) describes to determine what constitutes 'constitutional' legislation, but rather to act as a neutral umpire in the conduct of a referendum. Thus, governments still have not sought to enumerate which matters are to be submitted to referendum. Consequently, in the absence of a written constitution, the referendum rather than acting as a check upon government could serve to increase its power. The question thus becomes, if the calling of a referendum is to be at the discretion of the government of the day, how can such a power be limited or curbed? In reality, however, it is unlikely that governments would resort to the referendum when faced with parliamentary difficulties or differences within their own party which prevent them from carrying their legislation, since no government would wish to advertise such disagreements and acknowledge that the appearance of MPs on opposing platforms in a referendum campaign will do little to enhance credibility[2].

Moreover, the fundamental issue is that a government can never be sure of the outcome of a referendum as was demonstrated by the 'surprise' results of the French and Dutch votes regarding the EU Constitution in 2005. To call for a referendum, therefore, may unnecessarily risk its standing, as the French vote undoubtedly did to the already politically ailing Jacques Chirac. In terms of 1975, the outcome of the EEC referendum proved fortunate for the Wilson administration, but things could easily have been otherwise. Indeed, a mere four years later, the devolution referendums led to the fall of the Callaghan administration (Bogdanor, 1981).

Consequently, it is unlikely that governments would seek to add a referendum clause to a bill whenever backbench opposition surfaced. Rather it would be more likely that the referendum would be deployed on those occasions when the established party system is unable to provide clear or coherent solutions to major problems. However, even on such occurrences that they would only consider such a move as a last resort since it would be interpreted as a sign of weakness.

To date, UK referendums (excluding local referendums) have all been concerned with the legitimacy of irreversibly transferring the powers of Parliament suggesting that Parliament has decided that a referendum should be held on any proposal to transfer its powers (e.g. devolution). Although it would be difficult to assert that a referendum was constitutionally necessary in such circumstances, there are at the very least persuasive precedents, amounting perhaps to a constitutional convention for requiring a referendum and it would be very difficult for a government proposing a significant transfer of Parliament's power to avoid holding one (Bogdanor, 1981).

Furthermore, there is also a clear rationale for such a requirement whereby the transfer of the powers concerns the machinery by which laws are made, which citizens have previously entrusted to parliamentarians; but they give them no authority to transfer this

---

[2] The 1975 Referendum on continued EEC membership is, of course, the exception to the general rule.

power. Hence, such authority, it can be argued, can only be granted through a specific mandate in the form of a referendum.

Compatibility of Referendums with the British Constitution

Discussion of the constitutional implications has mainly dwelt upon the supposed conflict between the referendum and the principle of the sovereignty of Parliament, thus insofar as it conflicts with this principle, then the referendum is suggested to be incompatible with the British Constitution. Such an objection can be answered in that if it is held that Parliament is sovereign and able to do anything, then if it so wishes it can call for a referendum. However, what it cannot do is to allow itself to be bound by such a referendum. Hence, the referendum must be only advisory. In a wider context, the notion of a referendum possesses implications regarding the role of MPs, political parties and its role as an educative device (Bogdanor, 1981).

A specific area when the notion of a referendum is frequently regarded as incompatible with the British Constitution relates to the argument that it inevitably undermines an MP's independence and judgment. This derives from the traditional concept that it is the MP who, as a representative, must make up their mind on the issues of the day, and not the electorate (Dalyell, 2006). However, MPs are essentially elected as representatives of a political party with all that this entails within the modern party-driven system. Consequently, it would appear pedantic to suggest whether a referendum interferes with the independence and judgment of the MP.

Hence, Bogdanor (1981) argues that it is absurd to argue that the use of the referendum is incompatible with either the role of Parliament or the position of MPs. Indeed, a referendum may improve the position of the individual MP by providing them with an additional and powerful weapon to use against the tyranny of governments and the party machine. Moreover, the knowledge that the electorate will be able to pronounce upon legislation might strengthen the House of Commons, since MPs will seek to ensure that legislation is put to the people in an attractive and convincing form. Additionally, the government will have an incentive to accept reasonable amendments if they increase the likelihood of the legislation gaining public endorsement.

Furthermore, opinion poll evidence indicates that electors did not regard the introduction of referendums as an attack upon representative institutions and increased popular satisfaction rather then diminishing it. Indeed, the majority of the electorate was eager to be given the opportunity of expressing its opinion on the EEC (see Chapter 6).

Finally, the referendum does not necessarily indicate an attack upon representative government, but can be regarded as an instrument to remedy its defects, particularly in terms of weakening the domination of parties. Hence, it tends to be advocated by those who desire to loosen the authority of political parties and rejected by those content with the status quo of party government. In this context, the demand for a referendum arises not out of distrust of the efficacy of representative institutions, but more from a dislike of the rigidity of the party machine. Hence, it increases the influence of those not deeply pledged to the doctrines of the main political parties (Bogdanor, 1981).

From the above discussion it is clear that the issue of a referendum should focus not on its supposed incompatibility with the British Constitution, but on the consequences for party government. The 1975 Referendum and those scheduled for the EU Constitutional Treaty and EMU membership indicate that the referendum device is most likely to be called into play again because the party system is incapable of handling contentious issues which cut across traditional party stances.

Indeed, much of the division of opinion in British politics in relation to Britain's current and future membership of the EU has been within the parties rather than between them, paralleling the debate at the beginning of the 20th century when the referendum lay at the forefront of political debate regarding questions such as Home Rule and Tariff Reform. To this extent, it will be even less easy to claim that a vote for a party is also a vote for the particular line of policy recommended by the faction which happens to lead the party. Indeed, the central message of Chapters 3, 4 and 5 is the story of multiple shifts in attitudes and policy by each major political party and trade unions in relation to British membership of the EU.

Finally, in this discussion of the constitutional status of the referendum, there is the notion that a referendum could also improve the quality of the citizen's relationship to government, whereby in a democracy it is important that the citizens identify themselves with the public good, in terms of the interests of the nation as a whole. A referendum, therefore, should have a profoundly educative effect upon the electorate (Bogdanor, 1981).

Thus, the 1975 EEC Referendum encouraged a sense of social unity by enabling political activists to cross traditional party lines and establish contact with those holding similar opinions on the EEC, but widely differing opinions on other political issues (Butler and Kitzinger, 1976). As a consequence this appeared to develop a sense of public spirit that had previously evaded the mainstream political parties following the Second World War, which at the time was suggested to potentially spearhead a reversal of the popular alienation from politics. However, such an argument needs to be carefully qualified, for it is by no means certain that electors welcome frequent referendums, with turnout being generally lower than in general elections.

Thus where referendums are used sparingly it seems plausible to suggest that they are most likely to exert the greatest educative effect. Hence, it should be confined to major issues which cannot be solved otherwise and requires the endorsement of the electorate if the final decision is to acquire legitimacy.

UK Experience of Referendums

Britain experienced several types of local referendum with provision made for local polls on the establishment of free public libraries (1850) and on municipally sponsored legislation (1858–1947), whilst since 1932 the Sunday opening of cinemas could be put to a local vote. However, there were relatively few referendums under these headings and they failed to register on the national political radar. Thus it was Northern Ireland that brought the initial major referendum to Britain following the suspension of its government and parliament (Table 2.1). In an attempt at a new settlement, a referendum was held on 8 March 1973, asking the voters of Northern Ireland whether they wanted the province to remain part of the UK. Although this referendum did not settle the province's difficulties, it set a precedent that was to be important in the argument over whether to put British entry into Europe to a popular vote.

The subsequent 1975 Referendum highlighted the threat that the device could pose for orthodox British party politics, it also illustrated that a referendum could be conducted in a relatively tranquil and efficient manner to settle a contentious issue without leaving any serious constitutional repercussions. Hence, it was likely to remain as one practicable way out of future political or constitutional difficulties. Indeed, following the immediate aftermath of 1975, referendums were considered in several different contexts, including Scottish and Welsh devolution, conflict between the two houses of Parliament, to resolve conflict with trade unions and capital punishment.

Table 2.1 – Major UK Referendums (1973–75)

Theme	Date	Question(s)	Outcome	Turnout (%)	Government response
Whether Northern Ireland should remain part of the UK	8 March 1973	1. Do you want NI to remain part of the UK? 2. Do you want NI to be joined with the Republic of Ireland, outside the UK?	Option 1 – 591,820 (98.9%) Option 2 – 6,463 (1.1%)	58.1	No action since results in favour of remaining part of the UK
Whether the UK should remain part of the EC	5 June 1975	Do you think the UK should stay in the European Community (Common Market)?	Yes – 17,378,581 (67.2%) No – 8,470,073 (32.8%)	64.5	Membership retained on basis of renegotiated terms

Early History of Referendums in EU Integration

In light of the momentous changes following from the instigation of post-war European economic and political integration, referendums in the initial decades were notable by their absence. Indeed, as Hug (2002: 23) states, the development of an ever closer union 'was to be pursued by elites, fostering common ground, which later, presumably automatically, would be embraced by the common citizens'. Hence, it was not until the first round of enlargement with Denmark, Ireland, Norway and the UK that the notion of referendums entered the European Community psyche. However, by the end of the 20th century twenty two national referendums concerning European integration had occurred, whilst a further nineteen were held in the first five years of the 21st century. Hence, there appears to be a clear pattern of extreme acceleration in the recourse to referendums, although the certainty of outcome has diminished from an affirmative rate of 77.3% from 1973–2000, to one of 68.4% from 2000–05.

Table 2.2 – Referendums on European Integration (1972–75)

Country	Date	Theme	Yes vote (%)
France	23 April 1972	Enlargement	68.3
Ireland	10 May 1972	Membership	83.1
Norway	24–25 September 1972	Membership	46.5
Denmark	2 October 1972	Membership	63.1
Switzerland	3 December 1972	EC-EFTA Treaty	72.5
UK	5 June 1975	Membership	67.2
Source: Adapted from Hug (2002)			

Table 2.2 summarises the history of referendums in chronological order relating to the initial period of European integration until the UK's referendum in 1975. These initial six referendums concerned the first wave of EU enlargement which was endorsed by French voters in 1972 'in a legally ambiguous referendum' (Hug, 2002: 26), thereby inaugurating the subsequent sequence of referendums concerning European integration. This was initiated by President Pompidou under Article 11 of the French constitution which specified that based on a proposal of government or both chambers of parliament, the president may submit laws which authorise the ratification of treaties affecting the functioning of the national institu-

tions to a referendum. However, as several commentators have noted, it is questionable whether there was appropriate constitutional justification for the referendum since it is doubtful as to the effect of enlargement upon French institutions (Gallagher, 1997; Rideau, 1997; Hug, 2002). Thus a significant degree of ambiguity and political expedience surrounds the precursor referendum concerning European integration.

Subsequently, referendums took place in three of the four accession candidates (Ireland, Norway and Denmark) and although Norway's rejection of membership in 1972 signalled the first pause in the integration process this was largely overlooked given that Norway was seeking membership in the first instance. The missing country in this round of referendums was, of course, Britain which with its unwritten constitution had been largely immune to referendums (Bogdanor, 1981; Rourke *et al.*, 1992). Moreover, although during the 1970 General Election campaign Edward Heath indicated that further European integration would not happen 'except with the full-hearted consent of the Parliaments and peoples of the new member countries' no referendum was held upon accession. In contrast to the minimal ructions in the Conservative Party, the Labour Party was seriously divided at Shadow Cabinet level and beyond regarding EEC membership (Owen, 2006). Hence, its 1974 General Election manifesto included a pledge to renegotiate membership terms and then hold a referendum.

Although as Prime Minister Harold Wilson had himself sought British entry into the EEC in 1967, as a member of the opposition since 1970 he severely criticised the compromises accepted by his successor, the Conservative Edward Heath, at the time of ratification of the Treaty of Accession in 1972. Thus, on his return to power, Wilson immediately called into question the British conditions of entry into the EEC, whilst the Foreign Secretary, James Callaghan, in his first speech before the Council of Ministers on 1 April 1974, demanded a fundamental renegotiation of the conditions set by the treaties of accession negotiated by the previous Conservative administration. Hence, following Labour's election victories in February and October 1974, which eventually saw the attainment of a majority government, the manifesto pledge to renegotiate better terms and then hold a referendum on whether Britain should stay in the EEC was initiated[3]

---

[3] For a detailed analysis of the 1975 Referendum, see Butler and Kitzinger (1976), Goodhart (1976), King (1977) and Baimbridge (2006).

Although the new Labour Government did not challenge the principle of British membership itself, it nonetheless sought to obtain improvements and amendments in favour of the UK remaining within the EEC. In particular, it wanted to obtain an extension to the preferential terms agreed with regard to the transitional period to allow the entry of Caribbean sugar and New Zealand butter into Britain. The government also sought the reduction of the financial cost of membership and the renewal of direct subsidies, or deficiency payments, to small farmers in the poorest regions.

The UK's partners in Europe, in spite of French reservations, showed themselves ready to make certain concessions in order to avoid a victory for the opponents to European integration. Thus at the Paris Summit held on 9–10 December 1974, Wilson obtained the creation of the Regional Development Fund, which would generally be of benefit to Britain and a correction to the budgetary contribution mechanism. The UK also obtained partial reimbursement of its contribution on VAT at the European Council meeting in Dublin on 10–11 March 1975 (Donoughue, 2006). Consequently, on 27 March 1975, the Wilson Government recommended the electorate to approve the results of the renegotiation and published a new White Paper calling for continued British membership of the Community.

Subsequently, on 9 April 1975 the House of Commons voted 396 to 170 in favour of retaining Britain's membership of the EEC on the basis of the newly negotiated terms. Hence, the Referendum date was set for June 1975. An intense campaign then commenced to influence public opinion led by Britain in Europe (BIE), which supported continued membership of the EEC and the National Referendum Campaign (NRC), which opposed continued membership.

Given the longstanding and open division within Wilson's cabinet between strongly pro- and anti-Marketeers, the unprecedented decision was made to suspend the convention of collective Cabinet responsibility and permit ministers to publicly campaign against each other. In total, seven of the twenty-three members of the cabinet opposed EEC membership.

In addition therefore to most of the cabinet supporting the Yes campaign, it was also backed by the majority of the Conservative Party, in particular its newly-elected leader Margaret Thatcher, the Liberal Party, together with other minor parties. In contrast, the No campaign consisted mainly of the left of the Labour Party, including cabinet ministers such as Tony Benn, Michael Foot, Peter Shore and Barbara Castle, together with many Labour backbench MPs. Moreover, further support came from some members of the right of the Conservative Party, together with the Unionists parties of Northern Ireland, a prominent member being the former Conservative minister Enoch Powell. However, the No campaign also attracted support from the extreme right and left, such as the National Front and the Communist Party.

During the campaign, virtually all the mainstream national British press supported the Yes campaign, with the communist *Morning Star* being the only notable national daily to back the No campaign. However, this was seen by many on the No side as a 'kiss of death' and by those campaigning on the Yes side as a clear indication of the political stance of those advocating a No vote. Television broadcasts were used by both campaigns, under rules pertaining to General Election broadcasts, which attracted audiences of up to 20 million. However, the Yes campaign was much better funded from the outset with Wilson meeting several prominent industrialists to elicit support (Butler and Kitzinger, 1976).

Following announcement of the overwhelming result (see Table 2.1), Harold Wilson called it a 'historic decision'. However, the frequently shifting sands of politics has impacted upon the participants of 1975, with many of those who were strongly for (against) EEC in 1975 are now more sceptical (supportive) of the EU (Edmonds, 2006; Sked, 2006). Indeed, it is these movements in the trends and issues regarding British membership of the EU that the following chapters seek to evaluate in terms of the Labour Party, the Conservative Party, trade unions, public opinion, together with assessing relevant economic and political/sovereignty issues.

Conclusion

This chapter has sought to illustrate that, firstly, the arguments both for and against referendums share at least one important characteristic in that they are compounds of preferences for certain values and empirical causal statements. These are amenable to verification by the systematic analysis of experience, for example, the 1880s–1920s, when the adoption, repeal, or extension of the referendum and the initiative were live questions in, *inter alia*, Britain, the United States and Australia. Subsequently, in the late 1970s there was a major revival of interest in referendums, partly associated with the enlargement of the EU and use in Northern Ireland.

Secondly, we have seen that many of the arguments advanced against the referendum are problematic. Whilst the referendum remains an instrument of veto and not of initiative, the dangers of demagogy and extremism are likely to be remote. Nor need the referendum necessarily increase the power of government or permit the manipulation of public opinion. Moreover, it can be used without involving the upheaval of a written constitution or a judicial-type tribunal of interpretation.

Thirdly, to the extent that the referendum is an entrenching device, it acts as a deterrent to government in terms of being a disincentive to legislate in the particular area that it protects. Consequently, in most of the democracies that employ the referendum, as typified by EU member states, it is used sparingly rather than frequently. Therefore, it is possible to develop a rationale for the use of the referendum without laying down *a priori* rules for its use, or being committed to an overall constitutional settlement involving a written constitution. Indeed, Bogdanor (1981) suggests that the pragmatic use of the referendum device is much more in accordance with the British approach to constitutional matters than a new constitutional settlement would be.

Finally, the introduction of referendums into the European integration process was a belated development triggered by the initial enlargement process to both permit its occurrence (France) and by three of the four candidate countries (Denmark, Ireland and Norway). However, Britain's referendum followed post-membership based on the renegotiated terms. It was thus rooted on a significantly different basis in terms of confirming membership supported by all mainstream political parties, the majority of businesses and the media.

Three
The Labour Party and Europe

Introduction

The issue of European integration, and whether or not Britain should participate, has been a contentious and divisive one for the Labour Party. This chapter, divided into five sections, documents the shifts in Labour's European policy between 1945 and 2005. The first section summarises Labour's European policy. The second section charts the policy changes during the 1945 to 1975 period, the third section looks at the internal divisions during the 1975 Referendum, whilst the fourth section surveys the policy changes during the 1976 to 2005 period. The fifth section concludes, highlighting the five main features of Labour's European policy. It also contrasts the situation in 1975 with the present balance of power between anti- and pro-European Union (EU)[1] forces, before surmising what a future configuration of forces might look like.

The European Policy of the Labour Party

The *official* European policy of the Labour Party between 1945 and 2005, as agreed by the Annual Conference, together with the policy *actually pursued* by the Labour leadership plus the European policy adopted by the Foreign Office, is summarised in Figure 3.1.

---

[1] For simplicity, the post-war project of European economic and political integration is henceforth referred to as the European Union (EU), rather than its previous titles of Common Market, European Economic Community or European Community.

Figure 3.1 – European Policies of the Labour Party and the Foreign Office (1945–2005)

Year	Annual Conference Policy	Labour Leadership Policy	Foreign Office*
1945 (G)			Imperial third force
1946 (G)		Imperial third force	"
1947 (G)	Support for European integration		"
1948 (G)	Socialist third force**	Intergovernmental European co-operation	"
1949 (G)	"	"	Limited liability
1950 (G)	Intergovernmental European co-operation	"	"
1951 (G)	"	"	"
1952 (O)	"	"	"
1953 (O)	"	"	"
1954 (O)	"	"	"
1955 (O)	"	"	"
1956 (O)	"	Support for the FTA	Partial engagement
1957 (O)	"	"	"
1958 (O)	"	"	"
1959 (O)	"	Conditional support for the EFTA	Near identification
1960 (O)	"	"	Pro-entry
1961 (O)	Opposition to entry without safeguards**	Opposition to entry without safeguards	"
1962 (O)	Conditional support for entry	Conditional support for entry	"
1963 (O)	"	"	"

The Labour Party and Europe

Year	Annual Conference Policy	Labour Leadership Policy	Foreign Office*
1964 (G)	Conditional support for entry	Conditional support for entry	Pro-entry
1965 (G)	"	"	"
1966 (G)	"	"	"
1967 (G)	"	"	"
1968 (G)	"	"	"
1969 (G)	Conditional support for entry**	"	"
1970 (O)	"	"	"
1971 (O)	Opposition to entry on Conservative terms	Opposition to entry on Conservative terms	"
1972 (O)	Renegotiate the terms, hold a general election or referendum and boycott EU institutions	Renegotiate the terms, hold general election or referendum and boycott EU institutions	"
1973 (O)	"	Renegotiate the terms and hold a referendum	Pro-membership
1974 (G)	Renegotiate the terms and hold a referendum	Renegotiate the terms and hold a referendum	"
1975 (G)	Campaign for a No vote in the 1975 Referendum	Campaign for a Yes vote in the 1975 Referendum	"
1976 (G)	Withdrawal, plus opposition to Direct Elections	Pro-membership, plus support for Direct Elections	"
1977 (G)	Reform of the EU	Reform of the EU	"
1978 (G)	Reform of the EU, plus opposition to EMU	Reform of the EU, plus opposition to the ERM	"
1979 (O)	Reform of the EU, plus withdrawal from the CAP	Reform of the EU, plus support for EU enlargement	"

Year	Annual Conference Policy	Labour Leadership Policy	Foreign Office*
1980 (O)	Withdrawal commitment in the manifesto	Withdrawal commitment in the manifesto	Pro-membership
1981 (O)	"	"	"
1982 (O)	"	"	"
1983 (O)	"	"	"
1984 (O)	"	Support for co-ordinated European reflation	"
1985 (O)	"	Opposition to the Single Market	"
1986 (O)	"	"	"
1987 (O)	"	Pro-membership	"
1988 (O)	Pro-membership	"	"
1989 (O)	Support for EU enlargement, foreign policy co-ordination, EU institutional reform and the Single Market	Support for EU enlargement, the ERM, foreign policy co-ordination, EU institutional reform and the Single Market	"
1990 (O)	Support for EMU, EU enlargement, the ERM and EU institutional reform	Support for EMU, EU enlargement, the ERM and EU institutional reform	"
1991 (O)	Support for CAP reform, EMU, EU enlargement, the ERM and the Social Charter	Support for CAP reform, EMU, EU enlargement, the ERM and the Social Charter	"
1992 (O)	Support for CAP reform, EU enlargement, EU institutional reform and Maastricht Treaty ratification with the Social Chapter	Support for CAP reform, EU enlargement, EU institutional reform and Maastricht Treaty ratification with the Social Chapter	"

Year	Annual Conference Policy	Labour Leadership Policy	Foreign Office*
1993 (O)	Support for CAP reform, the CFSP, a co-ordinated employment and growth strategy, EMU, EU enlargement, a European Environment Agency, a European Investment Bank, EU institutional reform, JHA, the Social Chapter and EU-wide workers' rights	Support for CAP reform, the CFSP, a co-ordinated employment and growth strategy, EMU, EU enlargement, a European Environment Agency, a European Investment Bank, EU institutional reform, JHA, the Social Chapter and EU-wide workers' rights	Pro-membership
1994 (O)	Support for a co-ordinated employment and growth strategy, EU institutional reform, Maastricht Treaty revision, the Social Chapter and EU-wide workers' rights	Support for a co-ordinated employment and growth strategy, EU institutional reform, Maastricht Treaty revision, the Social Chapter and EU-wide workers' rights	"
1995 (O)	Support for the reform of the EU Budget, CAP and CFP, the CFSP, EMU, a co-ordinated employment and growth strategy, EU enlargement, an EU industrial policy, EU institutional reform, JHA, the revision of the Maastricht Treaty, plus the Social Chapter	Support for the reform of the EU Budget, CAP and CFP, the CFSP, EMU, a co-ordinated employment and growth strategy, EU enlargement, an EU industrial policy, EU institutional reform, JHA, the revision of the Maastricht Treaty, plus the Social Chapter	"

Year	Annual Conference Policy	Labour Leadership Policy	Foreign Office*
1996 (O)	Support for CAP reform, the CFSP, economic policy co-ordination, EMU, EU enlargement, EU institutional reform and a revised treaty with an employment chapter, plus the Social Chapter	Support for CAP reform, the CFSP, economic policy co-ordination, EMU, EU enlargement, EU institutional reform and a revised treaty with an employment chapter, plus the Social Chapter	Pro-membership
1997 (G)	Support for the Amsterdam Treaty, CAP reform, the European Employment Strategy, EU enlargement, plus conditional support for euro entry	Support for the Amsterdam Treaty, CAP reform, the European Employment Strategy, EU enlargement, plus conditional support for euro entry	"
1998 (G)	Support for EU Budget, CAP and CFP reform, the CFSP, economic reform across the EU, EU enlargement, environmental co-operation, the European Employment Strategy, EU institutional reform, JHA, plus conditional support for euro entry	Support for EU Budget, CAP and CFP reform, the CFSP, economic reform across the EU, EU enlargement, environmental co-operation, the European Employment Strategy, EU institutional reform, JHA, plus conditional support for euro entry	"
1999 (G)	Support for the CFSP, EU enlargement, plus conditional support for euro entry	Support for the CFSP, EU enlargement, plus conditional support for euro entry	"
2000 (G)	Support for the CFSP, EU enlargement, plus conditional support for euro entry	Support for the CFSP, EU enlargement, plus conditional support for euro entry	"

Year	Annual Conference Policy	Labour Leadership Policy	Foreign Office*
2001 (G)	Support for the CFSP, economic reform across the EU, EU enlargement, the Nice Treaty, plus conditional support for euro entry	Support for the CFSP, economic reform across the EU, EU enlargement, the Nice Treaty, plus conditional support for euro entry	Pro-membership
2002 (G)	Support for the CFSP, economic reform across the EU, EU enlargement, EU institutional reform, plus conditional support for euro entry	Support for the CFSP, Convention on Future of Europe, economic reform across the EU, EU enlargement, EU institutional reform, plus conditional support for euro entry	"
2003 (G)	Support for the CFSP, the Convention on the Future of Europe, economic reform across the EU, EU enlargement, plus conditional support for the euro	Support for CFSP, a European constitution, economic reform across the EU, EU enlargement, plus conditional support for the euro	"
2004 (G)	Support for economic reform across the EU, plus conditional support for euro entry	Support for the European Constitution, holding a referendum on the treaty, economic reform across the EU, plus conditional support for euro entry	"
2005 (G)	A new EU Budget, reformed 'European Social model', plus further EU enlargement (including Turkey) and conditional support for euro entry	Support for further EU enlargement (including Turkey), economic reform across the EU, plus conditional support for euro entry	"

Notes: G = Labour in government. O = Labour in opposition.

* Historically, the Foreign Office tended to dominate the formulation of the British State's European policy. For an account of the post-war European policy of the British State see Mullen (2005).

** 'Qualified acceptance' was a procedural device used by the Labour leadership to neuter Annual Conference decisions.

The 1945–1975 Period

Support for European Integration (1945–60)

Labour's 1945 General Election manifesto contained no reference to European integration. Thereafter, however, it featured significantly as a foreign policy objective, although the visions of the Annual Conference and the Labour leadership were at times quite different.

Imperial Third Force

The immediate post-war aim of the Foreign Office was to safeguard Britain's 'great power' status. However, Britain's economic weakness negated such a strategy. Instead, the Foreign office, supported by the Labour leadership, explored the feasibility of creating a European union to act as a third force between the two superpowers. However, the *imperial third force* policy, which was not ratified by the Annual Conference, was abandoned in 1948, for three reasons. First, the Labour government was beset by a number of problems, which considerably weakened its capacity to pursue an independent policy. Second, Britain was increasingly dependent on the United States (US), which was hostile to such a policy. Third, European federalists, encouraged by the US, began to challenge Britain's goal of European leadership.

Socialist Third Force

While the Labour leadership was pursuing its imperial third force policy, members of the Parliamentary Labour Party (PLP) promoted a federal United States of Europe as a socialist third force alternative, a policy adopted by the 1948 Conference. However, the *socialist third force* policy was limited in its impact, for two reasons. First, the 1948 resolution received only conditional support from the National Executive Committee (NEC), which deployed the procedural device of 'qualified acceptance' to neutralise it. Second, although there was a long history of support for federalism within the party,[2] it had no Cabinet-level champions.

Intergovernmental European Co-operation

The Labour leadership ignored the 1948 Conference decision, opting for a policy of *intergovernmental European co-operation*. It insisted that

---

[2] Federalist supporters included Clement Attlee, Fenner Brockway, GDH Cole, Richard Crossman, Michael Foot, Lord Philip Lothian, Richard Mackay, Ian Mikardo, RH Tawney and Harold Wilson.

the Organisation of European Economic Co-operation and the Council of Europe should operate on an intergovernmental basis, refused to participate in the Schuman Plan negotiations, opposed British participation in the proposed European Defence Community, and opted out of two articles of the European Convention on Human Rights. The NEC subsequently formalised the Labour leadership's position by publishing a policy statement, endorsed by the 1950 Conference, which opposed any moves towards federalism, arguing that European co-operation should not prevent the Labour government from implementing its national Keynesian programme.

Following the creation of the EU on a supranational basis in April 1951, the Conservatives promoted the concept of a Free Trade Area (FTA) in an attempt to supplant the Six[3] and reinstate the principle of intergovernmentalism. However, France and the US rejected the FTA proposal. Nevertheless, the Conservatives and six other European governments established the European Free Trade Association (EFTA) in November 1959. The Labour leadership supported the original FTA proposals, and offered conditional support to the EFTA. However, neither the EFTA, nor the principle of free trade, were debated or ratified by the Annual Conference.

In October 1961, the Conservatives initiated EU entry negotiations with the Six, having submitted a formal application in August. During this period, pro-EU forces began to promote entry within the Labour Party, through the cross-party Common Market Campaign and the Labour Common Market Committee. In the late 1960s, anti-EU forces, such as the Forward Britain Movement and senior party figures such as Douglas Jay and Peter Shore, promoted a number of alternatives to the EU.

Opposition to Entry Without Safeguards (1961)

At the 1961 Conference, the party united to support a policy of *opposition to entry without safeguards*, specifically the protection of British agriculture, Commonwealth and EFTA interests, plus the right to pursue economic planning and public ownership. However, as George Brown, the pro-EU Deputy-Leader of the party, explained, NEC support for the resolution was based on the understanding that if such guarantees were obtained, the party would consider joining the EU. Once again, the Labour leadership used the procedural

---

[3] The Six, as they were termed, referred to the six original members of the EU: Belgium, France, Italy Luxembourg, the Netherlands and West Germany.

device of 'qualified acceptance' to weaken an Annual Conference decision, so as to maintain the option of entry.

Conditional Support for Entry (1962–70)

The 1962 Conference agreed five conditions that would have to be satisfied before Labour would support entry: safeguarding Britain's Commonwealth trade, its freedom to pursue an independent foreign policy, its obligations to the EFTA, its ability to plan the economy and its commitment to British agriculture. However, the NEC policy statement declared that, if the five conditions were satisfied, Britain should join. During the Annual Conference debate, Party Leader Hugh Gaitskell warned that political integration would mean the end of a thousand years of history. Nevertheless, Brown argued that, on balance, the economic advantages of entry outweighed the costs, asserting that this view infused the NEC policy statement. The policy of *conditional support for entry* was therefore biased in favour of entry. Indeed, the Labour leadership tabled an amendment in the House of Commons in November 1962 stating that it would support entry, subject to the five conditions. However, French President Charles de Gaulle vetoed Britain's first application in January 1963.

At the 1963 Conference, in an attempt to avoid party division before the general election, the Labour leadership instituted the 'three-year rule' so as to prevent any debate on the EU. Consequently it was not debated again until the 1967 Conference.

The 1964 General Election manifesto stated that, although Labour would seek closer relations with the EU, its primary responsibility was to the Commonwealth. Back in power, Prime Minister Harold Wilson reaffirmed the commitment to the five conditions. However, under the influence of pro-EU civil servants, Wilson began to shift in favour of entry. In December 1965, he accepted Articles 25 and 46 of the European Convention on Human Rights, reversing the opt-outs negotiated in 1950. Taken as an executive decision using the Royal Prerogative, neither the Cabinet nor Parliament discussed the change, despite its constitutional significance.

The 1966 General Election manifesto declared that Labour would join the EU, provided essential British and Commonwealth interests were safeguarded. In November 1966, Wilson announced to the House of Commons that Labour, having reviewed its European policy, had decided to explore the potential for further negotiations.

Between January and March 1967, Brown and Wilson toured the EU to meet representatives of the Six.

In April 1967, the Cabinet voted 13 to 8 to re-open negotiations. Labour subsequently published a White Paper setting out its terms. These included transition arrangements for the implementation of the Common Agricultural Policy (CAP), plus safeguards on the balance of payments, Commonwealth trade and regional policy. In the House of Commons debate that followed, Wilson argued that, economically, industry would probably benefit from entry. However, he acknowledged the problems posed by the CAP and the end of Commonwealth Preference. It was estimated that the cost of living would increase between 2.5 and 3.5 per cent, that food prices would increase between 10 and 14 per cent, and that the net cost to the balance of payments would be between £175 and £250 million per year. Politically, he dismissed the idea of a federal Europe, whilst constitutionally, he stated that EU law would only take precedence in certain areas, claiming that most domestic law would remain unchanged. However, he conceded that entry would involve the surrender of sovereignty, and that, in future, Britain would have to refrain from enacting legislation inconsistent with EU law. During the debate, 37 Labour MPs tabled an amendment opposing the White Paper, arguing that it failed to uphold the conditions laid down by the Annual Conference. Despite a three-line whip, 35 Labour MPs voted against, while 51 abstained. However, due to Conservative support, the Labour motion was approved by 488 votes to 62. Britain's second application was formally submitted in May, without a mandate from the Annual Conference. During this period, anti-EU forces established the Labour Committee for the Five Safeguards on the Common Market.

Brown set out Labour's case for entry before EU representatives at a meeting of the Western European Union (WEU) in July 1967. He attempted to reassure the Six that the fundamental features of the EU would remain unchanged if Britain joined by declaring that Labour was willing to accept the EU objectives of economic and political union. Critically, only the problematic issue of agriculture was reserved for future negotiations.

The NEC presented a revised policy statement to the 1967 Conference, stating that the party's concerns about entry had been allayed. The Annual Conference endorsed the policy statement by 4.1 million votes to 2 million, whilst a resolution opposed to entry was defeated by 997,000 votes out of 6 million, as was a federalist resolution. However, de Gaulle vetoed Britain's second application in November 1967.

The 1969 Conference endorsed a Parliamentary Report declaring that Labour was committed to entry and was eager to engage in further negotiations. It adopted an NEC policy statement declaring that the result of any negotiations, and the final decision, would be subject to a parliamentary vote. The Annual Conference also carried a resolution containing additional safeguards, on foreign policy, health and the welfare state, and which opposed the development of a nuclear-armed federal EU. Facing the possibility of defeat, Brown endorsed the resolution, subject to qualification. He stated that the NEC would accept the resolution on the understanding that the safeguards set out in his WEU speech in July 1967 would be included in the resolution. Critically, it should be recalled that the only issue reserved for negotiation in this speech was agriculture; there was no mention of any other safeguards.

Labour published another White Paper in 1970, conceding that the consequences of entry would be even more adverse than the 1967 calculations. Food prices, for example, were expected to rise between 18 and 26 per cent cumulatively over any negotiated transition period, compared to the estimate of 10 to 14 per cent in 1967. Nevertheless, the second leg of Britain's negotiations opened in April, just two months before Labour's ejection from office.

Having lost the 1970 General Election, the NEC urged the 1970 Conference not to change party policy just because it was in opposition. It subsequently reaffirmed the decision of the 1969 Conference, and rejected a resolution that was opposed to entry by 140,000 votes out of 6 million.

Opposition to Entry on Conservative Terms (1971)

The Conservatives' principal objective upon gaining office in 1970 was to secure British entry. The Conservatives published a White Paper in 1971 conceding that food prices would rise and that Britain's contribution to the EU budget would become a burden unless the CAP was reformed. However, it neglected to mention Economic and Monetary Union (EMU), even though the Six had already pledged to create a single currency by 1980.

Labour held a Special Conference on the EU in July 1971. A resolution pledging that the NEC would produce a definitive resolution on entry, which the party could vote upon at the Annual Conference in October, was carried, whilst an attempt to hold an immediate vote was defeated. Although the Special Conference agreed the suggested procedure and timetable, the NEC pre-empted the Annual Conference by launching a 'No to Entry on Tory Terms' campaign.

The 1971 Conference endorsed the policy recommended by the NEC, namely *opposition to entry on Conservative terms*, by 5 million votes to 1 million. An amendment in favour of holding a referendum before joining was defeated by 4.2 million votes to 1.9 million, whilst a resolution advocating a United States of Europe was defeated by 3 million votes to 2 million. James Callaghan, the Shadow Home Secretary, concluded the debate on behalf of the NEC and pledged that, when re-elected, Labour would renegotiate the terms. The PLP followed the Annual Conference by voting to oppose the terms by 159 to 89.

The House of Commons debated a Conservative motion in favour of entry in October 1971. As a result of a secret alliance between the Conservatives and the 69-strong pro-EU wing of the PLP, 356 MPs voted for entry with 244 against in the final division on the 28th October. In January 1972, the government signed the Treaty of Accession and published the European Communities Bill. The Bill was passed on the 17th October 1972, and Britain joined the EU on the 1st January 1973.

Renegotiating the Terms (1972-74)

Labour's attacks on the Conservative government following accession focused on the fact that it possessed no mandate for entry, as the British people had not been consulted. During this period Tony Benn, who left the Shadow Cabinet to return to the backbenches, launched his campaign for a referendum on entry. In March 1972, following the French decision to hold a referendum, the Shadow Cabinet accepted Benn's proposal by 13 votes to 11. In April, the PLP voted 129 to 96 in favour, prompting pro-EU Cabinet members, including Roy Jenkins, to resign.

The 1972 Conference reaffirmed the party's opposition to entry, whilst agreeing a new policy of *renegotiating the terms*. The NEC policy statement listed the six issues upon which Labour would renegotiate: the CAP, the EU Budget, powers over fiscal, industrial and regional policy, capital controls, the protection of Commonwealth interests and value-added tax (VAT). The document stated that if renegotiations were successful, Labour would put the decision to the people at a general election or referendum. The policy statement was adopted by 3.4 million votes to 1.8 million. A resolution supporting a boycott of EU institutions was carried by 3.3 million votes to 2.8 million, whilst a resolution calling for a future Labour government to withdraw was defeated, by only 118,000 votes out of 6 million.

Given the scale of opposition within the party, Wilson was concerned that the 1973 Conference would vote in favour of withdrawal. He consequently threatened to resign if the party adopted such a policy and his threat was effective. The NEC supported a resolution in favour of a boycott and holding a referendum, which was carried by 5.2 million votes to 945,000. However, a resolution advocating withdrawal, followed by the construction of a socialist united Europe, was defeated by 516,000 votes out of 6 million. In December, the PLP voted to boycott EU institutions by 140 votes to 55.

The February 1974 General Election manifesto set out Labour's objectives for the renegotiations: reform of the CAP and EU Budget, opposition to EMU, the retention of powers over the British economy, the protection of Commonwealth interests and opposition to VAT harmonisation. Callaghan launched the renegotiations in April. The October 1974 General Election manifesto stated that, within 12 months, a Labour government would give the people the choice, through the ballot box, on whether to retain membership or withdraw.

The NEC supported a resolution at the 1974 Conference insisting upon balance in a future referendum, in terms of financial and media support, between the anti- and pro-EU campaigns. The resolution was carried. However, a second resolution advocating additional safeguards on capital controls, Commonwealth trade, defence, food subsidies, labour movements, parliamentary sovereignty, public ownership, taxation and state aid, was also carried, by a majority of 158,000 votes out of nearly 6 million.

The 1975 Referendum

A Divided Cabinet (1975)

Following the conclusion of the renegotiations in March 1975, the Cabinet debated whether to support continued membership or to withdraw. Ministers on the anti-EU left highlighted the threat posed by the EU to democracy and parliamentary sovereignty. Benn claimed that 'we have not achieved our manifesto objectives and indeed we did not even try.' He charged that 'the real case for entry has never been spelled out, which is that there should be a fully federal Europe in which Britain would become a province. It hasn't been spelled out because people would never accept it. We are at the moment on a federal escalator, moving as we talk, going towards a federal objective we do not wish to reach' (Benn, 1990: 345-347). Wilson, however, held a different view: 'I recommend that we should stay in and that is the view of the Foreign Secretary. We have substantially achieved our objectives, the Community has changed *de facto* and *de jure*' (Ibid.). The Cabinet voted by 16 to 7 to accept the revised terms of membership. In Wilson's absence, the Cabinet also agreed to allow ministers to vote against the government.

In March 1975, the NEC voted 18 to 11 against the outcome of the renegotiations, prompting Wilson to again threaten resignation. Policy-wise, the Labour leadership and the NEC were opposed, whilst the PLP was split. In April, a House of Commons motion in favour of staying in was carried by 396 votes to 170, mainly due to Conservative support. On the Labour side, 145 MPs voted against (including 38 ministers), 137 voted for and 33 abstained.

The Special Conference on the EU, held in April 1975, debated the NEC statement arguing that the terms, even as renegotiated, were unsatisfactory. The NEC therefore opposed continued membership, although it supported the freedom of ministers to dissent. During the debate, an unsuccessful attempt was made to prevent a vote. Instead, the NEC statement, in favour of *withdrawal*, was carried by 5,710,000 votes to 3,724,000. Nevertheless, the Labour leadership helped to co-ordinate Britain's third national pro-EU propaganda campaign to secure a Yes vote in the 1975 Referendum (see Chapter 6).

In the referendum on the 25th June, 67.2 per cent voted Yes and 32.8 per cent voted No. Wilson declared that 'the verdict has been given by a vote and a majority bigger than that achieved by any government in a general election in the history of our democracy.' It 'means that fourteen years of national argument are over' (Wilson, 1975). Wilson subsequently demoted Benn, whilst the PLP reversed its boycott and sent representatives to the EU Economic and Social Committee and the European Parliament.

The Post-1975 Period

Reform of the EU (1976–79)

The 1976 Conference debated the NEC policy statement on direct elections to the European Parliament. The document insisted that there was no mandate for direct elections, as it had not been mentioned during the 1975 Referendum. It further argued that the party should oppose such elections because the European Parliament constituted a threat to Westminster. It was carried by a majority of 4 million votes to 2.2 million.

The Cabinet discussed direct elections in February 1977 and was divided on the matter. In April, Labour issued a White Paper on alternative electoral systems for the European elections, making no explicit recommendation and agreeing to hold a free House of Commons vote. However, in July the bill was defeated by 394 votes to 147, with 124 Labour MPs against (including 32 Ministers), whilst in November, MPs voted by 319 to 222 to reject the government's preference of an open, regional list system in favour of 78 single-member constituencies. However, the Labour rebels abstained and the bill, reintroduced to parliament in 1978, was passed with the votes of Conservative and Liberal MPs.

The 1977 Conference adopted the NEC policy statement, which reaffirmed Labour's opposition to supranationalism and re-emphasised the threat posed by the EU to its industrial strategy. The policy statement reiterated the 1976 Conference decision to seek specific derogations from EU law on energy, regional and social policies, and transport. It pledged to reform the EU aid policy, the CAP and the CFP. It also pledged to oppose direct elections, the European Monetary System (EMS), EMU and tax harmonisation, including VAT. A resolution calling for the fundamental reform of the CAP was carried. However, following a plea to maintain party unity, the 1977 Conference rejected two amendments, one of which called for Britain's withdrawal from the CAP. It also rejected a resolution calling for another referendum on membership, and remitted a resolution in favour of amending the 1972 European Communities Act to restore parliamentary supremacy.

The European Council reaffirmed its commitment to EMU in 1978, launching a new system of monetary co-ordination: the EMS and its Exchange Rate Mechanism (ERM). Although Callaghan (1987: 493) supported the idea, he did not believe that the party would. Furthermore, 'this, coupled with my own and the Treasury's belief that sterling was too high to make our entry advantageous' led him to reject entry. In October the NEC rejected the EMS by 16 votes to 9.

The 1978 Conference rejected withdrawal in favour of a policy of *reform of the EU*. The Annual Conference carried a resolution calling for the next Labour manifesto to include a commitment to amend the 1972 European Communities Act so as to restore parliamentary sovereignty. The resolution rejected EMU and supported the reform of the EU. It was carried by 4.85 million votes to 1.64 million.

Callaghan used the leadership veto over policy, so often used by Wilson, to emasculate the policy decisions of the 1978 Conference when drafting the manifesto for the 1979 General Election. It declared that Labour would seek the fundamental reform of the EU. It supported EU enlargement, pledged to reform the CAP and the EU Budget, and promised to amend, if necessary, the 1972 European Communities Act so as to safeguard parliamentary sovereignty.

Under Benn's leadership, the NEC drafted the manifesto for the 1979 European Election. Carried by 19 votes to 4, it warned that, in the absence of fundamental EU reform, the party would adopt a policy of withdrawal. In the first direct elections to the European Parliament, three weeks after Labour's general election defeat, Labour polled 32 per cent of the vote and gained 17 Members of the European Parliament (MEPs), compared to the Conservatives' 48 per cent and 60 MEPs.

Withdrawal (1980–87)

The European policies of the Annual Conference and the Labour leadership converged under Michael Foot. The 1980 Conference supported a resolution declaring that there had been no progress in reforming the EU and that Labour should include a policy of *withdrawal* in its next manifesto. The resolution was carried by 5 million votes to 2 million. At the 1981 Conference, an attempt to introduce a commitment to hold a referendum before withdrawing was defeated by 5.8 million votes to 1 million. The 1983 General Election manifesto duly included the pledge to withdraw, within the lifetime of one parliament.

The manifesto for the 1984 European Election acknowledged that Britain would remain a member of the EU for the term of the next European Parliament, but pledged that Labour would aim to fundamentally reform the EU. In the second direct election to the European Parliament, Labour polled 35 per cent of the vote and gained 32 MEPs, compared to the Conservatives' 39 per cent and 45 MEPs.

The European Commission's plan to create a European single market by 1992 served to accelerate the process of European integration. Conservative Prime Minister Margaret Thatcher supported the creation of a single market, believing it would lead to a free market and a free trade area. With Labour officially opposed, the House of Commons voted by 149 to 43 to incorporate the EU Single European Act into British law in July 1986.

Labour's 1987 General Election manifesto contained no reference to withdrawal, although it remained official party policy. Instead, it stated that Labour's aim was to work constructively with the EU to promote economic expansion and to combat unemployment.

Pro–Membership (1988–)

The attempt to change the party's withdrawal policy began in 1983, following Labour's general election defeat. For Party Leader Neil Kinnock, 'the rejection of the withdrawal policy by the voters was clear and absolute.' However, 'because anti-Europeanism was quite deeply rooted in parts of the movement, particularly the trade unions, the change had to be achieved by degrees rather than by a sudden shift.' This was because 'as Labour had already demonstrated, parties were seriously in danger of cracking and then crumbling over the issue of Europe if the matter was not handled with care as well as determination.' [4]

Kinnock's chosen vehicle for changing party policy was the Policy Review, established following Labour's 1987 General Election defeat. Seven policy committees were created, including the Modern World Committee, which was responsible for European policy. Committee member Regan Scott revealed that Kinnock 'packed the committee with pro-Europeans' to achieve his 'new policy of conditional engagement.'[5] Pro-EU forces, having secured Kinnock's U-turn and marginalised potential opponents, were ready to change party policy. Their opportunity came in 1988 when the European Commission President, Jacques Delors, addressed the Trades Union Congress (TUC). The big trade unions, commanding a majority of TUC Congress votes and attracted to the promise of a 'social Europe', reversed the withdrawal policy. Three weeks later, they voted to change Labour's policy.

The 1988 Conference endorsed the first Policy Review report, which supported EU-wide employment standards, plus the co-ordination of member states' foreign, industrial, regional and social policies. It also carried a resolution stating that Labour, in conjunction with other parties, should use the EU to promote democratic socialism. A second resolution calling for a future Labour government to

[4] Correspondence from Neil Kinnock, 29 January 2003.
[5] Interview with Regan Scott on 8 October 2002.

amend the 1972 European Communities Act was remitted. It had taken several years, but the Labour leadership had finally secured a *pro-membership* policy.

Labour entered the 1989 European Election on a pro-EU platform, polling 40 per cent of the vote and gaining 45 MEPs, compared to the Conservatives' 35 per cent and 32 MEPs. The 1989 Conference endorsed the second Policy Review report advocating the democratisation of EU decision-making, whilst supporting EU enlargement, foreign policy co-ordination and the Single Market.

The European Commission's three-stage EMU project, agreed in June 1989, was translated into the 1991 Maastricht Treaty. It was originally envisaged that the treaty would include a social chapter. However, the British refused to accept it, leading the other 11 member states to adopt a separate Social Charter. Britain negotiated an opt-out from stage 3 of EMU, membership of a single currency, but participated in the first two stages. Britain duly joined the ERM in October 1990, supported by the Labour leadership and the TUC General Council, plus the Bank of England, the Foreign Office, the Treasury and much of the media.

The 1990 Conference endorsed the third Policy Review report, which supported EU enlargement and institutional reform. It also carried a resolution recommending membership of EMU and the EMS. The 1991 Conference adopted the final Policy Review report, which highlighted the need to strengthen the supply side of Britain's economy to meet the challenge of the Single Market. It claimed that EMU would reduce business costs and would eliminate currency speculation, and suggested that monetary policy-co-operation, manifest in the ERM, was both inevitable and desirable. It favoured a London-based European central bank, and supported the Social Charter. The Annual Conference also carried a resolution in favour of British membership of the single currency.

The Bill incorporating the Maastricht Treaty into British law was presented to the House of Commons in May 1992. Although MPs were not given the full text of the treaty, only 72 MPs voted against the Bill. During its passage, Benn presented his Treaty of Maastricht (Referendum) Bill, plus his Commonwealth of Europe Bill, as an alternative to the EU.

The Maastricht Bill's parliamentary journey witnessed several rebellions. In April 1993, Labour helped the Conservatives to defeat an amendment demanding a referendum on the treaty. The battle culminated in the third and final reading in May in which the Conservatives secured a victory of 292 votes to 112, with Labour officially abstaining. However, 65 Labour MPs voted against the treaty and 4 voted in favour. A further division in July on Labour's amendment to incorporate the Social Chapter produced a 317 draw, with the Speaker casting her vote in favour. The Conservatives then presented a motion to accept the Bill, and lost by 8 votes. The following day, Prime Minister John Major held a confidence vote to overturn the vote of the previous day and the Bill was passed by 39 votes.

Between 1990 and 1996, the Annual Conference followed the Labour leadership line on the EU. An exception to this consensus occurred at the 1992 Conference, when Benn submitted a resolution demanding a referendum on the Maastricht Treaty. It was defeated, as was a resolution calling for the fundamental revision of the treaty. Opponents of these resolutions insisted that if the treaty fell, Labour would lose the option of reversing the opt-out from the Social Chapter. In the 1994 European Election, Labour polled 43 per cent of the vote and 62 MEPs, compared to the Conservatives' 27 per cent and 18 MEPs.

One of New Labour's first acts, following its 1997 General Election victory, was to grant independence to the Bank of England, as required by stage 2 of the Maastricht Treaty. Stage 1 requires member states to abide by the EMU convergence criteria/Stability and Growth Pact, hence New Labour's decision to freeze public spending in its first two years in office, Chancellor Gordon Brown's 'golden rule' governing public finance and the expansion of the Private Finance Initiative. New Labour signed the Social Chapter. However, it delayed or blocked the implementation of several EU directives, including the working time directive.

New Labour supported the 1997 Amsterdam Treaty. In November 1997, at the end of the bill's second reading, the House of Commons voted by 392 to 162 in favour of ratification, with 31 Labour MPs abstaining. In the bill's third and final reading in January 1998, MPs voted by 370 to 145 to incorporate the treaty into British law. In the 1999 European Election, New Labour polled 28 per cent of the vote and gained 29 MEPs, compared to the Conservatives' 36 per cent and 36 MEPs. New Labour supported the 2001 Nice Treaty. A Conservative amendment in the House of Commons in July 2001, calling for a referendum on the Nice Treaty, was defeated by 378 votes to 129, with 4 Labour MPs voting in favour of a referendum and 9 abstaining. In October, the bill incorporating the treaty into

British law was carried by 392 votes to 158, with 2 Labour MPs voting against and 29 abstaining.

New Labour also supported the development of an EU foreign and security policy, plus EU enlargement. However, the policy where New Labour's enthusiasm was most evident is that concerning the euro. New Labour's 1997 manifesto set out three pre-conditions that would have to be satisfied before Britain could join the euro: the Cabinet would have to agree, Parliament would have to vote in favour, and the British people would have to say yes in a referendum. It subsequently decided against joining the first wave of euro members in 1999, and it opted to delay membership until a number of conditions, the five economic tests set out in October 1997, were met. During New Labour's first term, the Annual Conference followed the Labour leadership line on the EU. The first phase of the Partnership in Power (PiP) policy-making process (1997–2001), resulting in the *Britain in the World* document adopted by the 2000 Conference, set out the perceived benefits of euro entry.

Although the official policy in its first term was one of *wait and see*, the Labour leadership's unofficial policy was one *prepare and persuade* for euro entry (see Mullen and Burkitt, 2003). However, the main obstacle was public opinion, with a consistent majority opposed to the euro. Another obstacle was Rupert Murdoch. Peter Mandelson revealed that New Labour did not attempt a referendum during its first term because Murdoch's media empire would have campaigned against euro entry.

In June 2003, the Treasury published its assessment of the five economic tests, together with 18 additional documents, concluding that only one test, the impact on financial services, had been passed. New Labour subsequently set out a road map to euro entry, concluding that several reforms, both domestic and in the EU, would have to be instituted before Britain could join.

There was considerable opposition within the party to the euro. Labour Against the Euro was formed in 2002, gaining the support of 37 MPs and 62 councillors, whilst a 2002 survey for ITV found that 27 per cent of Labour MPs were opposed to euro entry. There was also opposition amongst Labour's supporters. An ICM poll in 2002 found that a substantial majority of Labour voters were opposed to euro entry.

During New Labour's second term, the Annual Conference again supported the Labour leadership line. The second phase of PiP (2002–2005) resulted in the adoption of the *Britain in the Global Econ-*

omy document by the 2004 Conference. It claimed that euro entry could benefit the British economy, by up to £3 billion per year. However, it warned that 'if we entered with the five economic tests not met at the wrong exchange rate, then—just as with the ERM in 1992—we could see unemployment rise, public service investment fall and growth stall. The discipline of the five tests is to ensure that there will be no repeat of the experience of the ERM' (Labour Party, 2004).

New Labour supported the 2002 Convention on the Future of Europe and the resulting European Constitution, which was agreed in June 2004. A Conservative motion in the House of Commons in March 2004, demanding a referendum on a future European constitution, was defeated by 328 votes to 212, with 36 Labour MPs abstaining. New Labour argued that there was no need for a referendum; indeed, one minister described the restructuring of the EU treaties as a mere 'tidying up' exercise. However, one month later, following a campaign by the Murdoch press, and another by Vote 2004, which gained the support of 60 Labour MPs, Blair performed a U-turn and agreed to hold a referendum. He also hinted that a second referendum would be held if the first one produced a No vote. It has been alleged that Blair's U-turn, a decision that was not discussed by the Cabinet, was also influenced by Murdoch's threat to withdraw his support from New Labour at the next general election unless he changed his policy.

Labour against a Superstate, which opposed the European Constitution, was formed in April 2004, claiming the support of over 80 MPs. In June, an ICM poll found that almost half of Labour voters would vote against it. However, in the summer of 2005, France and the Netherlands rejected the European Constitution in their respective referendums; New Labour subsequently shelved its 'game plan' to ratify the treaty. In the 2004 European Election, New Labour polled 23 per cent of the vote and gained 19 MEPs, compared to the Conservatives' 27 per cent and 27 MEPs. In August 2004, Mandelson was appointed as a European Commissioner, a prime position from which to sell the euro, the European Constitution and continued membership to a sceptical British public, whilst promoting the EU reform agenda on behalf of New Labour.

In a speech to the European Parliament in June 2005, following the No votes in France and the Netherlands, Blair set out his three goals for the British Presidency of the EU (the last two of which were achieved). He called for the 'modernisation' of the 'European social model', the agreement of a new EU Budget, and further EU enlargement to include Turkey—objectives that were endorsed by the 2005 Conference. In December, at the end of the British Presidency, Blair pledged to support Germany in resurrecting the European Constitution in 2007. However, he argued that, for ratification to succeed, it would be necessary to change the context of the debate about the treaty. He specifically recommended economic reform in the EU, a fundamental review of the EU Budget and further EU enlargement.

Conclusion

Labour's European policy during the post-war period exhibits five main features. The first feature was the difference in policy depending on whether Labour was in government or in opposition. In government, the Labour leadership tended to ignore the decisions of the Annual Conference, circumventing official party policy and adopting the pro-EU stance of the Foreign Office. However, in opposition, the generally more sceptical Annual Conference tended to reassert itself, thus circumscribing the Labour leadership's room for manoeuvre.

The second feature was the extent of internal division over European integration. Labour was divided from top to bottom on the issue of the EU, from affiliated organisations through to the NEC, the PLP, the Shadow Cabinet/Cabinet and the Labour leadership itself. Two main cleavages can be identified, the division between anti- and pro-EU forces, and that between the left and the right, creating four main aggregations: the pro-EU left, the pro-EU right, from which the Labour leadership was usually drawn, the anti-EU left, and the anti-EU right. These competed to control the policy-making process and its outcomes.

The third feature, flowing from the second, was the volatility of Labour's European policy: there were eight significant policy shifts over the post-war period. Likewise, many prominent Labour figures changed their position on the EU, some several times.

The fourth feature was the allegedly extensive and enduring links between the pro-EU Labour Right, the US Central Intelligence Agency and the European federalist movement. These external actors attempted to shape Labour's European policy (see Mullen, 2005). However, given the secrecy surrounding this area, assessing the impact of such operations is difficult to establish.

The fifth feature was the seismic change of attitude towards European integration that occurred in 1988. Although, post-1988, the party remained divided, for example over the euro and the European Constitution, support for withdrawal from the EU seems to have evaporated. However, the formation of organisations such as Labour Against the Euro and Labour Against a Superstate suggest that scepticism about further European integration has not dissipated.

European integration, or more precisely further European integration, looks set to remain a divisive issue for the Labour Party, in both the short and longer term. It is divided on the question of whether to adopt the euro, and there was substantial internal opposition to the proposed European Constitution. If the promised referendum on the euro is held, and if a referendum on the European Constitution is staged at some point in the future, these conflicts are certain to re-emerge. This begs the question, if referendums on these matters are called, what is the likely configuration of forces? To answer this question, it is useful to contrast the situation in 1975 with that in 2006.

More than thirty years on, it is possible to identify a number of important similarities and differences between the 1975 Referendum and the state of affairs in 2006. The most obvious similarities are that Labour is in power and that the party is still divided on the question of European integration. Another similarity is that, as in 1975, pro-EU forces enjoy the backing of the government and the considerable power resources of the British State. However, there are three important differences, which have implications for the future balance of power. First, during the 1975 Referendum, pro-EU forces were defending the status quo of continued membership. In the current period they are, or in the future they will be, seeking to change the status quo, advocating euro entry and, possibly, adopting a treaty that further entrenches the power of the EU *vis-à-vis* member states. Second, unlike in 1975, the business sector, the media, political parties and the trade union movement are more evenly divided on the question of further European integration. Third, in contrast to 1975, anti-EU forces have access to substantial financial resources.

In the longer term, conflict within the Labour Party about further European integration looks set to escalate, helping to tip the currently fairly equal balance of power between anti- and pro-EU forces firmly in favour of the former. There are three reasons for this. First, as the EU aggrandises more power over the British economy and policy-making process, the potential for clashes between Brussels and Westminster increases. This begs the question as to whether a future Labour government would accept rulings from the EU that effectively undermined its programme? Second, if the EU continues in a neo-liberal direction—manifest in policies such as the Single Market, the euro and the recent liberalisation of services directive—it is likely that left-wing and trade union opposition to the EU will grow. Third, the party faces the question of what is the ultimate objective of the European integration process? Will the EU develop into a single European state, a federal United States of Europe, or some form of hybrid of these? Neither Labour Party members, the British people, nor the public in any continental European country have been asked for their opinion on this fundamental matter, a fact which is sure to inflame anger and opposition if European integration proceeds.

Four
The Conservative Party and Europe

Introduction

European integration, in contemporary terms, is a contentious and divisive issue for the Conservative Party. However, it was not always so; in historical terms, the Conservatives were the 'party of Europe', submitting the first application to join the European Union (EU)[1] in 1962, overseeing accession in 1973, and signing the Single European Act (SEA) and Maastricht Treaty in 1986 and 1993 respectively. This chapter, divided into five sections, documents the shifts in the Conservatives' European policy during the 1945 to 2005 period. The first section summarises the Conservatives' European policy. The second section charts the policy changes during the 1945 to 1975 period, the third section looks at the party's efforts to secure a Yes vote in the 1975 Referendum, whilst the fourth section surveys the policy changes during the 1976 to 2005 period. The fifth section concludes, highlighting the four main features of the party's European policy over this period. It also assesses the present balance of power between anti- and pro-EU forces within the party, before speculating what a future configuration of forces might look like.

The European Policy of the Conservative Party

The *official* European policy of the Conservative Party between 1945 and 1981, as agreed by the Annual Conference, the sovereign policy-making body of the party, together with the policy *actually pursued* by the Conservative leadership, plus the European policy

---

[1] For simplicity, the post-war project of European economic and political integration is henceforth referred to as the European Union (EU), rather than its previous titles of Common Market, European Economic Community or European Community.

adopted by the Foreign Office, is summarised in Figure 4.1. Given that the party stopped publishing its annual conference report in 1977, Figure 4.2 summarises the Conservatives' *official* European policy between 1978 and 2005, as contained in election manifestos and other sources, plus the policy *actually pursued* by the Conservative leadership.

Figure 4.1 – European policies of the Conservative Party and the Foreign Office (1945–1977)

Year	Annual Conference Policy	Conservative Leadership Policy	Foreign Office*
1945 (O)			Imperial third force
1946 (O)		Three Great Circles (support for European integration excluding Britain)	"
1947 (O)		"	"
1948 (O)		"	"
1949 (O)	Support for Council of Europe and European unity	"	Limited liability
1950 (O)		"	"
1951 (G)		Intergovernmental European Co-operation	"
1952 (G)		"	"
1953 (G)		"	"
1954 (G)		"	"
1955 (G)		"	"
1956 (G)		Partial engagement	Partial engagement
1957 (G)		"	"
1958 (G)		"	"
1959 (G)		Partial engagement	Near identification

Year	Annual Conference Policy	Conservative Leadership Policy	Foreign Office*
1960 (G)	Support for closer economic co-operation between the Six and the Seven	Support for entry	Pro-entry
1961 (G)	Support for closer association with the EU	"	"
1962 (G)	Conditional support for entry	"	"
1963 (G)		"	"
1964 (O)		"	"
1965 (O)		"	"
1966 (O)		"	"
1967 (O)		"	"
1968 (O)		"	"
1969 (O)	Support for entry	"	"
1970 (G)	Conditional support for entry	"	"
1971 (G)	Support for entry	"	"
1972 (G)		"	"
1973 (G)		Support for membership	Pro-membership
1974 (O)			"
1975 (O)	Support for Direct Elections	Campaign for a Yes vote in the 1975 Referendum	"
1976 (O)	Support for Direct Elections		"
1977 (O)	Support for a stronger, united EU	Support for a confederation	"

Notes: G = Conservatives in government. O = Conservatives in opposition. * Historically, the Foreign Office tended to dominate the formulation of the British State's European policy. For an account of the post-war European policy of the British State see Mullen (2005).

Figure 4.2 – European Policies of the Conservative Party (1978-2005)

Year	Annual Conference Policy (other sources)/Conservative Manifesto Policy	Conservative Leadership Policy
1978 (O)		Support for the EMS and ERM entry
1979 (G)	Opposition to excessive bureaucracy and unnecessary policy harmonisation, plus reform of the CAP, EU Budget and CFP	Reform of the CAP and EU Budget
1980 (G)	Reform of the EU Budget, plus support for a pro-EU propaganda campaign	"
1981 (G)	Opposition to Labour's withdrawal policy	"
1982 (G)		"
1983 (G)	Opposition to Labour's withdrawal policy, reform of the EU Budget and support for the free movement of goods and services	Reform of the CAP and EU Budget, plus opposition to ERM entry
1984 (G)		
1985 (G)		Support for a single market
1986 (G)		
1987 (G)	Reform of the EU Budget, plus support for the free movement of goods and services	
1988 (G)		Opposition to EU federalism and ERM entry
1989 (G)		
1990 (G)		Support for ERM entry, plus opt-outs from stage 3 of EMU and the Social Chapter
1991 (G)		Ratification of the Maastricht Treaty

Year	Annual Conference Policy (other sources)/Conservative Manifesto Policy	Conservative Leadership Policy
1992 (G)	Opposition to any extension of EU competence, plus support for CAP reform, EU enlargement, completion of the Single Market and subsidiarity	
1993 (G)		
1994 (G)		
1995 (G)		
1996 (G)		Support for a referendum on euro entry
1997 (O)	Opposition to a federal EU and any extension of QMV, plus support for the abatement, Britain's opt-outs/ veto and a referendum on euro entry	Opposition to the Amsterdam Treaty
1998 (O)		No euro entry for two parliaments
1999 (O)		
2000 (O)		
2001 (O)		Opposition to the Nice Treaty
2002 (O)		
2003 (O)		Support for a referendum on the European Constitution
2004 (O)		
2005 (O)	Support for CAP reform, withdrawal from the CFP, EU enlargement, EU reform and the restoration of the Social Chapter opt-out, plus opposition to an EU army, euro entry and the European Constitution	Withdrawal of Conservative MEPs from European People's Party in the European Parliament

Notes: G = Conservatives in government.
O = Conservatives in opposition.

The Pre-1975 Period

Support for European Integration (1945–60)

Three Great Circles

The Conservatives' manifesto for the 1945 General Election contained no mention of European integration. Nevertheless, in opposition, Party Leader Winston Churchill pursued his *three great circles* policy, supporting the process of European integration, albeit without British participation. In his March 1946 'Iron Curtain' speech in the United States (US), Churchill lamented the Cold War division of Europe and called for European unity. In a further speech in September, Churchill specifically recommended the creation of a federal United States of Europe. However, he did not envisage that Britain would join this creation; Churchill favoured the projection of British power through its leadership of the Commonwealth, a 'close association' with Europe and its 'special relationship' with the US. These, for Churchill, were the 'three great circles' in which Britain would play a pivotal role. To realise part of his vision, Churchill established the United Europe Movement in May 1947.

Churchill, together with 24 other Conservative MPs, attended the Congress of Europe in The Hague in May 1948. The Congress called for the creation of a Council of Europe to devise plans for European integration. Although no formal proposals were adopted, with Churchill's support the Congress agreed to establish the European Movement to co-ordinate the different groups promoting European integration. Launched in May 1949, the European Movement was far from a unified force. The ensuing battle between supporters of federalism (principally the continental Europeans and the US) and advocates of intergovernmentalism (namely Britain and the Scandinavian countries) was settled decisively in favour of the former; the Council of Europe was established on an intergovernmental basis in May 1949.

Back in Britain, the Conservatives' 1949 Conference carried a resolution endorsing the three great circles policy and the work of the Council of Europe, with only two delegates opposed. Likewise, the party's manifesto for the 1950 General Election reiterated the three great circles policy, calling for closer association with Western Europe, whilst its manifesto for the 1951 General Election recommended a 'united Europe'.

Intergovernmental European Co-operation

Unexpectedly back in power following his 1951 General Election victory, Churchill modified his European policy. Although still committed to European integration, he adopted the *intergovernmental European co-operation* policy of the previous government. Churchill's aim was to thwart the 'small group of states which are moving towards political federation by the progressive establishment of organisations exercising supranational powers' (Cabinet Office, 1952). Accordingly, Foreign Secretary Anthony Eden published a plan in February 1952 that advocated the reform of the intergovernmental Council of Europe to incorporate the European Coal and Steel Community (ECSC) and the proposed European Defence Community (EDC). However, the plan was rejected by the Six[2], as was the EDC treaty (signed in May 1952 but rejected by the French in August 1954). Nevertheless, Eden succeeded in regaining the initiative by proposing the revision of the 1948 Brussels Treaty,[3] thus paving the way for the creation of the intergovernmental Western European Union (WEU) in May 1955.

In April 1955, Eden replaced Churchill as Prime Minister. Two months later, Eden attempted to wreck the Messina Conference[4] by sending a civil servant rather than a ministerial delegation. The reasoning was established by the Cabinet Mutual Aid Committee, which ruled out British participation in any supranational schemes in October. It believed that EU entry would 'increase the relative importance of our trade with Europe and reduce our economic links with the Commonwealth'. This would have a 'profound effect on the readiness of other Commonwealth countries to co-operate with us in the Sterling Area' and 'would damage the Imperial Preference system.' Furthermore, 'once we became members of a common market, we should be subject to strong political pressures to extend the 'harmonisation' of our policies with those of other members beyond the field of tariffs into other fields both of internal and external policy' (Cabinet Office, 1955). In November 1955, Eden withdrew the British

---

[2] The Six, as they were termed, referred to the six original members of the EU: Belgium, France, Italy Luxembourg, the Netherlands and West Germany.

[3] The 1948 Brussels Treaty, signed by Belgium, Britain, France, Luxembourg and the Netherlands, provided for collaboration in cultural, economic and social matters, plus collective self-defence.

[4] The purpose of the Messina Conference was to negotiate a common market among the Six, with an ECSC-type (supranational) institutional structure.

representative from the Spaak Committee[5], whilst the Six went on to establish the EU in March 1957.

According to Finer et al. (1961), during the 1955–1959 Parliament, pro-EU MPs were outnumbered by those who were loyal to the Commonwealth/Empire. The latter group was concerned about the impact of entry on agriculture (given that farmers constitute a core Conservative interest group), Commonwealth trade, sovereignty and the loss of the anti-EU working class vote. Although the party's modified policy was not debated or ratified by the Annual Conference, it thus enjoyed the backing of a majority of MPs.

Partial Engagement

The 1956 Suez crisis precipitated a significant policy shift, to one of *partial engagement*, as Eden attempted to re-capture the leadership of the European integration process. The Suez fiasco persuaded the Conservatives to abandon their role as an imperial party in favour of becoming the party that supported the process of European integration with British participation. One manifestation of the new policy was the plan for a free trade area in manufactured goods, presented to the Cabinet by Chancellor of the Exchequer Harold Macmillan in September 1956. 'Plan G' was one of the seven options devised by the Treasury in anticipation of Messina. It envisaged the creation of a 17-member Free Trade Area (FTA), in which the Six would constitute the core of a wider membership. In an attempt to reinstate the intergovernmental principle, and thus supplant the Six, the Conservative leadership recommended the integration of the FTA within the Organisation for European Economic Co-operation. However, France and the US rejected the FTA proposal in November 1956, prompting Eden to opt for the smaller European Free Trade Association (EFTA). Established in November 1959, the Conservatives preferred the EFTA to EU entry, as the former did not involve any commitment to supranational institutions or the imposition of a common tariff. Meanwhile, Macmillan (1959), who became Prime Minister in January 1957, decided to turn his attention to 'how to live with the Common Market economically, and turn its political effects into harmless channels for us.'

---

[5] The Spaak Committee was established as a result of the 1955 Messina Conference in order to devise concrete proposals for economic integration among the Six. The work of the committee laid the foundations for the 1957 Treaty of Rome.

Support for Entry/Continued Membership (1960-74)

In March 1960, an interdepartmental committee of senior civil servants, chaired by the pro-EU civil servant Sir Frank Lee, was established to review Britain's European policy. The Lee memorandum, published in May, argued that negotiating entry would involve 'difficult and unpalatable decisions', including some surrender of sovereignty (Cabinet Office, 1960a). It recommended a policy of near identification, that is, accepting many of its obligations without formal membership. Macmillan subsequently stated that the 'policies of 'near identification' and of joining [the EU] were so similar that one might well lead to the other, and if we were prepared to accept near identification, it might be preferable to contemplate full membership' (Cabinet Office, 1960b).

In June 1960, Macmillan circulated a memorandum to officials, asking them to answer 23 questions. The subsequent report stated that:

> We cannot join the Common Market on the cheap. First we must accept that there will have to be a political content in our action – we must show ourselves prepared to join with the Six in their institutional arrangements and in any development towards closer political integration. Without this we cannot achieve our foreign policy aims. Secondly, there must be a real intention to have a 'common market', in general we must accept the common tariff (Cabinet Office, 1960c).

The memorandum also considered the issue of timing, recommending a delay of between 12 and 18 months, rather than an immediate application to join.

The Cabinet discussed the Lee memorandum, plus the answers to the 23 questions, in July 1960. However, it was apparent that the Cabinet was divided on the benefits and costs of entry. Two weeks later, Macmillan restructured the Cabinet in favour of pro-EU ministers. Looking back on this period, Young (1998, p.123) noted that no ministerial paper was put to the Cabinet, making this 'an officials' operation'. In other words, Macmillan's new policy of *support for entry* was effectively made by civil servants. Denman (1996: 211) charged that 'it must be the only occasion in British history when a memorandum by an official was largely responsible for a momentous change in British foreign policy.' In public, Macmillan (1973: 22-23) stressed that 'in spite of the political overtones in the whole concept, [the EU] was an economic community', and that 'there is nothing in the Treaty of Rome that commits the members of [the EU] to any kind of federalist solution'. However in private, Macmillan (1972: 324) acknowledged 'the new economic, and perhaps political, state which is being created by the Six countries of continental Western Europe'. Likewise, Heath announced to a ministerial meeting of the WEU in April 1962 that 'we are looking forward to joining you as soon as possible in constructing a Europe united politically as well as economically'. Such an eventuality was never placed before the general public or the party.

In July 1960, the House of Commons debated a Conservative motion in support of European economic and political unity, carried by 215 votes to 4. Likewise, the 1960 Conference carried a resolution in favour of closer economic co-operation between the Six and the EFTA.

Between April and July 1961, several Cabinet committee meetings discussed the implications of entry, whilst in June and July, Macmillan consulted with the Commonwealth on Britain's intentions. In July, the Cabinet agreed to open negotiations with the Six. Macmillan announced his decision to parliament on the 31st July, giving an undertaking that he would consult parliament before any agreement. However, he refused to publish a White Paper.

Despite such manoeuvres, there was internal opposition to Macmillan's policy of entry. Sceptics included the likes of the Home Secretary, R. A. Butler, who was concerned about the impact of entry on agriculture and the Commonwealth. Likewise, Foreign Secretary Anthony Eden (1962a; 1962b) expressed doubts that 'the experiment of the Six can succeed without federation', warning that 'I am sure that it must be federation in the sense of one parliament, one foreign policy and one currency.' For Eden, 'the British people should know where they are going before they wake up and find themselves where they do not want to be'. Opposition was also manifest in the House of Commons motion put down in July, supported by 49 Conservative MPs, expressing fear about the loss of British sovereignty. Similarly, in the House of Commons vote on opening entry negotiations in August, one Conservative MP voted against entry, whilst 24 abstained. Nevertheless, Macmillan's European policy was endorsed by 313 votes to 5 in the final vote. On the 9th August, the Conservatives formally submitted Britain's first application to join the EU and the negotiations opened in October. While the negotiations were proceeding, Macmillan turned his attention to preparing public opinion for entry, launching Britain's first national pro-EU propaganda campaign (see Chapter 6).

The 1961 Conference carried a resolution in favour of a close association between the Six and the Commonwealth/EFTA, with only 40 delegates out of 4,000 voting against. Although the Annual Conference did not explicitly endorse entry, it rejected an amendment put down by anti-EU MPs that was opposed to the ceding of any British sovereignty.

Further opposition to Macmillan's European policy emerged in 1962 when 30 Conservative MPs put down a motion in the House of Commons in March urging the government to reject entry if special arrangements for the Commonwealth could not be secured. In June, two MPs (who claimed the support of 60 others) published a pamphlet setting out a Commonwealth-based alternative to entry, whilst in July, a second critical motion was put down in the House of Commons, supported by 36 Conservative MPs.

In an attempt to win round the sceptics, on the eve of the 1962 Conference Macmillan published a pamphlet aimed at party members that extolled the virtues of the EU. Conservative Central Office also produced a number of pamphlets and speakers in favour of entry. Conference delegates faced a clear choice: they could support Macmillan's resolution in favour of entry negotiations, or they could support a sceptical amendment urging the government to honour its pledges on agriculture and the Commonwealth. The latter was also opposed to any moves towards a European political union that would result in a loss of sovereignty. During the debate, sceptics warned of the 'hidden agenda' of the EU, that of political federation, whilst Butler, having shifted to a less sceptical position, reassured the delegates that the government would not agree to anything that undermined the powers of British courts and parliament. With little dissent, the Annual Conference supported the official government policy of conditional support for entry, subject to safeguards on British interests and those of the Commonwealth and EFTA. Looking back on this period, Macmillan (1973: 31) admitted that:

> I was under some apprehension that the Conservative Party would be deeply split by the decision that we should enter into negotiations with the Six. But I was gratified to find that the Conservative Party was fluid, ready to move with the times, and, especially with the younger men, anxious to seize new opportunities.

Nevertheless, scepticism remained. In December 1962, 47 Conservative MPs signed a motion urging the government to stand firm, even if it resulted in the failure of the negotiations. However, French

President Charles de Gaulle vetoed Britain's first application in January 1963.

The Conservatives' manifesto for the 1964 General Election declared that entry was not a viable option and that further negotiations were impossible at that time. However, it pledged to secure the closest possible relations with the Six, consistent with Britain's Commonwealth links. However, although still in opposition, by the time of the 1966 General Election the Conservatives were again in favour of entry. The manifesto stated that the party was determined to lead Britain into an enlarged EU, so that the country could exert its influence on a global scale and so that British industry could benefit from a bigger home market. When Labour's decision to re-open negotiations was put to the House of Commons in May 1967, the decision was endorsed by 488 votes to 62 with official Conservative support. Britain's second application was submitted on 10th May 1967. Although rejected by de Gaulle in November, the party held firm; the 1969 Conference carried a resolution in support of entry, by 1,452 votes to 475.

The Conservatives' manifesto for the 1970 General Election argued that, given the right terms, entry would be in Britain's long-term interest, on the basis that a bigger home market would increase economic growth and lead to a higher standard of living. However, it acknowledged the short-term disadvantages of entry, pledging that 'our sole commitment is to negotiate; no more, no less' (Conservative Party, 1970). However, the primary objective of Prime Minister Edward Heath, following his general election victory, was to secure entry. To achieve this, Heath encouraged the formation of the Conservative Group for Europe by pro-EU MPs. He also established the European Secretariat in the Cabinet Office, transferring responsibility for the negotiations from the Foreign Office to this new body. Having inherited Labour's team, Heath proceeded with negotiations between July 1970 and January 1972. The 1970 Conference carried a resolution offering conditional support for entry, subject to satisfactory terms, plus support for EU enlargement.

Following a meeting between Heath and Georges Pompidou in May 1971, the French President signalled that the veto would be lifted and that a third application would be successful. Heath duly published a White Paper in July, stressing the economic and political benefits of entry. It conceded that food prices would rise and that Britain's contribution to the EU budget may become a burden unless the CAP was reformed. However, it neglected to mention Economic and Monetary Union (EMU), even though the Six had already pledged to create a single currency by 1980. The White Paper also dismissed the notion that entry would undermine national sovereignty. That same month, the anti-EU Edward Taylor resigned in protest.

With the negotiations progressing well, and with public opinion moving in the required direction as a result of the Conservatives' second national pro-EU propaganda campaign (see Chapter 6), Heath decided to act. The House of Commons debated a motion in favour of entry in October 1971. As a result of the 69 Labour MPs defying their party whip, the motion was carried. In the final division on the 28th October, 356 MPs voted for entry and 244 against. However, 39 Conservative MPs voted against, whilst 2 abstained. In January 1972, Heath published the European Communities Bill. There were 104 votes during the Bill's passage, and although government majorities fell to single figures on 16 occasions, not one vote was lost. The biggest Conservative rebellion occurred in April, when 22 MPs supported an amendment calling for a referendum. However, supported by Labour, the government successfully defeated the amendment. Using the guillotine measure to expedite its passage, the bill was passed on the 17th October 1972. Britain joined the EU on the 1st January 1973.

At the 1971 Conference, a speech by the anti-EU Enoch Powell prompted Heath to call a vote of the delegates, resulting in a majority of 2,474 votes to 324 in favour of entry. The 1972 Conference carried a resolution urging the government to take positive initiatives in the EU, more specifically to shape the EU in Britain's 'national interest', whilst in February 1974, Powell, who had decided not to stand in the forthcoming general election, attacked Heath's European policy. He urged his supporters to vote Labour, on the basis that only the opposition had promised to renegotiate and to place the decision before the people. The Conservatives' manifestos for the 1974 general elections, however, favoured continued membership.

The 1975 Referendum

Several Conservatives played a key role in preparing for the referendum from early 1974 onwards (see Chapter 6). Although back in opposition, these figures continued their efforts in 1975. At Heath's request, the party's Deputy Chair helped to establish the cross-party Britain in Europe, whilst organising a series of one-day seminars to brief party activists. However, in February 1975 Margaret Thatcher replaced Heath as Party Leader and, although Thatcher had supported entry, she was not as vociferous as Heath in her enthusiasm.

Following Labour's renegotiation of the terms of continued membership in March 1975, the government published a White Paper on holding a referendum. In her maiden speech as Party Leader in the House of Commons, Thatcher challenged the principle of such a plebiscite on constitutional grounds. Nevertheless, MPs voted by 314 (including 5 Conservative MPs) to 262 in favour of a referendum, with the Conservatives officially opposed.

In April 1975, a government motion accepting the renegotiated terms was carried in the House of Commons by 396 votes to 170, with Conservative support. Thatcher insisted that continued membership would ensure peace and security, safeguard food supplies, and secure a future world role for Britain. However, there was some dissent: 8 Conservative MPs voted against the motion, whilst 18 abstained. Furthermore, two Conservative associations adopted an anti-EU position.

On the eve of the referendum, in which Thatcher had decided to campaign in *support of continued membership*, party agents were summoned to London and were instructed to use the constituency organisations to arrange meetings and to distribute literature. Thereafter, despite the efforts of Conservatives Against the Treaty of Rome, the infrastructure of the party was placed at the disposal of the Yes campaign. Following the vote in favour of continued membership in June, the 1975 Conference, acknowledging the result, called for the creation of a centre-right alliance in the European Parliament and urged the Conservatives to press the case for *Direct Elections*.

The Post-1975 Period

Support for a Stronger, United European Union (1976–77)

The 1976 Conference carried a resolution backing continued membership. However, it opposed unnecessary harmonisation proposals emanating from the European Commission. The Annual Conference also carried an amendment reiterating the party's support for Direct Elections.

Labour issued a White Paper on alternative electoral systems for the European elections in April 1977, making no explicit recommendation and agreeing to hold a free House of Commons vote. However, in July the bill was defeated by 394 votes to 147, whilst in

November, MPs voted by 319 to 222 to reject the government's preference of an open, regional list system in favour of 78 single-member constituencies. However, the Labour rebels abstained and the bill, reintroduced to parliament in 1978, was passed with the votes of Conservative and Liberal MPs, with only 9 Conservative MPs voting against. The 1977 Conference carried a resolution endorsing continued membership and calling for the Conservatives to help bring about a *stronger, united EU*, an objective reiterated by the 1978 Conference.

Meanwhile, Thatcher began to argue in favour of a confederation, insisting that 'we should continue to have a partnership of nation-states each retaining the right to protect its vital national interests' (in Biffen, 1977: 5). However, she repeatedly criticised the Labour government in 1978 for not joining the European Monetary System and its Exchange Rate Mechanism (ERM).

Reform of the EU (1979–84)

The Conservatives' manifesto for the 1979 General Election called for a 'common sense' EU that resisted excessive bureaucracy and unnecessary policy harmonisation. The party also pledged to *reform the EU*, specifically the Common Agricultural Policy (CAP), the EU Budget and the proposed Common Fisheries Policy (CFP). In the first direct elections to the European Parliament, three weeks after their general election victory, the Conservatives polled 48 per cent of the vote and gained 60 Members of the European Parliament (MEPs), compared to Labour's 32 per cent and 17 MEPs. Reflecting Thatcher's new confederal position, the 1979 Conference carried a resolution in support of close co-operation with other EU member states.

Thatcher's 1979 victory brought a change of style to Anglo-EU relations. Importantly, it was a stylistic rather than substantive change, for Thatcher, during her three terms in office, 'took Britain further into Europe than anyone except Heath' (Young, 1998: 306). The first objective of Thatcher's European policy was to revise Britain's contribution to the EU Budget, a policy endorsed by the 1980 Conference. The Annual Conference also carried a resolution in favour of a further national pro-EU propaganda campaign, which did not materialise, whilst the 1981 Conference condemned Labour's policy of withdrawal. After several years of negotiations, the 1984 Fontainebleau Agreement established a correction mechanism for dealing with budgetary imbalances, whilst Britain was granted an abatement.

The Conservatives' manifesto for the 1983 General Election condemned the Labour Party's policy of withdrawal, warning that 2 million jobs would be at risk, together with exports and foreign direct investment. However, it also condemned the uncritical policy of the Liberal-Social Democratic Party Alliance, stating that the Conservatives would secure a lasting solution to the EU Budget problem and would seek the removal of restrictions on the free movement of goods and services in the EU. Similar pledges were included in the manifesto for the 1987 General Election. In the 1984 European Election, the Conservatives polled 39 per cent of the vote and 45 MEPs, compared to Labour's 35 per cent and 32 MEPs.

Support for the Single Market (1985–)

Thatcher's second objective was the creation of a *single market*, which, through a policy of deregulation, she believed would lead to the formation of a 'free trade and free enterprise area' (Thatcher, 1992: 546). Lord Arthur Cockfield, appointed to the European Commission by Thatcher, was asked to prepare a plan for its implementation. Thatcher argued that a single market could be achieved through a non-legal agreement with implementation proceeding on the basis of unanimity, thus preserving the national veto, without any revision to the Treaty of Rome. At the 1985 EU Summit, the British proposal was defeated and an intergovernmental conference (IGC) was established to agree a new treaty. The price for the creation of the Single Market was the extension of qualified majority voting (QMV) to 12 new policy areas, plus a treaty commitment to introduce EMU. The bill incorporating the SEA into British law was presented to the House of Commons in April 1986, passing through all of its stages in six days. Following the imposition of the guillotine procedure in July, it was carried by 149 votes to 43, with 7 Conservative MPs voting against. In the late 1980s, the Conservatives launched Britain's fourth national pro-EU propaganda campaign, to sell the benefits of the EU and its Single Market (see Chapter 6).

Opposition to EMU and a Federal EU (1988–89)

Thatcher's third objective was to derail the federalist and social democratic plans of European Commission President Jacques Delors. She feared his 1988 prediction that 'in ten years, 80 per cent of economic legislation, and perhaps tax and social regulation', will be directed by the EU (quoted in Reynolds, 1991: 271). Furthermore, she opposed the European Commission taking advantage of its exclusive powers to initiate legislation, charged it with issuing directives using QMV where unanimity was required, and denounced Delors' speech at the 1988 Trades Union Congress at which he called for a social dimension to the Single Market. Thatcher's response to Delors was the 1988 Bruges speech in which she proclaimed that 'we have not successfully rolled back the frontiers of the state in Britain, only to see them re-imposed at a European level, with a European superstate exercising a new dominance from Brussels' (Thatcher, 1988).

Thatcher's fourth objective was to *resist EMU*. Following the Conservatives' abandonment of monetarism, some ministers began to view the exchange rate as the solution to the need for a new counter-inflationary strategy. Between 1983 and 1985, Foreign Secretary Geoffrey Howe and Chancellor Nigel Lawson lobbied the sceptical Bank of England and the Treasury to support the idea of ERM entry. Thatcher, however, opposed it. Nevertheless, Lawson began to secretly shadow the deutchsmark as if part of the ERM. Howe and Lawson produced a memorandum for Thatcher in preparation for the 1989 EU Summit, the main agenda item of which was Delors' plan for EMU. The memorandum argued that EMU would happen with or without British involvement, that ERM entry would provide Britain with some leverage over the future direction of EMU, and that British membership of EMU would preclude the development of a two-speed EU. Howe and Lawson threatened to resign if Thatcher did not reverse her opposition. She conceded defeat and duly announced that Britain would join the ERM. Following the Summit, Thatcher removed Howe from the Cabinet, whilst Lawson resigned. The new Chancellor, John Major, was fully committed to ERM entry but not to EMU. In a last ditch effort to forestall EMU, Major proposed a number of alternatives, which failed to elicit any support.

In the 1989 European Election, the Conservatives polled 35 per cent of the vote and gained 32 MEPs compared to Labour's 40 per cent and 45 MEPs. Pro-EU forces within the party became concerned at Thatcher's increasingly anti-EU populism. This rhetoric, together with the highly unpopular Poll Tax, led to her downfall.

Support for EMU and an Intergovernmental EU (1990–96)

Following Thatcher's succession by John Major in January 1990, anti-EU forces grew in number, exploiting Major's narrow majority of 21 after the 1992 General Election. Although the rhetorical aim of Major's European policy was to put Britain 'at the heart of Europe', his actual objectives were to create an intergovernmental and market economy-based EU. Major duly returned from the 1990–1991 IGCs having successfully lobbied for the partially intergovernmental Maastricht Treaty model and having negotiated opt-outs from the Social Chapter and stage 3 of EMU. Nevertheless, Britain participated in stage 1 of EMU and duly joined the ERM in October 1990. However in September 1992, Britain was ejected from the ERM following an attempt to defend the parity of sterling. Treasury papers released in February 2005 revealed that the debacle 'cost taxpayers a total of £3.3 billion' (Blitz and Newman, 2005).

The manifesto for the 1992 General Election declared that the Conservatives were the 'party of Europe'. However, it promised that the Conservatives would resist any further treaty changes that might damage business interests and would oppose the extension of EU competence. It endorsed the principle of subsidiarity and supported the defence of the British abatement, CAP reform, EU enlargement and the completion of the Single Market.

The Danish No vote in June 1992, coupled with the ERM disaster, encouraged anti-EU forces to stage a rebellion in an attempt to prevent the ratification of the Maastricht Treaty. The Danish No vote prompted a House of Commons motion, signed by 84 Conservative MPs, calling for the treaty to be abandoned. Major, however, was determined to ratify the treaty and thus *enable EMU*. Consequently, the parliamentary passage of the bill incorporating the Maastricht Treaty in British law witnessed several revolts. In April 1993, Labour helped the Conservatives to defeat an amendment demanding a referendum on the treaty. However, 38 Conservative MPs voted for a referendum, whilst 13 abstained. The battle culminated in the third and final reading in May in which the Conservatives secured a victory of 292 votes to 112, with Labour officially abstaining. A further division in July on Labour's amendment to incorporate the Social Chapter produced a 317 draw, with the Speaker casting her vote in favour. Major then presented a motion to accept the bill, and lost by 8 votes. The following day, Major held a confidence vote to overturn the vote of the previous day and the bill was passed by 39 votes.

Major attempted to quell the anti-EU rebellion in September 1993 by publishing an article re-emphasising his commitment to a Europe of nation-states. However, his U-turn on changing the rules governing QMV in February 1994 served to revive dissent, culminating in the withdrawal of the party whip from 8 anti-EU Conservative MPs in November. In the 1994 European Election, the Conservatives polled 27 per cent of the vote and obtained 18 MEPs, compared to New Labour's 43 per cent and 62 MEPs. Meanwhile, at the 1994 Annual Conference the former Chancellor, Norman Lamont (1995), attacked the EU declaring that 'if Britain was not a member of the EU today, I do not believe there would be a case to join'.

In an attempt to reassert his leadership, Major resigned in June 1995, challenging his critics to 'put up or shut up'. He refused to rule out future membership of the single currency, prompting the anti-EU John Redwood to make a bid for the leadership. However, Redwood was defeated and Major was re-elected. The Conservatives were increasingly under pressure from the Referendum Party during this period. Established in October 1995, this anti-EU party threatened to stand against pro-EU Conservative candidates in the forthcoming general election, prompting many candidates to issue sceptical personal manifestos. In December, Emma Nicholson MP defected to the Liberal Democrats as a result of the Conservatives' increasingly anti-EU rhetoric.

In April 1996, Major formally announced that a future Conservative government would not contemplate entering EMU without first holding a referendum. In June, the anti-EU Bill Cash, supported by 4 ex-cabinet ministers, submitted his Referendum Bill before parliament. Intended to establish 'who governs?' — and therefore answer the European question of whether Britain should be in or out of the EU once and for all — the bill was supported by 74 Conservative MPs.

The Conservatives' manifesto for the 1997 General Election, based on the theme 'we want to be in Europe but not run by Europe', defended the British nation-state and called for a partnership of nations. It specifically stated that a Conservative government would not allow Britain to be subsumed within a federal Europe, and pledged to defend Britain's abatement, its opt-outs, its veto power, and to oppose any extension of QMV. It supported participation in the talks about the launch of the European single currency, but was opposed to joining the first wave of countries to adopt the euro. It also promised to hold a referendum on euro entry if a future Conservative government believed that membership was in Britain's interest. Nevertheless, 20 candidates defied official party policy by supporting euro entry in their election addresses.

Opposition to Further European Integration (1997–)

As a result of the disastrous 1997 General Election result, Major resigned as Party Leader and was replaced by the anti-EU William Hague, who, together with subsequent party leaders, sought to halt any *further European integration*. In an effort to sideline pro-EU Conservatives, Hague conducted a ballot of party members to ascertain their views on the euro. Announced at the 1998 Conference, 85 per cent backed Hague's policy of ruling out euro entry for the 1997–2001 Parliament and the duration of the next. Nevertheless, the Conservatives' civil war over the EU generally, and the euro more specifically, persisted. Pro-EU figures such as Leon Brittan, Kenneth Clarke, Michael Heseltine, Douglas Hurd and Chris Patten openly attacked the party's euro policy, whilst anti-EU figures such as Norman Lamont, Michael Portillo, Norman Tebbit and Margaret Thatcher supported Hague in opposing the single currency.

In November 1997, in the second reading of the bill to incorporate the Amsterdam Treaty into British law, the House of Commons voted by 392 to 162 in favour of ratification, with 28 Conservative MPs abstaining. In the bill's third and final reading in January 1998, MPs voted by 370 to 145 to accept the treaty. For the first time, the Conservatives were officially opposed to signing an EU treaty. Nevertheless, despite a three-line whip, Clarke, Heath and Heseltine voted against official party policy.

Hague established the Policy Commission on the Pound Sterling in March 1999 to examine the implications for Britain's economy of joining the euro. The Commission reported its findings in September, stressing that euro entry was a political and not just an economic decision. Although it praised the Single Market and supported EU enlargement, it warned that euro entry would accelerate EU regulatory and tax harmonisation and thus further damage Britain's competitiveness. The report concluded that Britain should remain a member of the EU but stay out of the euro.

Before the 1999 European Election, two Conservative MEPs who were disqualified from standing because of their pro-EU stance launched the Pro-Euro Conservative Party. In the election, the Conservatives polled 36 per cent of the vote and gained 36 MEPs, compared to New Labour's 28 per cent and 29 MEPs.

On the eve of the 1999 Conference, Major delivered a speech in the US in which he predicted that British entry to the euro was inevitable if the single currency was a success. He also warned that Britain would face a decline in direct inward investment if it remained outside. At the 1999 Conference, Shadow Foreign Secretary John Maples stated that a future Conservative government would renegotiate the terms of continued membership, arguing that the only decisions that should be made at the EU level were those concerned with bringing about a free market and free trade. He specifically pledged to negotiate an amendment to the Treaty of Rome that would allow each country the freedom to decide whether or not to apply new EU legislation, arguing that this would stop the 'slide to a superstate'. He also promised to keep the pound, to oppose new regulatory burdens on business, to resist the erosion of the British veto and to reduce the power of the European Court of Justice. Meanwhile, Hague was careful not to entirely rule out joining the euro at some point in the future. Instead, he argued that Britain should not consider joining until at least the general election after next. At a fringe meeting at the 1999 Conference, Heseltine warned Hague not to listen to the 'incalculable folly' of those in the party who favoured withdrawal. Heseltine was joined by Kenneth Clarke who warned that the strategy of renegotiation was, for some, a 'cloak' for their real aim: withdrawal.

Hague delivered a speech in January 2000 in which he criticised the European Commission for seeking to produce a blueprint for a single European state. In March, a group of senior anti-EU Conservatives persuaded a US Senate committee to investigate the possibility of Britain joining the North American Free Trade Area (NAFTA), a move which would require withdrawal from the EU. However, the committee report, published in August, concluded that NAFTA entry would have 'minimal effects' on the British economy, whilst EU withdrawal from the EU would cause considerable damage.

The Conservatives' manifesto for the 2001 General Election pledged to veto any further transfer of power from Westminster to Brussels. It also promised to reduce the EU Budget, to resist euro entry, to oppose the development of an EU army outside of NATO, to form a transatlantic free trade area (incorporating the EU and NATFA) and to complete the Single Market. In the election, the party increased their number of seats by one in the 2001 General Election, prompting Hague's resignation. A new, two-stage selection procedure for choosing the Party Leader was introduced. In the first stage,

Conservative MPs would vote to decide which candidates should be included on the ballot papers. In the second stage, party members would vote on the MPs' selection. In September 2001, the anti-EU Iain Duncan Smith defeated Clarke by 155,933 votes to 100,864.

A Conservative amendment in the House of Commons in July 2001, calling for a referendum on the Nice Treaty, was defeated by 378 votes to 129, with one Conservative MP abstaining. In October, the bill incorporating the treaty into British law was carried by 392 votes to 158, with one Conservative MP voting in favour of ratification and 19 abstaining. The Tory Europe Network, committed to continued membership and euro entry, was launched in May of the following year.

At the 2003 Conference, Shadow Foreign Secretary Michael Ancram pledged that the Conservatives would deliver a petition to parliament demanding a referendum on the proposed European constitution. Meanwhile, Duncan Smith lost the confidence of the Conservative parliamentary party and in a ballot of MPs was defeated by 75 votes to 90. A contest was avoided when only one candidate was nominated; the anti-EU Michael Howard was declared Party Leader in November.

A Conservative motion in the House of Commons in March 2004, demanding a referendum on a future European constitution, was defeated by 328 votes to 212, with 19 Conservative MPs abstaining. In the 2004 European Election, the Conservatives polled 27 per cent of the vote and gained 27 MEPs, compared to New Labour's 23 per cent and 19 MEPs.

The Conservatives' manifesto for the 2005 General Election favoured the reform of the EU into a decentralised, flexible and liberal set of institutions. It rejected the euro and the European Constitution, offering a referendum on the latter within six months of the party being elected. It called for CAP reform and further EU enlargement (including Turkey). It opposed the development of an EU army outside of NATO, promised to withdraw from the CFP and pledged to restore Britain's opt-out from the Social Chapter.

The events of the 2005 leadership contest confirmed that the EU remains a divisive issue. A survey of 100 Conservative association chairs by *The Times* in September found that Clarke was the preferred leader by a majority of almost two to one over his nearest rival, David Davis. However, in November, in the first ballot among Conservative MPs, Clarke was ousted from the contest with only 38 out of the possible 198 votes. The final contest, decided by party members, was between David Cameron and David Davis. Cameron called for a Europe of nation-states, the return of employment and social policy to Westminster, and for the volume of new EU regulations to be reduced. He also pledged to withdraw Conservative MEPs from the federalist, centre-right European People's Party in the European Parliament. In December, Cameron was elected Party Leader by 67 per cent of the membership, compared to 32 per cent for Davis.

In December 2005, Conservative MEP Daniel Hannan organised the Congress of Brussels, attended by anti-EU right-wing politicians and think tanks from 30 countries. The event saw the launch of the Alliance for an Open Europe, a new grouping of MEPs in the European Parliament. Hannan announced that the new group opposed the current 'federal EU juggernaut', instead favouring the maximum devolution of power from the EU level and an EU based on free enterprise. That same month, the Conservative group of MEPs elected a pro-EU group leader rather than an anti-EU candidate by a two-thirds majority.

Conclusion

The Conservatives' European policy during the post-war period exhibits four main features. The first feature is that between 1945 and 1997, in contrast to the Labour Party, there was no difference in policy depending on whether the party was in government or in opposition. The Conservative leadership effectively shadowed the pro-EU policy of the Foreign Office during this period, whilst the Annual Conference, with the exception of a few minor rebellions (in 1961, 1969 and 1971), remained loyal to the Conservative leadership.

The second feature, again in contrast to the Labour Party, is the relative absence of internal division over European integration. Before 1992, although there were some modifications of policy, the Conservatives could indeed be described as the 'party of Europe'.

The third feature is the civil war over European integration that raged in the party between 1992 and 1996. Such a conflagration was widely believed to have contributed to the Conservatives' defeat in the 1997 General Election.

The fourth feature is the seismic policy shift that occurred in 1997 as the Conservatives entered their long period in opposition. Post-1997, anti-EU forces have tended to dominate the Conservative leadership (Hague, Duncan Smith, Howard and now Cameron) and hence the party's European policy.

Contrasting the state of affairs during the 1975 Referendum and the current situation is instructive in terms of assessing the present balance of power within the party. In 1975, the Conservatives were solidly in favour of European integration and the party dominated the Yes campaign. Current party policy, however, is to oppose further European integration, specifically euro entry and the European Constitution — although it remains committed to continued membership.

In terms of the future configuration of forces, the contours of Cameron's European policy remain unclear. In his quest for the 'centre ground' of British politics, he may curb the party's scepticism and attempt to re-establish the Conservatives as the 'party of Europe' in the eyes of the business sector and the electorate. However, defeating the anti-EU forces unleashed by Thatcher in her infamous Bruges speech in 1988 may not be easy, and he may fail. Much depends on the future direction of the EU itself. If the European Constitution is revived in 2007, and the process of further European integration continues (towards a single European state, a federal United States of Europe, or some form of hybrid of these), then the Conservatives may maintain their current opposition. If, however, the EU economy is further reformed in a neo-liberal direction and the EU continues to expand, necessitating a multi-speed and multi-level institutional framework, then the Conservatives may, once again, champion the cause of European integration.

Five
Trade Unions and Europe

Introduction

The British trade union movement is currently considered to be amongst the staunchest supporters of continued European economic and political integration amongst the British industrial and political elite. Certainly, TUC policy has remained firmly pro-European for the past seventeen years, and the closeness of links between British and European trade union leaders may be evidenced via the appointment of the former TUC General Secretary, John Monks, as General Secretary of the pan-European peak level organisation, the European Trade Union Confederation (ETUC).

There was, however, not always such apparent harmony amongst EU trade union organisations concerning support for further European integration. Indeed, trade union opposition towards EU membership was once as firmly rooted within the trade union movement as support for participation within integrationist projects now appears to be. Indeed, of all progressive organisations, one might anticipate that trade unions might be most sceptical about European economic integration due to the potentially damaging impact upon employment and social spending (Whyman, 2001). Thus, trade unionists tended to initially dismiss the EU as a 'big business' organisation, and thereby against the interests of workers and the wider citizenry, with subsequent policy stances oscillating between outright opposition to enthusiastic acceptance (see Table One).

Table 5.1 Chronology of British trade union policy towards European integration

Year	European Policy of the TUC	
1950	Opposition	Opposition to the Schuman Plan
1955	Support	Conditional support for European Integration
1962	Neutral	'Wait and see' approach, relating to the terms of entry
1971	Opposition	Opposition to Membership of EU on the terms negotiated by the UK Conservative government
1972	Opposition	Opposition to membership in principle
1974	Renegotiation	Renegotiation of the terms of UK membership of the EU
1975	Opposition; Reform	Advocated 'NO' vote in the referendum; thereafter, policy changed to acknowledge public opinion, but still promoted fundamental reform of the EU (i.e. budget, CAP)
1980	Withdrawal	Withdrawal from the EU — approved by Congress, but TUC leadership preferred offering support for integrationist initiatives conditional upon future reform of institutions and policies
1988	Support — based on social dimension	Following Delors speech at TUC Conference, policy shifted to support for European integration conditional upon the creation of a social dimension
1990	Support	Supported ERM entry (at lower central rate than the Conservative government)
1992	Support	Support for the Maastricht Treaty (EMU) without referendum
1995	Conditional support	Support for the revision of the Maastricht Treaty (EMU), complete with an employment chapter
1996	Conditional support	Support for an employment chapter to counter-balance EMU; supported EMU in principle
2000	Support	Support for enlargement of EU

This chapter seeks to describe the position taken by the British trade union movement at the 1975 referendum, detail the policy shifts that occurred thereafter, and thereby compare and contrast the shifting agenda over time.

The 1975 Referendum — Principal Issues

At the time of the 1975 referendum, the TUC had adopted a policy stance that rejected EU membership on the grounds that it had not been sufficiently reformed to be acceptable to trade unionists and their families. The terms of entry negotiated by the Conservative government were considered insufficient to counter the basic anti-worker bias inherent within the organisation and its priorities in terms of extending market allocation of scarce resources and the distribution of subsequent rewards. Nevertheless, this is not to obscure the fact that there existed a live debate within and between individual trade unions relating to the proper relationship Britain should have with the EU.

One method of teasing out some of the key issues which concerned trade unionists vis-à-vis non-union members involves the examination of speeches given at TUC Congress debates, concerning the issue of European integration and potential EU membership.

Pro-Membership

Arguments supportive of UK membership of the EU include the following:

- A larger 'home' market, established through the creation of the European SIM
- Stimulus to British trade — and hence jobs
- Entry would raise the British standard of living and create jobs
- The Treaty of Rome did not prohibit an interventionist economic policy
- Britain would lose influence outside the EU
- The EU was a means of controlling multinational capital
- Rejection of the EU would be an isolationist policy and betray internationalism
- 'Socialism in one country' was no longer possible
- Membership would benefit the British economy, and strengthen trade unions

This range of issues raised by ordinary trade unionists is quite impressive, despite the fact that the pro-membership referendum campaign preferred to concentrate upon issues such as the greater opportunities for trade leading to potentially higher living standards.

Anti-Membership

By contrast, counter arguments were more numerous, and included:

- EU membership would result in higher food prices—due to agricultural protectionism—and hence lead to higher inflation
- Membership would worsen Britain's balance of trade (hence balance of payments)
- EU membership would damage trade and links with the Commonwealth and other non-EU nations
- EU undermined parliamentary democracy
- EU membership *did* preclude an interventionist economic policy—hence it would limit a future Labour government's freedom of action
- Entry would favour the interests of capital and weaken organised labour
- EU membership was a barrier to creating socialism
- The objective of EU integration was political union
- EU membership threatened jobs and would undermine full employment
- The EU constituted a threat to trade union collective bargaining
- EU membership would threaten British public services
- EU membership would result in slower economic growth and damage the British economy

Once again, however, the vast majority of trade union speeches were concerned with the first four of these arguments, with the remainder being of minority interest. Hence, it is not surprising that the referendum campaign was fought on issues of price rises, more expensive food, the threat to jobs (through a worsening of the trade balance) and undermining of parliamentary democracy.

The balance of opinion, in 1975, tended to reach the conclusion that the EU was an undemocratic, bureaucratic extension of the interests of big business, designed to benefit multinational capital at the expense of citizens and workers (Nairn, 1972:7,66-73,147). A larger market facilitated economies of scale, which enhanced industrial profitability but also provided trans-national capital with the opportunity to threaten national workforces with dis-investment and the relocation of production abroad if wage concessions were not made or strikes abandoned. The free movement of capital, enshrined by the Treaty of Rome, could shift power resources in its favour against a trade union movement still primarily organised at national level, thereby creating the opportunity for capital exit and/or pressure for wage concessions in economies where trade unions were strongest. The location of trade unions within nation states implies that any weakening of democratic government autonomy potentially reduces the strength of national labour. Corporatist pacts in which organised labour exchanges wage moderation for increases in employment and an improved social wage are less feasible if governments have ceded control of their economic instruments. In addition, the free movement of labour would increase the potential supply of available workers, thereby undermining existing negotiated wage rates, whilst these immigrants, despite most economic studies concluding that long term benefits are likely to exceed long term costs, they may place (at least temporary) pressure upon welfare benefits, housing stock and other public services (Sinn and Ochel, 2003).

Regional economic integration would weaken the UK economy, as it would reinforce the UK's contemporary uncompetitive position relative to other EU member states, causing deterioration in the UK balance of payments position. This, in turn, would undermine UK attempts to maintain a fixed exchange rate under conditions of full employment and rapid economic growth. This characterisation mirrored what Thirwall (1982) described as balance of payments constrained economic development, as successive governments would be caused to deflate the economy, causing unemployment and slowing economic growth rates, to prevent the balance of payments deficit from growing out of control. Admittedly, the UK's subsequent experience has proven that floating has removed the immediacy of this problem for policy makers. Nevertheless, a persistent balance of payments deficit remains a problem which governments will have to ultimately deal with through devaluation, hence reducing the relative living standards of UK citizens, or else persist with a high interest rate policy to encourage the necessary inflow of long and short term capital movements into the UK to balance the equation — hardly the basis for a long term economic strategy characterised by a high level of domestic investment and capital formation. Thus, sooner or later, British manufacturing jobs would be lost.

Joining the EU was also considered to have a negative inflationary impact. This was due to a largely one-off upward shift in agricultural prices, together with the effect of higher tariffs that the UK would have to impose upon non-EU trade in other goods and services, including especially semi-finished manufactured products. Furthermore, the EU's agricultural protectionism would fracture the UK's close relationship with many Commonwealth nations, where preferential trading relations stimulated desirable economic development in lesser developed countries (LDC's). Indeed, the fact that EU membership would result in the UK having to raise tariffs against the LDC's in general would undermine internationalism in its wider sense of promoting mutual understanding and co-operation between nations (Nairn, 1972:7,66–73,147).

The constraints upon government policy autonomy, imposed by EU membership, were additionally perceived as proving problematic for the type of 'Keynes-plus' interventionist economic policy strategy at that time favoured by the British trade union movement. The free movement of capital undermines the maintenance of full employment as high rates of fiscal expenditure and the pursuit of a 'cheap money' strategy may cause capital to flow out of the economy in search of better returns and to avoid the risk of currency depreciation, thereby causing a currency crisis and decline in investment. Furthermore, trade unionists argued that EU membership would limit the scope for a Labour government to create democratic socialism within the UK, through the extension of public ownership, and active industrial policy and prioritisation of full employment through macroeconomic policy — Keynesianism — later personified in the Alternative Economic Framework in the early 1980s. This sought to extend national control over economic forces and secure a sustainable reflation strategy through a combination of protectionism, active industrial policy and expansionary Keynesian demand management (Hill, 2001:167; Daniels, 2003:227).

Finally, the timing of the referendum, in 1975, coincided with the height of British trade union power. The miners had recently succeeded with a strike that ultimately witnessed the downfall of the Heath Conservative government, and the TUC was sufficiently confident that British trade unions were sufficiently strong to protect their members and advance their interests. Moreover, a perception of divisions across continental European trade unionism, along political and religious grounds, detracted from the proposal that British trade union members' interests could be better advanced through common cause with continental union movements. The TUC General Secretary, Len Murray, was cited by John Edmonds, in the sister volume to this book, as arguing that 'the most important decisions about our future can only be taken here in Britain' (Edmonds, 2006).

The Aftermath of the Referendum — From Opposition to Conditional Support

The result of the 1975 referendum was a set-back to trade union policy towards the regional integration project. Unions had sought to mobilise members behind the defence of a 'Keynes-plus' economic programme and protection of public services and British jobs, and yet had decisively lost the argument. Admittedly, the 'Yes' campaign benefited from a vast superiority in terms of campaign resources, both financial and availability of paid campaign staff (Mullen and Burkitt, 2004). Moreover, the fact that senior figures in the Labour government opposed party policy and spoke at pro-membership rallies probably blunted the TUC message. Nevertheless, the result highlighted the problems that the trade unions were having in influencing the hearts and minds of their own membership — a factor highlighted by the fact that the election of the 1979 Thatcher government would not have been possible without the support of a large swathe of trade union members at the time.

The response from the trade union movement was a reluctant acceptance of the referendum verdict, but continued criticism of the worst aspects of the EU organisation and policy, from a trade union perspective, such as continued agricultural protectionism, undemocratic and bureaucratic organisation, the absence of a macroeconomic strategy aimed at securing full employment and so forth (Strange, 1997:16). The increasingly positive nature of the Labour Party leadership towards EU membership and continued regional integration, with the short exception of the Michael Foot term of office (1980–1983), no doubt influenced trade union opinion — particularly those moderate unions whose strategy emphasises loyalty to the political wing of the labour movement ahead of perhaps more perceptive criticism on a range of issues. Furthermore, there had arisen a powerful hegemony within the British labour movement that globalisation posed a serious threat to 'traditional' forms of social democracy, and therefore that deeper regional integration provided at least one means of re-imposing control over trans- national capital and hence providing the foundations for a 'Euro- Keynesian' agenda (Baker et al, 1996). Euro-scepticism therefore appeared to be concentrated amongst a small group of the 'old' Left, thereby forming a 'declining legacy of Labour's past' with the party's 'centre of gravity ... shifted decisively in favour of Europe and EMU' (Strange, 1997:15).

The turning point for the TUC came at its 1998 Congress when Jaques Delors, the then Head of the EU Commission, outlined his vision of a 'social Europe' which embraced labour rights as core elements. This vision of a social democratic Europe proved extremely tempting to a trade union movement marginalised from political influence by successive Conservative governments, and having haemorrhaged membership due to mass unemployment and laws restricting major aspects of trade unionism. Furthermore, it was seen by many trade unionists that the process was inevitable, and that, despite reservations, they may as well accept this fact and therefore seek to deal with the consequences (Verdun, 2000:143-6,170-1). Hence, Ron Todd, General Secretary of the Transport and General Workers Union (T&GWU), moving the TUC General Council report, felt able to state that, whatever the weaknesses with it in terms of trade union interests, that European integration was 'the only card game in town'.

Factors Influencing the Shift in Trade Union Policy

Economics

An initial factor in the marginalisation of the Euro-sceptics within organised labour, derives from a change in the economic strategy supported by the leading figures in the labour movement, namely a shift from a more 'traditional' form of social democracy, emphasising full employment (to be secured through Keynesian policy) and social solidarity, and a neo-liberal form of 'new' social democracy, characterised most recently by discussion of the 'Third Way' (Whyman, 2006). As a result, the economic programme articulated by the trade union movement has undergone a similar evolution. Whereas policy used to emphasise the importance of competitive exchange rates, typically ensured through managed floating, the maintenance of full employment through active labour market and fiscal policies, together with the easing of monetary policy to encourage long term investment in productive industry, the TUC economics has more recently adopted an alternative, more orthodox strategy. Devaluation is rejected as 'anti worker' because it reduces real incomes and therefore makes employees pay for the failures of British industry to maintain their competitiveness through reductions in spending power. Moreover, neo-liberal analysis is partially accepted in so far as changes in nominal exchange rates are not *necessarily* reflected in changes to *real* values, suggesting that changes in exchange rates are not necessarily very effective at adjusting the real economy of employment and output.

Fixed exchange rates are considered preferable to variable, floating exchange rates, as they reduce uncertainty and should theoretically create an optimum climate for business decision-making, thereby boosting long-term investment. This change of emphasis caused the TUC to advocate membership of the Exchange Rate Mechanism (ERM) two years prior to UK participation (Strange, 1997:18). This involved the acceptance of the loss of monetary policy sovereignty together with the readjustment of the remainder of macroeconomic policy to secure a similar inflation rate to that of Germany. Failure to match or better German inflation rates would reduce UK competitiveness and, under conditions of fixed exchange rates, this would require considerable sacrifice to regain the former position, involving increases in unemployment, company bankruptcies and/or real wage cuts. The GMB and MSF, two of the largest and forward-thinking TUC-affiliated unions, were firm supporters of the ERM introducing a 'new realism' into pay bargaining by disciplining all participants to reach appropriate agreements. The union suggested that companies and governments would be additionally forced to recognise the fact that the main cause of UK competitiveness was due to under investment in productive capacity (Strange, 1997).

In view of the loss of monetary and exchange rate policy independence associated with ERM membership, the further step towards EMU membership is perceived as less threatening than it would be had the previous policy of competitive exchange rates been maintained. Supporters of EMU argue that it will produce a higher growth, more dynamic economy. The transparency of prices for goods and services now denoted in a single currency should intensify competition and lead to downward pressure on prices. The operation of the European Central Bank (ECB) should further eradicate inflationary pressure due to its sole operational objective being to achieve price stability. Lower inflation should feed through into lower long-term interest rates, with a consequent stimulus to investment, output and economic growth. To the extent that this scenario is produced by participation in EMU, trade union members should benefit through enhanced employment opportunities and rising living standards.

Fears that unwarranted exchange rate 'discipline' would result in deflation and higher levels of unemployment were at least partly assuaged by a commitment from the EU Commission to place greater emphasis upon employment matters, cumulating in the Luxembourg jobs summit in November 1997 (Monks 2000,186–7). Thus, despite the Luxembourg 'jobs summit' producing little of any consequence, the trade union viewpoint was that concerted action by all EU partners would reflate the European economy with fewer negative side effects, irrespective of whether such co-operation was truly on the political agenda. Unfortunately, the persistence of mass unemployment across most EU member states has yet to stimulate an adequate strategy to resolve the problem. Neither has it proved of sufficient importance for an unemployment target to be enshrined in an international treaty obligation, similar to the objectives of price stability as specified in the Maastricht Treaty.

European Social Model (ESM)

A second, and altogether more important factor encouraging British organised labour to support further European integration was the belief that EMU was 'part of the EU package' which included the establishment of a 'European Social Model' (ESM) (Verdun, 2000:143-6). In effect, the proposal made by Delors was that if trade unions:

> ... put up with the competitive pressures of a single market ... the social dimension will protect you from the worst excesses of laissez-faire capitalism. That is the deal and trade unionists have bought into it (Edmonds, 2000:194).

A variant of the post-war German 'Social Market Model', a fully developed ESM is intended to counter-balance the disruptive effects which can emanate from a successful, competitive market economy, through the provision of generous welfare provision and labour protection (Glasman 1997; Harding 1999). It is by means of this social pact or class compromise that the co-operation of employees can be successfully sought in relation to industrial restructuring when required by changes in global demand patterns. If workers have to bear the full cost of industrial restructuring, through loss of income through unemployment, relocation costs and loss of seniority (hence lower income), they are rational to oppose industrial change. However, continual innovation is necessary to maintain international competitiveness in the long run. Thus, society can strike a bargain with its citizens to absorb a substantial proportion of costs associated with the disruption inherent within a dynamic economy. The emphasis upon the inclusion of workers and their unions in the working of the economy facilitates an expression of 'voice' rather than 'exit'. This, in turn, leads to co-operation in adapting to change, superior morale resulting in enhanced productivity and lower employee turnover, and finally the prevention of low-skill, low investment competitive alternatives stimulates productive investment and innovation (Streeck 1992,5; Hutton 1994; Coates 1999,654-5).

Compensation can take the form of generous unemployment benefit replacement ratios, mobility grants and government sponsored retraining programmes. Moreover, to encourage risk-taking behaviour from normally risk-averse employees, society can subsidise investment in human capital on the grounds that society itself benefits from a more educated workforce in addition to those private benefits accruing to individual workers and firms. Comprehensive medical care can improve economic efficiency by removing many causes of lost working time and ensuring a healthy workforce. Childcare and social services for the elderly can release individuals of working age to contribute to the paid economy. The combination of a more universal system of social policy with increased labour regulation should produce partial labour de-commodification and thereby enhance trade union power resources (Korpi 1985; Esping-Andersen 1990).

A fully developed ESM should additionally incorporate trade unions as a legitimate social partner and counterpoint to organised business organisations, thereby promoting employee involvement in relevant aspects of working life at both local and super-national level. This feature was particularly attractive during the late 1980s, when unions were excluded from political influence and legal restrictions weakened their ability to deliver traditional industrial benefits to their members. The substitution of an alternative sphere of influence thus provided a new legitimate role for unions to fulfil and thereby justified continued membership. Accordingly, the

ETUC has been given a direct involvement in the design of social legislation for the EU. Moreover, if it can reach agreement with its federal counterparts, Union of Industrial Employers' Confederation of Europe (UNICE) and European Centre of Enterprises with Public Participation (CEEP), representing business opinion in the private and public sector accordingly, this unified position will form the basis of a Directive. This procedure should have two effects; the improvement of legislative operational flexibility and the simultaneous establishment of a precedent for further initiatives in Euro-corporatism (Edmonds, 2000:194).

The EU Commission has provided significant material support to facilitate social partnership between trade unions and employer organisations, whilst simultaneously promoting a European version of collective bargaining. This support has proved highly significant for the ETUC, rising from 5-8% of its total income in the early years of integration, to approximately 13% as the single internal market programme was introduced (Knutsen, 1997). The EU additionally supplies the ETUC with free meeting venues and interpreters, together with providing travel subsidies and technical assistance as a means of facilitating consultative processes in which it has an interest (Abbott 1997,472). UNICE has estimated that the level of subsidies between 1992 and 1994 totalled approximately Euro57 million, whilst the establishment of European Works Councils (EWCs) will have further increased union subsidies (Knutsen 1997,300) Consequently, the ETUC has a direct financial interest in supporting further European integration since a significant proportion of its activities are financed by EU sources and would otherwise not take place.

One final aspect of an ESM concerns its construction upon the basis of international treaty. This provides considerable protection for its matrix of social protection measures from the election of radical, neo-liberal government intent to dismantle what it would regard as an impediment upon work incentives. For British trade unions, so battered by the radical conservatism of former Conservative Prime Minister, Margaret Thatcher, an ESM, created within the protective boundaries of international treaty, provides a bulwark against the potential of the re-election of national governments intent upon the elimination of market imperfections, such as the trade unions themselves, and dismantling significant elements of the corporatist-welfare state model. Thus, John Edmonds (2000,191), former GMB General Secretary, felt able to claim that the ESM offered workers an alternative to worsening job insecurity and the uncertainty created by 'flexible' labour markets.

The combination of material support for a beleaguered trade union movement, and the possibility of the EU establishing its distinct variant of an ESM, together provide powerful reasons for the union leadership to overlook a degree of scepticism concerning the European integration project and to embrace EMU. Of-course, the case for joining EMU would be more compelling had the EU actually established a comprehensive ESM as outlined, above. In reality, such a social construction remains an unrealised aspiration. There is not, as yet, a European industrial relations system, nor a comprehensive European social policy. By contrast, the current form of social dimension being constructed across the EU is a minimalist version of a fully-fledged system of social protection of the kind operated by Germany or Scandinavian member states. However, even this minimalist scheme has delivered some notable benefits to employees, including the provision of a degree of protection for workers involved in company take-overs, improved health and safety protection, and has given workers a small but nevertheless significant influence over the strategies of European Trans-National Corporations (TNCs).

Counter-Arguments and the Contemporary Debate

The available evidence points towards the existence of a clear majority of trade unionists, in addition to UK citizenry at large, that accepts continued membership of the EU, whether due to a belief that it is in the national interest or due to a reluctant feeling that there is little alternative. Consequently, the trade union debate has become focused upon arguing over the merits of current and future initiatives, such as whether the UK should participate in EMU and/or the fate of the European Constitution (presently indeterminate). Indeed, the TUC appears to have adopted a stance consistent with avoiding internal conflict over these issues by deferring debate and thereby allowing the current relationship to continue developing subject to little scrutiny and accountability to the wider membership. One reason for this position may reflect the internal acknowledgement of a deeper split amongst trade union rank and file, and indeed between individual trade unions themselves, on these issues. It may additionally reflect the fact that the dominant trade union strategy, that of qualified support for continued European integration, may itself be called into question for failing to deliver the required results for working people. Instead, qualified acceptance of new initiatives as part of an overall, sophisticated bargain is all too often perceived as unqualified support for the process due to its own merits. Though critics are willing to expose this weakness in relation to EMU and *further* integration initiatives, few have done so in recent years in relation to membership of the EU itself. Yet, this is not to say that this will not happen — particularly if one or more of the arguments utilised by supporters of regional integration are found to be wanting.

The trade union stance supporting regional economic integration appears to be essentially rational if a number of assumptions are made. Firstly, the economic case for continued participation in wider and deeper EU integration depends upon an assessment that this has proved to be a net economic benefit for the nation in the past, and is likely to continue to be so in the future. Whilst there is disagreement over the measurement of many related phenomena, it seems reasonably certain that net *historical* costs to the UK economy relate to the large net budgetary contributions (circa £55 billion), a net trade deficit with EU member states (circa £100 billion), price inflation stemming from agricultural subsidies (through CAP), and the costs of regulation arising from EU sources (Burkitt *et al.*, 1996; Deva, 2002; Milne, 2004; Minford et al., 2005; Baimbridge and Whyman, 2006). The impact of the completion of the European single market (SIM) is difficult to discern, although it is probable that benefits arising from economies of scale, industrial rationalisation and lower prices due to competitive pressures may indeed outweigh costs associated with increased unemployment (at least in the short run transition period). However, even this evidence is not so clear cut, because the distribution of the benefits is skewed towards big business whilst workers may suffer job losses and smaller potential for wage increases as a result of the changes. Furthermore, reliance upon current and future initiatives to provide a clear net benefit to the UK is itself unwise, as estimates of the impact of participation in EMU looks equally problematic for supporters of further European integration (Holland, 1995; UNCTAD, 1996; Strange, 1997; Arestis and Sawyer, 2000; Baimbridge and Whyman, 2006).

Secondly, the shift made by the British labour movement in economic policy stance must be justified on the basis that more 'traditional' forms of Keynesianism is no longer workable under contemporary conditions of globalisation (Hall, 1987; Teeple, 1995; Mishra, 1999:95). Indeed, it has been suggested that the space available for different models of capitalism has so narrowed that institutions are no longer able to make a significant difference, and therefore sustaining alternatives to market-led capitalism are proving extremely difficult, if not impossible (Monbiot, 2000). This implies that 'luxuries' such as full employment, redistribution and the development of a universalistic welfare state can no longer be afforded due to greater economic constraints (Hay, 1999:29). Nevertheless, although it appears to have been persuasive within labour movement circles, this view is not universally accepted. For example, counter arguments embrace claims that globalisation is overstated (Hirst and Thompson, 1996; Berger and Dore, 1996). Moreover, Rodrik (1996) has demonstrated that, far from those economies that are the most integrated into the world economy suffering a 'shrinkage' of government, there is actually a positive correlation between openness and the share of government expenditure in GDP, due to the ability of government to act as an insulator against external shocks.

There is additionally little convincing evidence to indicate that globalisation has undermined the efficiency of institutional frameworks within which economic policy operates (Garrett, 1995). Globalisation does not have the depressing impact upon taxation and public expenditure that some theorists may claim, whilst there exists a *positive* and statistically significant association between capital mobility and the effective tax rate (Kopits, 1992; Swank, 1998). Furthermore, Wade (1996:108) notes that the vast bulk of a nation's resources are relatively immobile, including physical and human capital, and therefore governments can invest in education, infrastructure, targeted industrial support and facilitation of the development of business networks in order to enhance the advantages of immobility and proximity for individual companies. The 'embeddedness of companies in national institutions' provides information and a means of co-ordination between firms to secure common objectives, facilitates the development of a cluster of skilled labour and a technical supply chain specialising in the specific activity of the firm, thereby reducing the uncertainty arising from a dynamic business environment (Hirst and Thompson, 2000:306; Zysman, 2000:120-3). A 'national system of innovation' can be extremely successful in developing international competitive advantage (Porter, 1990; Patel and Pavitt, 1991). Indeed, a number of studies have pointed to capital market integration being associated with growing divergence in fiscal policy between nation states due to the continued influence upon domestic economic policy resulting in large part from the strength of organised labour (Garrett, 1995, 1998 and 2000). Thus, not only have national economies far more room for manoeuvre than they may themselves realise, but that the strength and determination of national labour movements is itself a key influence upon whether governments take advantage of this possibility and realise progressive policy goals.

The conclusion reached by this critical literature is that, although globalisation may have imposed minor constraints upon the operation of Keynesian macroeconomic measures, it has not fatally undermined the strategy. Rather it has been the 'fear of globalised capital' that has led to the retreat of the progressive-Left (Hirst and Thompson, 1996; Hirst, 1999:88; Watson, 1999a:155; Grant, 2002:49). Consequently, Aspinwall (2003:146) is correct in his assertion that:

> the question of whether to sacrifice domestic autonomy in favour of European integration is one of the most volatile and passionately discussed issues in British politics.

Thirdly, that whatever sacrifices the trade union movement is forced to make in order to help to legitimise the European integration project, it results in the creation of an ESM sufficient to counterbalance excessive pressures on employees emanating from a combination of the single market and EMU. Existing directives have ensured a degree of protection for employees in cases of collective redundancies, restrictions on working hours, the establishment of European Works Councils, minimum maternity rights, enhanced health and safety protection and equal treatment for workers on irregular contracts. However, whilst unfair to dismiss such achievements as meaningless, nor treat the social dimension as though it were a complete and coherent approach, it is nevertheless grossly insufficient for the EU Commission to portray this as a distinct ESM (see Table Two).

The high fragmentation of social policy within, and between, EU member states implies that European regulation is only possible for non-contentious issues, where nations share common interests and goals, such as health and safety matters. Otherwise, social protection will occur only at the lowest common denominator (Eichener, 1996; Keller and Sorries, 1997:93). Thus, the presentation of the EU's social dimension as the basis for a social citizenship is premature, as the existing minimalist safety-net framework has little measurable impact outside member states with particularly weak regulation. Indeed, Barnard and Deakin (1997:131) suggest that the ESM is noth-

Table 5.2 – Comparison Between Fully Developed ESM and Current EU 'Social Dimension'

	EU Social Dimension	European Social Model
Welfare State		
– Type	Minimalist	Comprehensive
– Coverage	Safety net	Universal
– Replacement Ratio	Low	High
– Association with labour market	Re-commodification	De-commodification
– Response to globalisation	Competitive – improve labour market skills	Protective – social citizenship requires non-market income source to make effective choices
Industrial Relations		
– Recognition of collective bargaining	Patchy	High/Comprehensive
– Corporatist	Diverse – some member states deregulated wage formation, whilst others rely upon social contracts to secure budget cuts	Established – facilitates superior inflation:employment trade-off
– Euro-level IR	Minimum – EWC, consultation only	Developed – framework bargaining between federal-level social partners
– Labour regulation	Minimum – complements single market; over-regulation impedes competitiveness	Fundamental – basis of social accord, combining industrial adjustment with employee protection

ing more than an 'eclectic body of employment law', whilst others claim the approach has a 'hollow core' (Leibfried, 1994:246; Leibfried and Pierson, 1995). Although it may have been successful in enticing trade union support for further European integration (Keller and Sorries, 1997:78), Streek (1992:218-9) considers the 'retarded advancement of European-level political rights' and the 'almost complete absence of an European system of industrial citizenship' as indicating that there is little reason to anticipate these initiatives to prove particularly successful.

It is possible to criticise this rather negative conclusion by suggesting that gaps in the EU social dimension will be progressively filled and it will ultimately evolve into a variant of an ESM. However, this ignores the increasingly vocal neo-liberal critique of the high taxes and supposed welfare dependency associated with welfare states, the labour market rigidity and costs for business arising from labour regulation and centralised wage bargaining, as causes of 'Eurosclerosis' and a decline in relative economic performance (Feldstein, 1974 and 1976; Lawrence and Schultz, 1987; Minford, 1990). Despite the evidence being rather mixed (Korpi, 1985 and 1996; Jackman et al, 1990:483; Barr, 1992; Rhodes, 1992:29), this neo-liberal argument has been at least partially adopted by leading European politicians, as demonstrated by British Prime Minister, Tony Blair, emphasising the need for all EU member economies to restructure their traditional approaches to social welfare and labour regulation. Indeed, in a recent speech[1], Blair pointedly rejected the 'old social model' in Europe, and argued that 'our welfare systems and labour markets will require fundamental reform'. This is consistent with a recent statement made by the ECB's senior economist, Otmar Issing, who blamed the poor performance of the Euro on 'the adverse impact of minimum wage and employment protection legislation', which can only be overcome by a 'comprehensive programme of structural reform'.[2]

In practice, this consists of creating what Cerny (1990) describes as a transition from welfare state to 'competition state', in which policies are determined by the perceived demands of survival in the global economy. Yet, this is in direct conflict with the ESM approach, as universal welfare provision is replaced by education, training and

---

[1] Blair, A. (2000), *Managing Change: A National and International Agenda of Reform?*, speech given at the World Economic Forum, Davos, Switzerland, 28 January.
[2] Cited in *The Guardian*, 13 May 2000, pg. 24.

mobility measures designed to enhance productivity and increase employment levels. Moreover, it would re-commodify individuals, albeit provide them with the opportunity to develop more skills and therefore be better placed in the labour market. Consequently, it appears paradoxical that British trade union leaders are relying upon the completion of an ESM to provide them with a preferable system of social protection and employee participation in the work process, when EU governments are increasingly questioning the future of this very model. Whether due to concerns over the future ability to afford generous levels of welfare expenditure, or due to a desire to restructure social policy to aid international competition rather than provide a sanctuary from commodification, the ESM approach looks less viable as a future model for Euro-land than in previous circumstances.

The final element of a fully-fledged ESM, namely the Europeanisation of industrial relations and wage bargaining, remains problematic. Whilst the EWC initiative does provide a potential basis for facilitating co-operation and the pooling of information between EU trade unions, this looks unlikely to lead onto a form of pattern bargaining, particularly since employer groups and big business are equally determined that this type of co-ordination of the market will not occur (Teague, 1991; Rhodes, 1992:45). It is, moreover, possible that the creation of a European labour market may be limited to certain key groups of workers, possessing specific technical and managerial skills, and for particular categories of highly mobile labour, notably managers, construction workers, labourers and young people (Walsh *et al*, 1995:85). This would further exacerbate income inequality and fracture national systems of wage bargaining (Marsden, 1992:593). In such circumstances, it is possible that workers adopt group egoist rather than class solidarity perspectives and unions may fragment along supranational company lines, with unions risking becoming 'partners ... of regional capital trying to survive in inter-regional free market competition' rather than 'agents of inter-regional redistribution' (Streeck and Schmitter, 1991:55).

There are, additionally, a second group of factors, which may cause a general decentralisation of industrial relations systems. The intensification of international competition has led many companies, particularly TNCs, to focus upon internal labour markets to establish multiple cost centres and implement initiatives to tailor working conditions to their specific business requirements in order to react flexibly to changing patterns of demand. Advances in information technology have facilitated a shift from administrative to performance-based control, with responsibility and accountability devolved to business units at lower levels of large organisations (Sisson and Marginson, 1995). These systems of 'managed autonomy', in which central management maintains control through an extensive web of formal and informal performance measures, place a premium on the bottom-line responsibility of individual business unit managers for labour as well as other costs. Multi-employer bargaining is ill suited to this process (Marginson and Sisson, 1996:177-8). Furthermore, there is a claim that deregulatory pressures are the consequence of a 'paradigm shift' from Fordist to post-Fordist industrial organisation, implying a duality of labour markets split between core and periphery workers. Thus, trade unions face being marginalised due to an employers preference for company-level 'productivity coalitions' rather than centralised concertation or sectoral bargaining (Lash and Urry, 1987; Windolf, 1989). According to this viewpoint, Euro-bargaining is irrelevant to the needs of post-Fordist flexible production (Rhodes, 1992:28).

The divergent tensions, threatening to further complicate European industrial relations, are likely to persist into EMU because current arrangements show no clear evidence of converging to a uniform pattern across Euro-land. Demands for greater firm-centred flexibility fit very poorly with the macroeconomic imperative of maintaining wage moderation and thereby international competitiveness. Hence, the most likely prediction is for an uneven and spasmodic development of industrial relations, with the eventual emergence of an ad hoc, partly institutionalised system of pan-European labour relations (Rhodes, 1992:43-44). Irrespective of the eventual evolution of industrial relations throughout Europe, trade unions face increasing challenges. One problem concerns the changing composition of the European labour market and lower unionisation amongst groups being increasingly represented in the labour force and in the expanding sectors of the manufacturing and particularly service sectors. Another relates to the tension between union objectives of social solidarity and maintaining membership through delivery of real material benefits. The former may be better served by national or sectoral wage formation, where employers and government may participate to secure aggregate wage moderation, whilst the latter may be best achieved by decentralised bargaining for workers in the most profitable companies.

Conclusion

The contemporary trade union perspective has evolved significantly from its position in 1975. Opposition to EU membership has been gradually relegated to a minority position, whilst the major current debates concern the future direction of the EU itself — i.e. whether to develop as a market-dominated or 'social model' form of society. Disagreements persist concerning whether or not the UK should join EMU, and whether the EU should have a formal constitution. Moreover, strategic differences hamper the development of trade union strategy towards issues like the development of a European labour market, and if this was to occur, concerning the precise activities of the trade union movement within this new institutional creation.

There are, however, a number of themes that, although not featuring in mainstream trade union discourse at present, may potentially arise if the integrationist 'project' fails to deliver the type of ESM that the trade unions desire, and have made the basis for their qualified support for further regional economic integration.

Six

Public Opinion and Europe

Introduction

Contrary to expectations, the referendum on continued European Union (EU)[1] membership in June 1975 did not settle the European question—whether Britain should be in or out of the EU. More than thirty years later, the European question remains to be settled, whilst the battle for British hearts and minds on European integration goes on.

This chapter, divided into nine sections, surveys the state of public opinion on the EU since its formation, highlighting the volatility of British attitudes towards European integration. The first eight sections discuss the state of public opinion from the 1950s to the present, whilst the ninth section concludes, contrasting the current state of public opinion with that during the 1975 Referendum. These changes are discussed within the context of Britain's shifting policy on the EU and the many attempts that have been made to influence public opinion. The political elite—more specifically the civil service and the leaderships of the Conservative Party and the Labour Party—has repeatedly resorted to propaganda campaigns in an attempt to manufacture consent for British participation in the European integration process. Propaganda is understood in the sense outlined by Carey (1995: 20): 'Propaganda refers to communications where the form and content is selected with the single-minded purpose of bringing some target audience to adopt attitudes and beliefs chosen in advance by the sponsors of the communications'. Carey advanced a two-level model to explain how such campaigns seek to influence

[1] For simplicity, the post-war project of European economic and political integration is henceforth referred to as the European Union (EU), rather than its previous titles of Common Market, European Economic Community or European Community.

public opinion. 'Grassroots' propaganda campaigns seek 'to reach as vast a number of people as possible in order to change public opinion', whereas 'treetops' propaganda, is 'aimed at the leaders of society'. The former aims to directly shape the attitudes, beliefs and values of the general public, whilst the latter seeks to influence public opinion indirectly. As we shall see, anti- and pro-EU forces attempted to utilise both national and targeted 'grassroots' and 'treetops' propaganda campaigns in their quest to influence public opinion on the EU. These propaganda campaigns are summarised in Table 6.1.

Table 6.1 — Anti- and Pro-EU Propaganda Campaigns in Britain (1945–2004)

Year	Campaign	Objective	Main Organiser(s)
1940s/1950s	Targeted	European Federation	American Committee on United Europe/European Movement/European Youth Campaign/Federal Union
1962	National	Securing British entry	Conservative Government
1971	Targeted	Resisting British entry	Labour Party
1971	Targeted	Resisting British entry	Trades Union Congress
1971	National	Securing British entry	Conservative Government/European Movement
1975	National	Maintaining British membership	Labour Government/Britain in Europe
1975	National	Securing British withdrawal	National Referendum Campaign/Trades Union Congress
1982	Targeted	Securing British withdrawal	Trades Union Congress
1983	Targeted	Opposing British withdrawal	European Movement
1988	National	Promoting Single Market	Conservative Government
1989	Targeted	Promoting Social Chapter	Trades Union Congress

Year	Campaign	Objective	Main Organiser(s)
1990	Targeted	Promoting Single Market	Ken Coates MEP with Michael Barratt Brown and Stuart Holland
1993	Targeted	Promoting Social Chapter	Trades Union Congress
1998	National	Promoting euro entry	New Labour Government
1999	National	Promoting euro entry	Britain in Europe
1999	Targeted	Promoting euro entry	Trades Union Congress
2000	National	Resisting euro entry	No Campaign
2001	National	Promoting euro entry	New Labour Government
2003	Targeted	Promoting 'Social Europe'	Trades Union Congress
2004	National	Opposing European Constitution	No Campaign
2004	National	Promoting European Constitution	Britain in Europe

Public Opinion and the Launch of European Integration (1950s)

Having flirted with a restoration of empire strategy and an imperial third force policy in the immediate post-war period (see Mullen, 2006), the political elite conceded they did not possess the necessary economic and political resources to pursue such ambitions. Instead, following the creation of the European Coal and Steel Community (ECSC) in 1951, they turned their attention to the leadership of the European integration process. The political elite supported the objective of European integration, but unsuccessfully attempted to lead it in an intergovernmental rather than supranational direction. It acknowledged that the latter posed a risk to Britain's economy, more specifically the system of Imperial (later Commonwealth) Preference and the Sterling Area. Meanwhile, the American Committee on United Europe, the European Movement, the European Youth Campaign and the Federal Union launched the first *targeted* pro-EU propaganda campaign, to undermine the resistance of sections of the business community, the Conservative Party and the Labour Party to federalist ideas. It seems to have been a success: the Communist Party of Great Britain, the Co-operative Party and the

Labour Party adopted a pro-federalist position in 1948, whilst the 1948 Trades Union Congress (TUC) and the 1949 Conservative Party Conference adopted resolutions in favour of European unity. Paradoxically, while the political elite stood aside from the ECSC and the formation of the European Economic Community and European Atomic Energy Community in 1957, the United States Information Agency found that public opinion was highly favourable to European integration, including Britain (see Table 6.2).

Table 6.2 — Public Support for European Integration (1952–57)

	For very much	Against to some extent	No reply
	%	%	%
1952	58	15	27
1954	78	4	18
1955	67	10	23
1956	65	16	19
1957	64	12	24

Q: Are you in general for or against making efforts towards uniting Western Europe?

Source: United States Information Agency in European Commission, 1995.

These polls suggest that the 1950s represent the zenith of public support for European integration in Britain.

Public Opinion and the Two Entry Attempts (1960s)

Having stood aside from the launch of European integration, the political elite attempted to shift the EU in an intergovernmental direction in the late 1950s. The Treasury promoted its 'Plan-G' proposal for a 17–member Free Trade Area, which would have incorporated the original six members of the EU. However, opposition from France and the US led to the formation of the more limited European Free Trade Association in 1959. Fearing a loss of influence outside the new bloc, and seeing the EU market as a means of reviving British industry, the political elite subsequently turned their attention to securing entry to the EU. Between April and July 1961, the Cabinet discussed the benefits and costs of entry. No ministerial paper was presented during these meetings; instead the Cabinet discussed a number of documents prepared by Sir Frank Lee, a pro-EU civil servant, finally agreeing to submit an application in July. On the 9th August, the Conservative Prime Minister, Harold Macmillan, formally submitted Britain's first application to join the EU and the entry negotiations opened in October. There was a significant decline in public support for entry whilst negotiations were proceeding. A Gallup poll in September 1961 found that 51 per cent supported entry. However, by June 1962 support had fallen to 36 per cent (see Table 6.3).

Table 6.3 – Public Support for Entry to the European Union (1960–63)

	Approve	Disapprove	Don't know
	%	%	%
Jul 1960	49	13	38
Jun 1960	44	20	36
Jul 1961	40	24	36
Aug 1961	49	19	32
Sep 1961	51	18	31
Oct 1961	48	18	34
Nov 1961	52	19	29
Dec 1961	53	19	28
Jan 1962	47	22	31
Mar 1962	49	23	28
Apr 1962	47	27	26
May 1962	47	21	32
Jun 1962	36	30	34
Jul 1962	42	25	33
Aug 1962	40	34	26
Sep 1962	46	30	24
Oct 1962	58	22	20
Nov 1962	50	23	27
Dec 1962	37	29	34
Jan 1963	41	30	29

Q.: *If the British Government was to decide that Britain's interest would best be served by joining the European Common Market, would you approve or disapprove?*

Source: Gallup, 1968: 49–50.

In July 1962, the Cabinet agreed that it 'would be necessary for the government to undertake as soon as practicable a campaign to present membership of the Common Market in a fairer light' (Cabinet Office, 1962a). In September, the Cabinet decided that 'public opinion was getting dangerously sceptical and needed correction' (Cabinet Office, 1962b). To counter public scepticism, the Conservative leadership enlisted the services of Lee, who set about devising a propaganda campaign to sell the concept of entry. As noted by Kitsch (1964: 163):

> At the Treasury, Sir Frank Lee held the national purse strings. He controlled public expenditure. He was at the nerve centre of Britain's communications; in an exceptional position to orchestrate and manipulate the entire complex of Britain's government and civil service communications system with the machinery of private enterprise. The situation was unique. It was the first observable example of the entire machinery of Britain's public and private communications system being co-ordinated and geared for a single objective.

That objective was joining the EU. Kitsch revealed that 'the planning and co-ordination of the exercise had been intensively organised during the final 12 months of the negotiations' (Kitsch, 1964).

The Conservative government subsequently launched Britain's first *national* pro-EU propaganda campaign. For Macmillan, facing the difficulty of projecting one intention to EU member states and another to its domestic and Commonwealth constituencies, the issue of presentation was critical. For the domestic audience, the Conservative leadership highlighted the economic benefits of entry whilst minimising its political consequences. The campaign included the publication of a government booklet and another produced by the Central Office of Information, plus the widespread distribution of leaflets and 'fact-sheets' to the business sector, the media, politicians, trade unions and the general public.

Macmillan's campaign was augmented by a number of others. They included campaigns by the Conservative, Labour and Liberal parties, the Federal Union, the United Europe Association, the business sector, and by the EU itself. Furthermore, Foreign Office officials were instrumental in establishing the cross-party Common Market Campaign. Although no official record of the first pro-EU propaganda campaign exists, making it difficult to assess its cost, Kitsch estimated that millions of pounds had been spent (Ibid.). The campaign's aim was to swing the business sector, the media, political parties, trade unions and ultimately the general public behind entry. It appears to have been a success. A Gallup poll in February 1963 found that 42 per cent supported entry. A further poll in March 1965 found that support had increased to 57 per cent. Although French President Charles de Gaulle vetoed Britain's first application in January 1963, the downward trend in public support was reversed (see Table 6.4).

Table 6.4 – Public Support for Entry to the European Union (1963–65)

	Try to join	Drop the idea	Don't know
	%	%	%
Feb 1963	42	37	21
Jun 1963	46	25	29
Sep 1963	46	36	18
Nov 1963	49	32	19
Dec 1963	42	34	24
Jan 1964	36	40	24
Feb 1964	42	33	25
Jul 1964	41	37	22
Nov 1964	44	28	28
Jan 1965	48	30	22
Feb 1965	53	25	22
Mar 1965	57	22	21

Q.: *If any opportunity occurs for Britain to join the Common Market, would you like to see us try or drop the idea altogether?*

Source: Gallup, 1968: 233.

Following the Labour Party's 1964 General Election victory, Prime Minister Harold Wilson reaffirmed the party's five conditions for entry. However, under the influence of pro-EU civil servants, Wilson began to shift in favour of entry. The second leg of entry negotiations began in May 1967, following the formal submission of Britain's second application to join the EU. According to Gallup, public opinion was generally favourable to entry at the start of the negotiations, with 49 per cent in favour (see Table 6.5).

Table 6.5 — Public Support for Entry to the European Union (1965-67)

	Approve	Disapprove	Don't know
	%	%	%
Apr 1965 (Q.1)	51	25	24
May 1965	60	19	21
Jun 1965	56	20	24
Jul 1965	56	22	22
Aug 1965	47	18	35
Sep 1965	55	15	30
Oct 1965	54	18	28
Nov 1965	60	17	23
Dec 1965	66	15	19
Jan 1966	60	15	25
Feb 1966	59	18	23
Mar 1966	68	14	18
May 1966	70	10	20
Jun 1966	61	16	23
Jul 1966	71	12	17
Aug 1966	70	12	18
Sep 1966	67	13	20
Oct 1966	68	14	18
Nov 1966	67	17	16
Dec 1966	66	16	18
Jan 1967	65	18	17
Feb 1967	61	20	19
Mar 1967	57	27	16
Apr 1967	43	30	27
May 1967 (Q.2)	49	34	17
Nov 1967 (Q.3)	37	44	19
Dec 1967 (Q.4)	36	51	13

Q.1: *If the British Government were to decide that Britain's interests would best be served by joining the European Common Market, would you approve or disapprove?*

Q.2: *The Government has decided that Britain's interest would best be served by applying to join the European Common Market; do you approve or disapprove?*

Q.3: *Do you approve or disapprove of the Government applying for membership of the European Common Market?*

Q.4: *Do you think that the British Government should press on with its application to join the Common Market, or should it withdraw the application?*

Source: Gallup, 1968: 246.

However, in November 1967 de Gaulle vetoed Britain's second application.

Public Opinion and Accession (1970s)

The primary objective of the Conservative leadership, following the 1970 General Election, was to secure entry to the EU. To achieve this, Prime Minister Edward Heath transferred responsibility for the negotiations from the Foreign Office to the new European Secretariat in the Cabinet Office, and the third leg of entry negotiations began in July 1970. The Labour leadership, however, under pressure from the more sceptical party membership, shifted its position to one of opposition to entry on the terms negotiated. In July 1971, following its Special Conference on the EU, Labour's National Executive Committee launched the first *targeted* anti-EU propaganda campaign, 'No to Entry on Tory Terms', in order to bolster opposition within the party. The TUC followed suit in October, launching a second *targeted* anti-EU propaganda campaign to convince trade unionists that Britain's economic prospects would be better outside than inside the EU. Heath, meanwhile, turned his attention to winning support for entry within the two main political parties, plus the backing of the general public. The fourth task was particularly problematic given the collapse of support for entry in the second half of 1967 (see Table 5). According to Gallup, opposition continued to grow throughout the late 1960s and stood at 66 per cent in November 1970, with only 16 per cent supporting entry (see Table 6.6).

In an attempt to turn around public opinion, the Conservative leadership enlisted the assistance of the Information Research Department (IRD), a covert Foreign Office unit with close links to MI6. Additional funding for the campaign, provided by the US Central Intelligence Agency (CIA), was allegedly channelled through the cross-party Economic League for European Co-operation (ELEC) (Dorril, 2000). Following extensive survey research commissioned by the European Movement, the Conservative leadership, together with other pro-EU forces, decided to concentrate upon several themes for the campaign, found to be effective in influencing opinion. These included the notions that entry would deliver higher standards of living, better social welfare, strengthen trade links, safeguard peace and security, and protect Britain's national interest whilst enhancing its global role. The Conservative government subsequently launched Britain's second *national* pro-EU propaganda campaign, which incorporated three stages.

Table 6.6 – Public Support for Entry to the European Union (1970-1)

	Approve	Disapprove	Don't know
	%	%	%
Feb 1970	22	57	21
Apr 1970	19	59	22
Jul 1970	24	55	21
Sep 1970	21	56	23
Oct 1970	22	56	22
Nov 1970	16	66	18
Jan 1971	22	58	20
Mar 1971	19	60	22
Apr 1971	22	60	19
May 1971	23	59	18
Jun 1971	27	58	15

Q.: Do you approve or disapprove of the Government applying for membership of the European Common Market?

Source: Gallup in Zakheim, 1973: 192.

The first stage began in the spring of 1971 when the government issued 12 'fact-sheets' and distributed 6 million copies of a booklet outlining the benefits of entry. Pro-EU campaigners flooded the press with letters, whilst ministers made 280 speeches on the issue between July and October. Furthermore, a special IRD organisation, the European Unit, was created to work closely with pro-EU forces to rebut the claims of the anti-EU campaign, which enjoyed less funding and fewer resources.

The second stage witnessed the lobbying of Conservative MPs by the parliamentary Conservative Group for Europe and party whips, plus the negotiation of a secret alliance with the 69-strong pro-EU wing of the Parliamentary Labour Party to ensure a successful House of Commons vote. Conservative Central Office, the Conservative Research Department and the Conservative Political Centre targeted Conservative associations, through constituency chairs, party agents and officers.

The third stage of the campaign was a national one, aimed at influencing the general public through the media. To this end, Geoffrey Tucker, a public relations expert who had worked for the Conservative Party, organised a series of cross-party breakfast meetings of between 20 and 30 people at London's Connaught Hotel. Business leaders, civil servants, media representatives and politicians attended these IRD-funded meetings. Furthermore, Geoffrey Rippon and Crispin Tickell, from the British negotiating team, reportedly attended some of these meetings (British Management Data Foundation, 2000). Radio and television media were particularly targeted, including such programmes as News at Ten, Panorama, Today, 24 Hours, Woman's Hour and World at One. The national campaign was augmented by specific ones organised by the Conservative Party for Europe, the Labour Party for Europe, the Liberal Party for Europe and the European Movement, co-ordinated by a government committee.

The European Movement campaign involved the recruitment of over 200 speakers, who addressed over 1000 public meetings, the publication of over 10 million leaflets and the distribution of the British European newsletter. It also included major advertising in the British press, billboard advertising, the distribution of prepared articles and letters to local and national newspapers, plus the release of a pop record called 'We've got to get in to get on'. As with the first campaign, no official record of the second campaign exists, making it difficult to estimate its expenditure. However, Wistrich (2001) reported that the European Movement alone spent over £1 million, in stark contrast to the anti-EU campaign, which only spent £50,000 (Evans, 1975). This campaign also seems to have been a success; support for entry increased, standing at 43 per cent in April 1972, according to Gallup (see Table 6.7), as the European Communities Bill made its way through Parliament.

Table 6.7 — Public Support for Entry to the European Union (1971-2)

	For	Against	Don't know
	%	%	%
Jul 1971	25	57	18
Aug 1971	39	43	17
Sep 1971	35	47	18
Oct 1971	32	51	17
Dec 1971	38	47	16
Feb 1972	42	41	17
Apr 1972	43	43	14
May 1972	41	45	14

Q.: *On the facts as you know them at present, are you for or against Britain joining the Common Market?*

Source: Gallup in Zakheim, 1973: 192.

The bill passed its final stage in October 1972 and Britain joined the EU on 1st January 1973.

Public Opinion and the 1975 Referendum

The hope that accession would settle the European question was not realised. According to Gallup, public opinion returned to a position whereby a majority opposed continued membership (see Table 6.8).

Table 6.8 – Public Support for European Union Membership (1973–4)

	Very sorry	Indifferent	Relieved	No reply
	%	%	%	%
Sep 1973	20	33	37	10
May 1974	24	28	40	8
Nov 1974	31	22	38	9

Q.: *If you were told tomorrow that Britain was leaving the EEC would you be very sorry about it, indifferent or relieved?*

Source: Gallup in Butler and Kitzinger, 1996: 247.

Claiming that the Conservatives possessed no mandate for entry, and eventually backing Tony Benn's campaign for a referendum, Wilson went into both general elections in 1974 with a pledge to renegotiate the terms of membership and to put the decision to the British people. Meanwhile, in anticipation of such a poll, pro-EU forces reconstituted the propaganda infrastructure that had been effectively dismantled upon entry. In the spring of 1974, an elite group known as 'the principals' launched a series of secret meetings to co-ordinate the campaign, led by Tucker and ELEC. Ernest Wistrich, who was then the national organiser of Britain in Europe, reported that:

> Within a month of the February 1974 election, we had set up a campaign committee involving not just the European Movement but representatives of political parties and others. We conducted a major attitude survey in June. In July we distributed 6.5 million leaflets to try and recruit the troops to conduct a referendum, as a result of which we got about 12,000 people involved (cited in Broad and Geiger, 1996: 89).

These preparations presaged Britain's third *national* pro-EU propaganda campaign, which was launched by the Labour government before the 1975 Referendum.

There were three stages to this campaign: the first whilst the Labour government was renegotiating the terms, the second during the passage of the Referendum Bill, and the third during the final weeks of the referendum campaign. The No and Yes campaigns broadly coalesced around two organisations: the National Referendum Campaign (NRC) brought together opponents of the EU, whilst Britain in Europe (BiE) united most of the pro-EU forces. BiE published *Why you Should Vote Yes*, the NRC issued *Why You Should Vote No*, whilst the Labour government distributed a pamphlet in favour of continued membership, *New Deal for Europe*, to every household in Britain. Recalling the themes and strategy of the pro-EU campaign, MORI's Robert Worcester stated that polls at the time indicated that economic rather than political issues were decisive: 58 per cent of those polled said the issue of the cost of living was central to how they would decide. Others said that food prices (37 per cent) and unemployment (15 per cent) were key, whilst only 9 per cent felt independence and sovereignty were important (cited in Broad and Geiger, 1996). Butler and Kitzinger (1996) argued that the electorate was divided into three roughly equal groups: pro-EU, anti-EU and the 'hesitants'. Yes campaigners concluded that the 'hestitants' were more likely to be persuaded by another hesitant rather than a pro, and this belief became central to their strategy.

BiE recruited 17 regional co-ordinators and trained 600 speakers who addressed thousands of public meetings. It created cross-party committees, leading to 374 local campaigning groups, developing a network of campaigning groups for professionals such as doctors and solicitors. High profile public personalities were enlisted, millions of leaflets, posters and other promotional materials were distributed, and shops in prominent locations in many town and cities were rented. The campaign also included the staging of mass public meetings, the screening of Party Political Broadcast-style television programmes, the launch of a newspaper campaign using the local and national press, plus billboard advertising.

The NRC, composed of several organisations, launched Britain's first *national* anti-EU propaganda campaign. The TUC contribution, which was based on the slogan 'Better Out Than In', argued that continued membership was damaging to the British economy and to Britain's democratic freedoms. In January 1975, Gallup found that 55 per cent supported withdrawal and 45 per cent supported continued membership. By early March these figures had reversed, with 66 per cent supporting continued membership and only 34 per cent supporting withdrawal (Worcester, 2000). In the referendum on the 5th June 1975, 67.2 per cent voted Yes and 32.8 per cent voted No. However, the hope that the 1975 Referendum would settle the European question was not realised. By June 1977, Gallup found that public opinion had returned to a position whereby a majority opposed continued membership (see Table 6.9).

Table 6.9 – Public Support for European Union Membership (1976–79)

	Good	Bad	Neither	Don't know
Jan 1976	50	24	17	9
Jun 1977	33	42	18	7
Jul 1978	25	48	20	7
May 1979	34	36	22	7

Q.: *Generally speaking, do you think that Britain's membership of the Common Market is a good thing, a bad thing or neither good nor bad?*

Source: Gallup in King, 2001: 301–302.

Public Opinion and the Single Market (1980s)

Following the Conservative victory in the 1979 General Election, Labour swung decisively to the left, pledging itself to withdrawal from the EU without a referendum. The TUC supported such a policy by launching the third targeted anti-EU propaganda campaign in 1982. The first stage of the campaign focused upon EU policy areas that trade unions were universally opposed to. It resulted in the production of a leaflet on the EU Budget and the Common Agricultural Policy, entitled 'The EEC's Crazy Finances: Time to Cry Halt!' The second stage explored the possibilities of alternatives to continued membership.

Before the 1983 General Election, the European Movement launched the second targeted pro-EU propaganda campaign to focus on the Labour Party, claiming that 2.5 million jobs were dependent upon continued membership. Wistrich, then Director of the European Movement in Britain, believed that the campaign 'certainly neutered the call for withdrawal because if you look back at the 1983 General Election, such a policy was hardly talked about.'[2] The empirical evidence supports Wistrich's claim. In terms of their

---

[2]   Interview with Ernest Wistrich, 9th September 2002.

election addresses, 100 per cent of Labour candidates mentioned unemployment, 92 per cent mentioned defence, 88 per cent mentioned education and 84 per cent mentioned housing, whilst only 57 per cent mentioned the EU (Butler and Kavanagh, 1984: 258–261).

Prime Minister Margaret Thatcher's response to the state of malaise in European politics in the 1970s was to attempt to reshape the EU in the British 'national interest'. Thatcher succeeded in reforming the EU Budget and obtained an agreement to establish a single European market, arguing that its implementation could proceed without the revision of the Treaty of Rome. However, the British proposal was rejected by other member states and the price for the creation of the Single Market was the extension of qualified majority voting, plus a treaty commitment to introduce Economic and Monetary Union (EMU). Thatcher railed against the federalist, social democratic plans of Jacques Delors, the European Commission President. Thatcher was also opposed to EMU and British entry to the European Monetary System. Nevertheless, under her leadership, the Conservative government launched Britain's fourth *national* pro-EU propaganda campaign when the Department for Trade and Industry organised the 'Europe: Open for Business' campaign,[3] spending £25 million in 1988 in order to sell the benefits of the EU and its Single Market (Macshane, 2005). The primary objective of the campaign was to galvanise support for the Single Market and, according to Eurobarometer, it seems to have been a success (see Table 6.10).

---

[3] Correspondence from Denis MacShane, 6th June 2005.

Table 6.10 – Public Support for the European Single Market (1988–96)

	Very hopeful	Rather hopeful	Rather fearful	Very fearful	Don't know
	%	%	%	%	%
Nov 1988	12	50	19	6	13
Mar 1989	12	45	25	6	12
Jul 1989	14	39	17	3	27
Nov 1989	12	49	18	5	16
Apr 1990	12	45	18	4	21
Nov 1990	8	47	20	4	21
Mar 1991	13	50	23	5	9
Oct 1991	12	44	19	6	19
Apr 1992	11	42	20	5	21
Oct 1992	8	39	27	10	16
Apr 1993	7	44	26	7	16
Nov 1993	6	48	25	6	14
May 1994	7	46	22	8	15
Dec 1994	6	47	23	6	17
Jan 1995	6	49	22	8	14
Dec 1995	6	46	23	9	16
Jan 1996	5	42	27	10	16
Nov 1996	5	44	26	10	13

Q.: *Personally, would you say that the Single European Market, which will come about by 1992, makes you feel very hopeful, rather hopeful, rather fearful or very fearful?*

Source: Eurobarometer.

The secondary objective of the campaign was to reverse the general public's opposition to continued membership. Again, the campaign secured some modest gains (see Table 6.11).

Table 6.11 – Public Support for European Union Membership (1980–89)

	Good	Bad	Neither	Don't know
	%	%	%	%
Apr 1980	22	57	13	8
Mar 1981	24	52	21	4
Mar 1982	23	48	23	7
May 1983	43	30	22	5
Mar 1984	25	48	20	7
Jan 1985	32	39	21	7
Jul 1987	28	39	25	8
Sep 1988	36	36	18	9
Mar 1989	36	30	27	7

Q.: *Generally speaking, do you think that Britain's membership of the Common Market is a good thing, a bad thing or neither good nor bad?*
Source: Gallup in King, 2001: 301–302.

Following Delors' speech to the 1988 Congress, the TUC reversed its support for withdrawal (as did the Labour Party some weeks later) in favour of a 'social Europe'. The third targeted pro-EU propaganda campaign, launched by the TUC in 1989, specifically backed the ratification of the EMU treaty, the Maastricht Treaty, with the Social Charter and was based on the theme of 'Europe: Free-For-All Or Fair-For-All'. The TUC commissioned a poll in 1989 that found that 65 per cent of the public endorsed the Social Charter.

In 1990, Ken Coates, who was an ally of Delors and a member of the European Parliamentary Labour Party (EPLP), lobbied his colleagues to support the 'Delors II' package, which proposed a substantial increase in the EU Budget to finance a new EU cohesion fund. Coates suggested to Delors 'that there should be a campaign to win public opinion on this matter.'[4] Coates, working with (academics) Michael Barratt-Brown and Stuart Holland, duly organised the fourth targeted pro-EU propaganda campaign, focusing upon the Labour Party, utilising church-based, peace movement and trade union networks across Europe in order to promote the development of a 'social dimension' to EMU. The campaign's goals included full employment as an EU treaty objective, an expanded EU Budget, new EU borrowing instruments, plus the development of a 'social

---

[4] Interview with Ken Coates, 4th October 2002.

Europe' via the Social Chapter and the 'social partnership' procedure.

The TUC established the European Commission-funded European Information Service at its headquarters in 1990 in order to disseminate pro-EU propaganda within the trade union movement. It also participated in the 1993 European Trade Union Confederation Day of Action against EU unemployment, launching an advertising campaign based on the theme of 'We're Part of Europe, So Let's Get It Working'. The TUC's fifth *targeted* pro-EU propaganda campaign, which promoted the virtues of the Social Chapter and the benefits of continued membership more generally, reportedly cost £200,000.

Public Opinion and the Euro (1990s)

Despite the campaigning activities of the TUC and Coates et al. during the Maastricht Treaty negotiations in 1990–1991, the Conservative Prime Minister, John Major, negotiated two opt-outs from the treaty: joining the European single currency and adopting the Social Chapter. Major successfully steered the European Communities (Amendment) Bill, incorporating the Maastricht Treaty, through Parliament, before announcing in 1996 that a Conservative government would not contemplate adopting the single currency without holding a referendum. The Labour Party duly followed suit.

During New Labour's first term, following its 1997 General Election victory, Prime Minister Tony Blair and Chancellor Gordon Brown granted independence to the Bank of England, as required by the Maastricht Treaty, and adopted the public spending plans of the previous Conservative government, in order to comply with the treaty. They also announced that Britain would abandon one of its opt-outs and would adopt the Social Chapter. However, the most controversial policy area was euro entry. The *official* policy was one of 'wait and see'; in October 1997, Brown set out his five economic tests that would have to be satisfied before Britain would join the single currency. Although Blair and Brown favoured euro entry, there were two significant obstacles. The first obstacle was opposition from the Rupert Murdoch's media empire (including titles such as *The Sun*). The second obstacle was the state of public opinion, which, according to MORI and ICM, was consistently opposed to euro entry (see Tables 6.12 and 6.13).

MORI conducted a further 28 polls on euro entry between January 2000 and February 2005. These found that, on average, 57 per cent opposed entry, whilst only 28 per cent supported entry.

Table 6.12 — Public Support for Joining the European Single Currency (1991–99)

	In favour	Against	Don't know
	%	%	%
Nov 1991 (Q.1)	33	54	13
Nov 1994 (Q.3)	33	56	11
Jun 1995 (Q.2)	29	60	11
May 1996 (Q.3)	23	60	17
Nov 1996	22	64	14
Apr 1997	22	58	19
Oct 1997	27	54	19
Jan 1998	32	52	16
Mar 1998	30	54	15
May 1998	31	54	16
Jul 1998	33	50	17
Sep 1998	30	49	20
Dec 1998	29	53	18
Jan 1999	33	51	16
Feb 1999	32	52	15
Mar 1999	31	56	13
Apr 1999	31	53	15
Jun 1999	24	57	18
Jul 1999	27	58	15
Sep 1999	30	56	14
Nov 1999	27	56	17

Q.1: *There have been calls for a national referendum on the issue of a single European currency to replace the pound sterling. If you voted in such a referendum, would you vote for or against Britain joining a single European currency?*

Q.2: *If there was a referendum on whether or not Britain should be part of a single European currency, how would you vote?*

Q.3: *If there were a referendum now on whether Britain should be part of a Single European Currency, how would you vote?*

Source: MORI.

Table 6.13 — Public Support for Joining the European Single Currency (1992–99)

	Vote to join	Vote not to join	Don't know
	%	%	%
Oct 1992	27	59	14
May 1994	23	66	11
Feb 1995	26	51	23
May 1996	29	64	7
Apr 1998	26	61	13
May 1998	34	48	17
Jan 1999	29	52	19
Feb 1999	36	52	12
Mar 1999	31	53	16
Apr 1999	34	53	13
May 1999	35	52	13
Jun 1999	27	61	13
Jul 1999	25	62	13
Aug 1999	24	60	16
Sep 1999	30	57	13
Oct 1999	27	58	14
Nov 1999	28	59	13
Dec 1999	24	61	15

Q.: *If there were to be a referendum, would you vote to join the European Single Currency (the Euro) or would you vote not to join?*

Source: ICM.

ICM conducted a further 56 polls on euro entry between January 2000 and December 2004. These found that, on average, 61 per cent opposed entry, whilst only 26 per cent supported entry.

In an attempt to counter such opposition, the New Labour government launched Britain's fifth *national* pro-EU propaganda campaign in 1998 to persuade business and the general public to back the euro. This was followed, in 1999, by the sixth *national* pro-EU propaganda campaign, organised by BiE, the sixth *targeted* pro-EU propaganda campaign, organised by the TUC, and the seventh *national* pro-EU propaganda campaign, organised by the New Labour government — all of which promoted euro entry. The TUC campaign seems to have had some impact; in 1999, a MORI poll of trade unionists found that 61 per cent opposed the euro, whilst a 2002 ICM poll found that only 49 per cent were opposed. In response to these campaigns, the second *national* anti-EU campaign was launched in 2000 by the No Campaign (a coalition of academics, business leaders and politicians). In addition to using traditional propaganda methods — such as the publication of flyers, leaflets and reports, letter writing, advertising in the media and on billboards — these campaigns adopted a number of new methods, including cinema adverts, interactive web sites and regular electronic information bulletins. The attempts to influence public opinion were becoming ever more sophisticated and costly, with many millions of pounds spent by both sides.

While the propaganda battle over the euro raged, the New Labour government actively prepared for euro entry. In conjunction with the European Movement, it devised a strategy for winning a referendum on the euro. It also introduced a number of institutional and legislative measures, contravening its official policy of 'wait and see'. These measures included its response to Lord Neill's report on referendum funding, the National Changeover Plan and the creation of a new Cabinet-level 'European enforcer' post. They also included the development of the 'Eurogrid' media rebuttal unit, the Political Parties, Elections and Referendums Act 2000, the funding of Euro-Info Centres and the formation of regional euro forums (see Mullen and Burkitt, 2003). However, with public opinion consistently opposed, the New Labour government postponed its objective of euro entry. In June 2003, the Treasury published its assessment of the five economic tests, concluding that only one had been met. Blair and Brown then set out a road map to euro entry, arguing that several (domestic and EU) reforms would have to be implemented before Britain could join. Meanwhile, Gallup found that opposition to continued membership had increased, rising from 13 per cent in November 1991 to 24 per cent in June 1999 (see Table 6.14).

Table 6.14 — Public Support for European Union Membership (1990–99)

	Good	Bad	Neither	Don't know
	%	%	%	%
Nov 1990	56	13	21	10
Nov 1991	49	22	20	9
Jun 1992	49	22	20	10
Jan 1993	41	29	19	10
Mar 1994	40	23	28	8
Feb 1995	36	29	22	13
Jun 1996	34	34	22	9
Dec 1998	36	31	27	6
Jun 1999	43	24	29	4

Q.: *Generally speaking, do you think that Britain's membership of the European Community is a good thing, a bad thing or neither good nor bad?*

Source: Gallup in King, 2001: 301–302.

Public Opinion and Enlargement (2000s)

In December 2003, the European Council agreed to the fifth enlargement of the EU, a policy objective long supported by the British State and the Conservative and Labour leaderships. However, according to Eurobarometer, a substantial section of the public was concerned about the implications of enlargement for Britain's standing and influence in the EU (see Table 6.15).

Table 6.15 — Public Opinion on Enlargement

	Tend to agree	Tend to disagree
	%	%
Nov 1997	46	34
May 1998	43	37
Nov 1998	51	33
Jan 2001	44	31
May 2001	44	32
Nov 2001	42	34
May 2002	45	33

> Q.: *After the enlargement of the EU to include these new countries, do you think Britain will become less important in Europe?*
> Source: Eurobarometer.

Despite these concerns, the New Labour government supported enlargement, and following a series of referendum votes in favour of entry, nine Central and Eastern European countries, plus Malta, joined the EU in May 2004.

Public Opinion and the European Constitution (2000s)

The New Labour government supported the 2002–2003 Convention on the Future of Europe, and the resulting draft European Constitution, agreed in June 2004, which combined and built upon the existing treaties of the EU. The New Labour government was initially resistant to holding a referendum on the treaty, with Peter Hain, the government's chief negotiator in the Convention, describing it as a mere 'tidying up exercise'. However, following a concerted campaign by the Murdoch media and Vote 2004 Blair performed a U-turn in April 2004 and agreed to hold a referendum. However, according to ICM, MORI and YouGov, a majority of the British public was opposed to ratifying the European Constitution (see Tables 6.16, 6.17 and 6.18).

Table 6.16 — Public Support for the European Constitution (ICM)

	Vote to join	Vote not to join	Don't know
	%	%	%
Apr 2004 (Q.1)	25	55	19
Jun 2004 (Q.2)	28	57	14
Nov 2004 (Q.3)	24	69	7
Feb 2005 (Q.3)	26	54	20

Q.1: Do you believe Britain should sign up to the new EU constitution?
Q.2: Will you vote in favour or against going in to the new EU constitution?
Q.3: If there was a vote tomorrow, would you vote for Britain to sign up to the new EU constitution or not?
Source: ICM.

Table 6.17 — Public Support for the European Constitution (MORI)

	Strongly support	Generally in favour, but could be persuaded against	Generally opposed, but could be persuaded in favour	Strongly opposed	Don't know
	%	%	%	%	%
Jul 2004	8	23	23	27	19
Nov 2004	8	22	28	27	15
Feb 2005	10	21	27	25	15
Q.: Which of the following best describes your own view of adopting the new European Constitution?					
Source: MORI.					

Table 6.18 — Public Support for the European Constitution (YouGov)

	Vote No	Vote Yes
	%	%
Apr 2004	53	16
May 2004	47	21
Jun 2004	49	23
Jan 2005	45	24
Q.: If a referendum were held now, how would you vote, in favour or against a new EU constitution?		
Source: YouGov.		

In an attempt to counter such opposition, the TUC launched its seventh targeted pro-EU propaganda campaign in 2003 to promote the benefits of a 'social Europe' and the incorporation of the Charter of Fundamental Rights in any new treaty. The following year, BiE launched the eighth national pro-EU propaganda campaign, in favour of the ratification of the European Constitution. In response, the third national anti-EU campaign was launched in 2004 by the No Campaign (an alliance of the Centre for a Social Europe and Vote No).

In May 2005, it was reported that the government had started work on a 'game plan' for securing victory in a referendum on the European Constitution. Senior ministers and Foreign Office officials agreed that 'recommending the benefits of EU membership should be a central theme of the campaign to win acceptance for the treaty'. BiE, meanwhile, proposed 'decoupling the treaty from the issue of euro membership' (Adams, 2005). That same month, Blair announced that he would appoint a high-ranking minister to spearhead the drive for a Yes vote (Newman, 2005). However, there was disagreement over whether the responsibility for a referendum should remain with the Foreign Office or whether it should be transferred to a specific unit, as happened in the 1975 Referendum. However, following the No votes in the referendums in France and the Netherlands in May and June 2005, all propaganda campaigns were suspended and the government's 'game plan' was shelved. Meanwhile, a Eurobarometer poll in April 2004 found that opposition to continued membership had increased to 29 per cent and was level with the number of those who supported continued membership (see Table 6.19).

Table 6.19 — Public Support for European Union Membership (2000–04)

	Good	Bad	Neither	Don't know
	%	%	%	%
Jun 2000	25	24	29	22
Jan 2001	28	22	29	20
May 2001	29	24	27	20
Nov 2001	33	22	31	14
May 2002	32	21	32	15
Apr 2004	29	29	n/a	13

Q.: *Generally speaking, do you think that Britain's membership of the European Community is a good thing, a bad thing or neither good nor bad?*

Source: Eurobarometer

Conclusion

It is clear from the polling evidence presented above that public opinion on European integration, in both historical and contemporary terms, has been volatile. It is suggested that such variability is, in large part, a consequence of repeated interventions by anti- and pro-EU forces and their deployment of propaganda campaigns in an attempt to influence public opinion.

It is beyond the scope of this chapter to investigate the actual impact of such campaigns (whether 'grassroots' or 'treetops', national or targeted) on the intended recipients (whether individuals or institutions). Nevertheless, these campaigns were deployed at critical junctures in the relationship between Britain and the EU, and the evidence suggests that there is a positive correlation between the timing and duration of these campaigns and the changes in public opinion. The high levels of spending on these campaigns — by the business sector, political parties, trade unions, the British State and other actors — is a further indication of their efficacy.

Historically, there was a considerable imbalance between these opposing forces. Until the 1990s, pro-EU forces enjoyed substantial financial and other resources, plus the backing of successive governments and, therefore, the considerable power resources of the British State. Generally speaking, pro-EU forces were far more successful than their anti-EU opponents in influencing public opinion during this period. However, the situation changed significantly in the late 1990s, as anti-EU forces increased their financial resources and their organisational capacity. Furthermore, business organisations, political parties and trade unions have become more evenly divided on the question of whether or not to support further European integration, specifically whether to adopt the euro and whether to ratify the European Constitution. These developments have important consequences for the future configuration of forces, and balance of power, should Britain hold a referendum on euro entry or on a new EU treaty.

There is a great deal of uncertainty about the future of the EU following the French and Dutch no votes in 2005. It is also unclear when Britain will stage a referendum on euro entry. What seems beyond doubt, however, is Tucker's assertion that 'the battle' for British hearts and minds on European integration 'will never be over' (British Management Data Foundation, 2000).

Seven

Economic Issues of Membership

Introduction

Economic issues have long dominated the debate concerning UK membership of the European Union (EU) and/or participation in further regional economic integrationist initiatives such as the creation of the Single Internal Market (SIM), European Exchange Rate Mechanism (ERM) and its successor Economic and Monetary Union (EMU). This is perhaps not surprising since EU membership has always been portrayed in primarily economic terms to the British electorate. Thus, whilst certain of the founding fathers of European integration openly stated their aim to create a federal European state[1], the British debate over membership primarily concerned issues of prices and incomes, fish and agriculture, together with trade and employment, and only subsequently relating to the impact upon the political and economic autonomy of the nation (Butler and Kitzinger, 1976; King, 1977; Broad and Geiger, 1996:98).

This is perhaps not surprising given that, in 1975, the British people were asked to vote on the retention of membership in what was then described as the Common Market. This has only subsequently evolved into the EU that exists today, with its wider remit and representing four times the number of nations that was the case upon British accession. Indeed, the narrowness of the British debate over the desirability of participation in wider and deeper European integration has tended to be conducted as an elite-level argument over economic theories and the interpretation of data. Nevertheless,

---

[1] The preamble to the European Coal and Steel Community (ECSC), ratified in 1951, stated that it perceived the organisation as 'the first step to the federation of Europe', whereas the Treaty of Rome, signed six years later, had obfuscated this desire somewhat with the statement that it promoted 'an ever closer union of the peoples of Europe' (Broad, 2001:25).

it is fascinating to look back at those early debates, surrounding the 1975 referendum, to discern which economic issues were prevalent at the time, and to compare these concerns with the contemporary debate over Britain's future relationship with the EU. This exercise indicates those issues which have proved to be of only temporary significance and those of more long-standing importance.

Economic Issues Raised in 1975

Pro-Membership

Advocates for UK membership in the Common Market, in 1975, concentrated upon three main economic arguments. These were:

- Superior economic development opportunities
- Greater potential for international trade
- Hence higher standards of living

The first argument employed in favour of UK participation in European integration relies upon the fact that the original six EU member states had enjoyed faster economic growth rates than had the UK for a number of years, the implication being that UK adoption of the same institutional arrangements would deliver a similar bounty in terms of faster rising living standards.

This basic thesis was contradicted by a 1970 National Institute study, which concluded that the six founder members of the EU had enjoyed more rapid economic development in the decade before the establishment of the EU than they had in the decade afterwards. This is contrary to the experience of other OECD nations, where growth was on average faster during the latter period than the former (Major and Hays, 1970). Nevertheless, it remained true that, between 1958 and 1973, the original six members enjoyed a combined average growth rate of 5.1% per annum (Nevin, 1990). This was a rate far in excess of that achieved by the UK economy. However, by the time the UK joined, the underlying conditions creating this preferable development had become exhausted. Indeed, due to a combination of factors[2], the EU's restrictive policies have in fact resulted in *lower* growth and higher unemployment than is the norm across the global

---

[2] Neo-liberal economists point towards the level of regulation adopted by the EU, in particular relating to the over-regulated labour market, together with the overall level of public spending (particularly welfare state benefit payments), resulting in Euro-sclerosis, thus leading to a reduction in EU growth rates in recent years. Keynesian economists, by contrast, focus upon

economy. This is particularly the case for the majority of those initial member states of the EU, who now represent the core of the EMU economies. Hence, World Bank (2000) figures indicate that, between 1990 and 1998, UK growth averaged 3.7% per annum, a figure slightly exceeding global GDP growth of 3.3%, whereas the EMU economy grew by a mere 1.8% per year.

This claim, based as it is upon an observation of growth rates over a relatively short time span, was always likely to prove to be a weak argument, based upon temporary statistical coincidence, and so it has proven. Rapid growth rates may reflect a period of 'catching-up', where GDP-per-head advances rapidly in a less developed nation, without ever actually reaching that of a slower-growing, but richer nation. It may also reflect a period when labour switches from relatively unproductive agricultural production to more productive manufacturing industry. Neither of these stimuli are sustainable in the long run, and therefore growth rates are likely to level-out at lower rates of expansion in the future.

In more recent years, indeed, as the EU has expanded, it has become a *slow growth area* relative to the global economy taken as a whole. Moreover, during the last decade, the EU's share of world trade has fallen by one quarter. Thus, Baimbridge and Whyman (2006) feel able to conclude that the European economy is pursuing integration as a defensive not offensive measure, by seeking to offset its economic weakness through greater economies of scale. Unfortunately, the economic framework adopted as part of EMU is likely to militate against this policy objective due to its deflationary fundamentals. Thus, Baimbridge and Whyman (2006) conclude that, if the UK decided to lock itself within a trading bloc, it could choose one more successful than the EU.

The second argument advanced in favour of EU membership concerned the possibility of enhancing the volume of international trade. Essentially, the argument here is that the ultimate creation of a single internal market, created by EU member states, involves the eradication of all tariffs and other barriers to trade between these participating economies and the erection of a common external tariff against the imports of goods from outside the common market. The

---

the deflationary macroeconomic policies adopted by EU member states during the past two decades, whether relating to the discipline imposed by ERM membership or that inflicted by the convergence criteria that must be met for individual economies to participate within EMU, and the subsequent restraint arising within monetary union from the Stability and Growth Pact (SGP).

dismantling of protectionism within the SIM therefore creates trade between member states, as the cost of purchasing goods falls, but it also diverts trade that would otherwise have taken place with more efficient outside producers whose goods and services are now rendered uncompetitive due to the common external tariff. The former increases economic efficiency in the world economy, whereas the latter reduces it. However, for the benefit of EU workers, it should create jobs by encouraging more trade to occur within the union, and will benefit consumers if the impact is to lower prices overall.

For Britain, which had a lower level of tariff rates for external economies than most EU member states, the net benefits of the creation of the SIM are less certain than for the EU as a whole. Prices will have likely risen for goods and services formerly imported from commonwealth nations—particularly cheap foodstuffs from New Zealand—and therefore trade diversion may be far larger for the UK relative to the EU average. Trade creation has undoubtedly occurred, leading to a growing proportion of the UK's overall traded goods arising from inter-EU trade patterns—a value presently representing approximately half of all UK trade. However, the *balance* of such trade has been persistently negative for the UK ever since it attained EU membership.

In the early years of membership, Britain's balance of trade deficit with the EU(6) has risen from a surplus of £385 million (1970), the last pre-entry year, to a deficit of £181 million (1971), widening to £499 million (1972) and £1,1167 million (1973), despite a gradual devaluation against these countries currencies, thereby denoting the UK's initial lack of competitiveness at the given exchange rate against its new EU partner economies. UK government reports had predicted this net cost to the UK in advance of membership, but the *scale* of the trade deficit was underestimated. According to the governments' own figures, published in the annual Balance of Payments Accounts (*The Pink Book*), the UK suffered a total accumulated trading deficit exceeding £100 billion with the EU during its more than three decades of membership, whereas it has enjoyed a trading surplus of approximately £80 billion with the rest of the world over the same period. In fact, the accumulated deficit is larger than official statistics suggest because these figures are not adjusted for inflation and neither do they take account of the Antwerp-Rotterdam effect, which incorrectly allocates approximately 10% of British exports to the EU rather than to the rest of the world, because they go initially to the Continent for containerisation before being dispatched internationally.

Such a substantial volume of resources, drained from the British economy, has led to deflationary budgetary and monetary policies to restore balance of trade equilibrium by lowering relative production costs. However, output and employment simultaneously fall, which in turn generates less favourable investment prospects. The resulting loss of efficiency further worsens the balance of trade, which necessitates more deflationary policies, causing lower growth. It is difficult for this spiral of relative decline to be reversed whilst the UK remains subject to a very large trade deficit with other EU member states. Orthodox policies to reduce trade deficits involve the deflation of the economy, thereby relying upon rising unemployment to choke off demand for imported goods. Unfortunately, this leaves the UK economy growing more slowly, and carrying higher rates of unemployment, than would otherwise have occurred, thus contradicting the economic advantages that were advocated in the 1970s relating to the trade benefits of EU membership. This process is what Thirwall (1982) referred to as balance of payments constrained growth.

The creation of the SIM was, additionally, intended to create a larger market for EU companies to export to, and thereby lead to a rationalisation of European industry to take advantage of economies of scale and encourage specialisation in industries whereby competitive advantage had been achieved. The resulting reductions in unit costs and intensified competition were supposed to reduce prices for consumers and therefore lead to a more efficient allocation of scarce resources across the single EU economic space. Indeed, a report commissioned by the EU Commission suggested these benefits would facilitate greater economic activity and this, in turn, would provide increased resources for reflationary government expenditure, the combination of the two factors increasing EU GDP by 7% and creating 5 million new jobs across the Union (Cecchini, 1988).

Unfortunately, Cecchini's conclusions have been proven overly optimistic as his assumption of concerted reflation amongst EU nations was always implausible amidst the hegemony of neo-liberal economics adopted by most EU governments and has been further stymied by the deflationary imperatives demanded by ERM membership and EMU's stability and growth pact. Without co-ordinated reflation, a considerable proportion of Cecchini's predicted benefits flowing from the SIM would be far lower, if indeed they would materialise at all (Burkitt and Baimbridge, 1990, 1991). Furthermore, alternative predictions for the effects of the SIM, based upon more restrictive (but arguably more realistic) assumptions than those used by Cecchini, anticipated the rationalisation of European industry to cause the loss of 300,000 manufacturing jobs in the UK, possibly offset by a gain of about the same number of service jobs, and causing rising regional disparities across the UK (Cambridge Econometrics, 1990). Another study, undertaken by Bakhoven (1989), predicted that employment across the EU as a whole will *fall* by some 0.1% over the first six years of SIM operation, implying that approximately 400,000 people will lose their jobs as a direct result of the SIM.

One final point, relating to the impact of the SIM upon the UK economy, relates to its predicted advantages arising from the creation of a single market, characterised by no tariff or other barriers, stimulating the creation of additional production and international trade. However, prior to EU membership, British companies were already favoured with access to a no-tariff market comprising 120 million customers, due to membership of EFTA and maintenance of previous preferential trading relations with commonwealth nations. As a result, British companies had a pre-existing opportunity for specialisation and the possibility to glean economies of scale from this former market arrangement, and thus the shift to an EU model would have had fewer benefits for UK companies than for most of their EU member state competitors.

Anti-Membership

Opponents of UK membership of the Common Market have tended to rely upon a wider range of economic arguments in support of their preferred policy position. Interestingly, however, the policy debate in 1975 focused heavily upon issues of:

- Higher food prices due to agricultural protectionism
- Higher cost of living (largely, through not entirely, resulting from agricultural support)
- Lack of British competitiveness leading to job losses and higher unemployment
- Budget contributions to the EU would drain the UK economy of scarce resources

Analysis of contemporary opinion poll data led Broad and Geiger (1996:98) to state that the two most significant issues for UK voters in the 1975 referendum were related to the cost of living and the development of food prices. This is perhaps a surprising finding, given that the ultimate result of the referendum was a 2:1 majority in favour of continued EU membership, yet both of these issues were most closely associated with the anti-EU campaign. The 1970 White Paper itself estimated that food prices were likely to rise by 18–26% cumulatively over the transitional period, leading to the full impact of membership being experienced by the UK economy in 1977 (Broad, 2001:73). The prime cause of this upward shift in food prices, and accordingly the overall level of inflation, relates to the Common Agricultural Policy (CAP) operated by the EU. This fixed a common minimum price for all foodstuffs covered by the scheme irrespective of the existing world level of prices for these agricultural commodities, by manipulating the quantity to which consumers enjoy access. This subsidy for less efficient European producers led to an excess supply of many foodstuffs, resulting in 'wine lakes' and 'butter mountains', later often dumped upon developing markets and further destroying the competitiveness of their indigenous producers. At UK entry to the EU, CAP expenditure represented 85% of total EU budgetary expenditure, whereas after decades of demands for reform, at the time of writing, the CAP still represents approximately half of a much larger EU budget.

The constraints imposed by the CAP raised the British cost of living, whilst encouraging an inefficient transfer of resources into agricultural output away from more productive manufacturing and services. Moreover, because the UK has traditionally been a net importer of foodstuffs, higher food prices represented a deterioration in the UK's terms of trade, whilst the inflationary impact upon UK exports damaged the balance of payments. Throughout the 1980s EU food prices were on average 7% greater than those prevailing on the world market (Burkitt *et al.*, 1992). The CAP is, moreover, an expensive, inefficient method of supporting agriculture; for every £100 that farmers gain from it, consumers and taxpayers' pay £160. Total CAP agricultural support, including the taxpayers' contribution to farming via the EU budget and the expense of destroying surplus produce, cost the average British family £36 per week. Combining the effect of the higher prices caused by the CAP with the impost upon the taxpayer of maintaining the system, the average burden upon British employees is one quarter the size of their income tax and national insurance contributions (Burkitt *et al.*, 1996).

Issues relating to the lack of competitiveness and a resulting deterioration in inter-EU trade, leading to slower rates of economic growth and rising unemployment, were discussed in the previous section. However, a second element leading to a significant deterioration in UK balance of payments is associated with net budgetary payments arising from EU membership (Broad, 2001:73). Moreover, in terms of the British debate, there have been four main issues arising from the fiscal drain upon the UK budget:

- the equity of the forms of taxation selected by the EU to raise its resources
- the breakdown of the distribution of budgetary expenditure
- the size of the net contribution
- the maintenance of the UK's budgetary rebate

The EU budget is financed through four mechanisms; agricultural levies, customs duties, a proportion of VAT receipts based on a nationally harmonised basket of goods and services, and a calculation based upon the size of each nations' GDP. These means of raising tax revenues are defined as the EU's 'own resources', accounting for 2.2%, 22.6%, 15.1% and 60.1% respectively towards the EU budget in 1999. As recently as 1990, VAT receipts made the largest contribution. However, this method of raising EU revenues is biased against members like the UK, since a greater proportion of British imports arose outside Europe, it was clear that Britain's gross contribution to the EU budget would be both absolutely and proportionately greater than any other member state. In addition, the UK's historically higher-than-average consumption rates caused overpayment to the EU in comparison to the GDP per capita calculation. Furthermore the EU ignores VAT-exemption, requiring member states to transfer the same amount of revenue to the EU budget whether or not the commodities paid full rates of VAT.

This method of funding was neither fair nor transparent, so that the EU eventually restructured its revenue collection by ensuring that the fourth resource became the principal contributor to financing the budget. Nevertheless, the other three 'own resources' remain significant in terms of revenue collection, and therefore EU taxation policy is remains biased against the UK's interests. The pattern of EU expenditure and the sources of its revenue are structured so that the UK consistently contributes a greater proportion of EU finances than it receives in return or than is warranted by its national income relative to that of other member states. This phenomenon did not arise by accident, but from the inherent structure of the EU budget. Therefore, without significant reform, it will persist in the future.

In terms of the overall size of the fiscal drain upon the UK economy, the 1970 White Paper estimated that the EU budget revenue contributed by the EU(6) would approximate $2.89bn, during a five year transitional period ending in 1978, whilst the contribution from the UK would be $1.38bn. This mean that it was recognised, at an early stage, that UK budgetary contributions were to be disproportionately high relative to the nations populations size and GDP-per-head. Furthermore, budgetary planning is not assisted by the fact that annual contributions to the EU budget vary considerably due to the volatility inherent within international trade (hence customs duties), agricultural production (levies), domestic consumption (VAT) and economic growth rates (GDP). This instability would be reduced by relying more heavily upon calculations based upon the so-called 'fourth resource' (i.e. GDP).

Most recently, UK contributions to the EU budget have varied between £7 billion and £11 billion (gross). These figures take account of the 'Fontainebleau rebate', which refers to a reduction in UK budget contributions was secured in 1984, by then Prime Minister Mrs Thatcher, as partial compensation for the excessive net payments Britain was making to the EU budget. The original agreement was intended to run until 1999, but is still in operation. The rebate has been a continued form of irritation to other net contributors to the EU budget, and this position has intensified in the aftermath of the latest round of enlargement of the organisation, with the addition of ten new member states, all of whom have GDP-per-capita below the EU average, and agricultural sectors larger than the EU average. Indeed, the most recent British Presidency of the EU was dominated by budgetary issues, and pressure caused Prime Minister Tony Blair to concede a reduction of part of the rebate. This caused accusations of Blair's acting against the national interest and failing to maintain the terms of earlier public policy announcements.

The UK's contribution is not a constant amount of a static total, because the EU budget grew over the period of UK membership. EU expenditure rose by an average of 9% per annum between 1979 and 1998, when annual inflation across the EU was just 5.7%. This represents a substantial real increase in EU resources at a time when national governments were restraining their budgets; from 1995 to 1998 the EU budget increased by 13.7%, far above the 5.4% average EU inflation rate. Over the 27 years to 2000 the UK's net contribution (i.e. total payments minus total receipts) came to £47.8 billion (not allowing for inflation), of which £4.7 billion was paid in 2000 alone. The magnitude of these sums is highlighted by the average cost of building an NHS hospital at £180 million.

The distribution of EU funding has changed over the years, with agricultural support declining from over two-thirds to just half of EU expenditure, whilst various redistributive transfer schemes (such as the regional, cohesion and social funds) increased in value. The UK receives relatively little from agricultural support, due to its greater concentration on non-agricultural sectors, whilst the entry of a large number of poorer nations during the recent round of EU enlargement means that the UK is expected to lose most of the relatively small amount of regional development funds that it receives from the EU budget. Consequently, in addition to the UK paying a disproportionately large share of tax revenues to the EU budget, it additionally receives a disproportionately small proportion of EU expenditure.

British taxpayers, individual and corporate, through the mechanism of contributions to the EU budget, paid an effective disguised tariff on UK exports to the EU of 6.8% (gross) or 3.4% (net) in 1998. If Britain's net payments to the EU ceased immediately, the Chancellor could cut 2p off the standard rate of income tax without increasing the public sector borrowing requirement.

Contemporary Economic Arguments

Pro-Membership

Whilst the debate concerning the UK's continuing relationship with the EU remains active, and retains the ability to polarise public opinion to a greater extent than most economic and/or political issues, perhaps three economic arguments have been utilised particularly prominently by advocates of continued membership of the EU. These are:

- benefits created by the completion of the SIM
- the 'new Europe' acting as a world power—creating a sufficiently large economic bloc to create a distinctive model of capitalism
- net benefits arising from participation in EMU

The first of these points has been dealt with in an earlier section of this chapter. The second, however, relates to an argument advanced by many on the social democratic Left, namely that membership of an increasingly integrated Europe provides 'the only force capable of countervailing the sovereignty of the global market-place' (Marquand, 1999:15) because the objectives of national economic management could be better achieved at super-national level (Baker et al, 2002:414). The failure of the French 1981–83 Mitterrand administration to maintain a strong form of 'Keynesianism in one country' came to be viewed as a pivotal episode in international political economy, whereby national Keynesianism was increasingly viewed as obsolete as its instruments lost their power due to the opening-up of national economies, leading to leakages from reflation strategies confined to national boundaries — difficulties magnified by currency crises provoked by international financial markets (Hall, 1987; Sassoon, 1996:548–61; Callaghan, 2000:108). According to this perspective, European integration could provide the means to develop a Euro-Keynesianism, at least partially insulated from the destabilising actions of international financial markets, whilst import penetration of the common market was a far smaller percentage than for each individual member state, thereby facilitating a more effective used of aggregate demand management. In addition, pressures upon national social policy and industrial relations systems may be resolved at European level due to the lower level of international penetration, whilst common levels of social support prevent strategies of social deconstruction to secure competitive advantage. Thus, the economic space created by regional integration has the *potential* to facilitate progressive economic policies designed to create a different form of capitalism from the market-orientated, flexible labour market form of 'American model' held to be the inevitable result of globalisation.

Critics of this position point to a number of potential weaknesses in the argument, not least of which is the fact that, although this argument might have been supported by the Delors leadership of the EU Commission, times have changed and the current balance of political forces is opposed to this type of interventionist alternative economic strategy. 'Third Way' political leaders, including British Prime Minister Blair, argued that 'we need to curb the European social model, not play around with it' (Blair, 1998). His preference was for a market-adapting economic strategy, combining elements of neo-liberal and New Keynesian economic policies, which see little need for the management of aggregate demand and other central tenets of the Euro-Keynesian proposition. Indeed, on a wider basis, the Blair position towards the maintenance of a 'European Social Model' (ESM), incorporating distinctive elements of labour protection, the regulation of capital and decommoditisation through social policy, need to be replaced by a more market-orientated, supply-side policy, aimed at empowering individuals through education and training, combined with improving economic performance through increasing the flexibility of the labour market. British Chancellor of the Exchequer, Gordon Brown, likewise rejects the 'old European model, which stifled job creation with over-regulation and inflexibility' (cited in Callaghan, 2000:xi). This argument has been more or less accepted by the EU Commission, as social policy is increasingly viewed as a means of promoting adaptability and flexibility across the European economy (Vaughan-Whitehead, 2003:516–7).

The third argument advanced by supporters of continued UK participation in European integration involves UK participation in the Economic and Monetary Union (EMU), established between twelve of the then fifteen (now twenty five) EU member states on 1 January 1999. For a detailed discussion of the merits and disadvantages posed by UK participation in this initiative, a large literature exists, and full discussion of each of the points lies beyond this present chapter (Healey, 2000; Michie, 2000; Layard, 2000; Minford, 2000; Arestis and Sawyer, 2000; Currie, 2000). Nevertheless, it is worth summarising the main points made both for and against UK membership (Baimbridge et al., 2000):

- Greater nominal exchange rate stability will occur, which reduces the risk associated with fluctuating exchange rates and is therefore assumed to encourage greater trade and investment, which, in turn, should result in higher growth and employment in the longer run.

- A reduction in transaction costs should occur since firms exporting or importing goods and services to another participating country will no longer have to exchange currency to complete the sale, thereby saving upon commission charges. Whilst less onerous for large companies than tourists changing small amounts of foreign currency, the removal of this small but significant charge upon international trade should encourage exports and thereby stimulate economic growth. Even a small annual boost to economic activity may become significant if its effects are cumulative over time.

- Price transparency should increase, because goods, services and labour are priced in the same currency, facilitating traders to make cheaper purchases and increase competition across the *Euro*-zone, thereby exerting a downward pressure upon prices to the benefit of European consumers. It is further argued that this price transparency is a precondition to the final completion of the single market.

- The ECB is charged with ensuring price stability above all alternative economic goals and therefore many proponents of EMU entry argue that inflation is likely to be lower for those countries with the single currency, particularly in the longer run. Accordingly, interest rates might be lower, thereby boosting investment and economic growth.

- Creation of the *Euro* would establish a major world currency capable of rivalling the US dollar and Japanese Yen, which could confer certain economic advantages in addition to providing political prestige based upon the EU's combined economic strength and greater world political influence. This might, or might not, involve closer political integration between EU member states, which would rival the USA in terms of population and wealth.

- Advocates of EMU participation argue that failure to join will leave nation states vulnerable and incapable of influencing the monetary policy of the EMU-zone from the outside. Potential threats are suggested to include the risk of losing markets due to some sort of 'unofficial' protectionism preventing the free passage of domestically produced goods and services across the rest of the EU and the risk of losing political influence within the EU.

- Arguments that membership of EMU reduces national sovereignty are rejected on the grounds that sovereignty is not absolute any more, due to the globalisation of financial markets and voluntary limitations imposed by international treaties such as membership of NATO, the Geneva Convention, the United Nations and the World Trade Organisation. Sovereignty is not given away because nations are still able to influence decision-making through the European Council, but as one voice amongst fifteen. Thus, sovereignty is shared, or pooled, within the EU, with decision-making subject to the collective viewpoint of participating member states.

- Advocates of further European integration often point out that many critics of the single currency are content in supporting continued EU membership and the Single Internal Market

(SIM), despite the fact that both reduced national independence to a greater degree than EMU may require. The Treaty of Rome required the freedom of movement of labour and capital, thereby undermining the potential for isolating individual economies from international financial markets. This is a move exacerbated by the Single European Act (SEA) which required the abolition of exchange controls and gave the European Court of Justice jurisdiction over domestic law where a contradiction occurs. The apparent inconsistency amongst many single currency critics may undermine their arguments or require them to reassess continued EU membership, a policy which appears to be less popular than opposition to EMU.

- Finally, the argument which caused the majority of national trade unions to accept EMU entry is based upon their desire to achieve the European 'social model'. The example of recent Conservative government in the UK convinced many trade union leaders that locking the economy into a European model, which embraces a social dimension, is an improvement upon the *laissez-faire* alternative variously supported by Labour and Conservative leaderships. The conditionality of this support distinguishes trade unionists from other advocates of EMU, because of their concern that the social dimension may be abandoned in favour of fiscal rectitude.

Anti-Membership

Opponents of continued membership of the EU, although a minority amongst the political elite, nevertheless have continued to voice their arguments more visibly in the past decade than has been the case after the set-back for their point of view arising from the 1975 referendum result. Partly this may reflect the fact that a number of years has passed and therefore it might be regarded as reasonable to take the political temperature of this issue once again. It might additionally reflect the fact that the EU has itself changed dramatically during the UK's three decades of membership, and therefore a second referendum might be justified to ascertain whether the British electorate mandate, given to continued membership a mere few years after first joining the organisation, remains valid. Thus, a number of publications have sought to evaluate issues as diverse as the cost of the CAP, fiscal drain resulting from budget contributions and international trade considerations (Burkitt *et al.*, 1996; Milne, 2004; Minford *et al.*, 2005; Baimbridge and Whyman, 2006). Nevertheless, more generally, Euro-sceptics have focused upon opposing additional initiatives taken to pursue a wider and deeper regional economic integration amongst EU member states. Thus, the two primary issues upon which this work focuses, relates to EU initiatives in the field of exchange rate management, namely:

- the Exchange Rate Mechanism (ERM)
- Economic and Monetary Union (EMU)

The European Monetary System (EMS) was created after the break-up of the Bretton Woods fixed exchange rate system, and the Exchange Rate Mechanism (ERM) was established in 1979 within the EMS. The ERM involved participating countries fixing their currencies against each other, with bilateral rates circulated against all others and consequently against the central European Currency Unit (ECU) rate, with each currency allowed to fluctuate between 2.25% (under the 'hard ERM' system) and 15% (after the 1992 ERM crisis) of their central rate to other members'. The desire was to create enhanced currency certainty and thereby facilitate the creation of the SIM and encourage further European integration. Initially protected by exchange controls and with frequent realignments permitted if currencies became fundamentally misaligned, the ERM performed quite adequately. However, in the run-up to establishing the single currency exchange controls were withdrawn and realignments ended, leading to the so-called period of 'hard ERM'.

The idea was to condition currencies to the reality that would exist once EMU was introduced. Moreover, it was at this point the UK decided to become a member of the ERM in October 1990, at a fixed central parity of 2.95 deutschmarks to the pound, a rate intended to put pressure upon the UK economy to reduce inflation rather than setting a competitive exchange rate. Unsurprisingly, this chosen rate proved to be grossly over-valued and contributed to forcing the UK into a recession. Organising a common reflation package across the ERM participants was complicated by the fact that Germany was, temporarily, enjoying an inflationary boom in the aftermath of reunification, whilst most other member states were suffering from deflation. Rising German interest rates therefore exacerbated the problems for other ERM member states, forcing their currencies to the margins of allowed fluctuations from the Deutschmark, and thereby encouraging destabilising speculation against those currencies perceived as over-valued. This included Sterling, the Swedish krona, Finnish marka, Spanish peseta, Italian lira, Irish pound and the French franc—indeed, it was only the latter currency, with the benefit of large short term financial loans, that managed to withstand speculatory pressures without having to widen its range of permitted fluctuations, devalue or otherwise leave the ERM altogether.

The period of ERM membership, from October 1990 to September 1992, represented a difficult period for the British economy. From expanding at a rate of 2% per annum prior to entry, the restraints imposed upon productive activity due to an over-valued currency were so severe that the economy headed into recession. During the two years of membership, GDP shrunk by 3.8%, being associated with six out of eight quarters of negative growth. Under these circumstances, unemployment rose by 1.2 million to a total of 2.85 million on official government figures.

Whilst it would be exaggerating to claim that this period of economic decline was caused solely by ERM membership, it is worth noting that the economy expanded by an average of 2% per annum immediately prior to membership and also in its aftermath. Moreover, the unemployment rate was 5.5% before sterling joined the ERM, rose sharply afterwards, but started to fall again once the UK departed. Of course, other factors influenced these developments (e.g. German reunification), but it was the restrictions imposed upon macroeconomic policy by the ERM, which prevented the UK from responding to deflationary pressures by expansionary fiscal and monetary policy to limit the damage inflicted upon jobs and output. One estimate suggested that, adding the costs borne by the UK Treasury (£10.8 billion), lost output (£53.4 billion) and the fall in value of the UK's official reserves (£3 billion), the ERM experiment cost £67.2 billion or 11.3% of 1992 UK GDP (Burkitt et al., 1996).

The second area where Euro-sceptics have concentrated most of their efforts, in more recent years, has been to seek to prevent UK participation in EMU. Critics have made much of the fact that in its present form, EMU is without precedent in the history of the civilised world, since there has never been an economic and monetary union between a group of countries without a simultaneous movement towards political union. Even the most successful fixed rate regimes, the Classical Gold Standard together with that arising from the post-WWII Bretton Woods conference, which facilitated the establishment of an international economic environment that each encouraged around three decades of economic expansion, were each terminated due to a combination of political and economic factors. Moreover, EMU involves a step-change in regional economic integration in Europe, as it involves 'one of the most-far-reaching transfers of sovereignty to European level' that EU member states have thus far experienced (Verdun, 2000:1).

Therefore, to balance the earlier list of potential benefits that advocates claim may arise from participation in EMU, the principal arguments advanced by those critical towards EMU, include:

- The loss of control over monetary policy and of influence over the exchange rate weakens national economic management, which is further constrained by the restraints upon fiscal policy resulting from the Maastricht Convergence Criteria (MCC) and Stability Pact rules on government borrowing. This combination reduces the potential capacity of a country to respond to internal or external shocks, exacerbating the danger of national destabilisation.

- The lack of prior cyclical and structural convergence amongst all participating member states will create strains within EMU. Consequently, unsynchronised business cycles and/or structural differences magnify the effects of asymmetric external shocks (i.e. oil price rises), whilst a unified monetary policy will be unable to meet satisfactorily the needs of all economies, concentrating upon the 'average' member state as it is likely to do. Thus, incorrectly set interest rates may damage individual economies, increasing their initial misfortunes rather than moderating them.

- The 'generous' interpretation of the MCC in order to ensure as many countries as possible participated in EMU implies that the majority of participants must continue to deflate their economies by raising taxes or cutting government spending in order to meet the rigid financial criteria established by the MCC and Stability Pact. The combination of these measures will result in higher unemployment and slower growth within the single currency zone.

- The absence of any substantial fiscal redistribution mechanism, which could stabilise EMU by transferring resources from favoured to weaker regions, means that less competitive areas may suffer declining incomes and persistent mass unemployment, thereby increasing inequality and social tension across the single currency area.

- Many of the economic objectives claimed by single currency advocates could be achieved through effective national economic management, such as price stability, high economic growth and full employment. Moreover, since the ECB will include Mediterranean countries as well as Germany, it is unlikely that it will initially possess the anti-inflation credibility that the Bundesbank enjoyed, meaning that the *Euro* might be a weak currency.

- The costs of transition to the new currency may be in the region of £18.5 billion, thereby cautioning against participation unless the benefits can be demonstrated to be substantially higher over time.

- The private financial sectors in certain countries (i.e. UK) are more sensitive to changes in interest rates since a higher proportion of mortgage debt is denominated in flexible rather than fixed interest rate stock. Consequently, were the ECB to vary interest rates in order to stimulate or restrain average EMU economic activity, nations including the UK would bear a disproportionate brunt of the corrective measures, causing the economy to diverge further from the EMU average. Thus, a uniform monetary policy would be likely to create fluctuating boom-bust cycles in the UK economy rather than a smooth and sustainable rate of economic development.

- Individual nation states have competitive advantage in different sectors of production — i.e. Germany has an advantage in medium-level technological metalworking, whilst Britain has an advantage in high technology, aeronautical, pharmaceutical and energy sectors. The latter grouping, however, are typically priced in US dollars and compete principally with US and Japanese companies even when exporting to other EU member states. Thus, the sterling-dollar exchange rate will remain far more important to this key element of British manufacturing than sterling-*Euro*, and hence participation in the *Euro* might increase exchange rate volatility for a crucial sector of the UK economy. This is not the case for DM-*Euro*.

- Opponents of EMU dismiss the threat of loss of markets through protectionist measures enacted by single currency members against non-participants in the project since these would flout the Treaty of Rome, the Single European Act, the 'Maastricht' Treaty on European Union and the rules of the World Trade Organisation.

- Critics of European integration generally reject the view that sovereignty can be pooled, suggesting that it refers to a national authority using every means at its disposal to achieve its objectives, within the constraints imposed by international markets and treaty obligations. Thus, sovereignty can be exercised *either* by national government *or* by the EU, but not by both. EMU would result in the loss of economic sovereignty to the ECB, with national authorities losing autonomy.

- The ECB is undemocratic because it is deliberately insulated from all political influence; the authors of the Maastricht Treaty believed that such insulation would enhance its ability to secure price stability. Thus, electors would no longer be able to influence monetary and exchange rate policies, whilst fiscal policy is also tightly constrained through the Growth and Stability Pact. These policies deeply affect individual citizens' lives, from setting the cost of their mortgage to the possibility of losing their job.

- In an ever-changing economic environment, the optimal value of the exchange rate, which facilitates full employment of domestic resources and an external trade balance simultaneously, will vary, and therefore it is crucial for each country to retain control over all national policy instruments. Badly constructed fixed exchange rate systems, on the other hand, such as the 1920s return to the Gold Standard on pre-First World War parities, or the ERM crisis of 1992 when shifts in economic fundamentals combined with economic policies harmful for some member states, were associated with economic recession, bankruptcies, house price collapses and mass unemployment. Consequently, whilst a properly constructed system can be a benefit to participating countries, a badly designed regime can cause untold damage to its members.

- One final criticism is that, rather than EMU creating a European super-state, it is in fact designed to 'roll back' the state and reduce its ability to regulate the actions of the owners of private capital and the international financial markets in the interests of their citizens. Increased constraints placed upon government economic autonomy reduce the choices available through the democratic process, whilst limiting the ability of one country to pursue a significantly unorthodox economic strategy intended to meet nation-specific goals.

Critics of EMU claim that fundamental structural differences between individual European economies preclude an easy 'marriage'. This has heightened the problem that federal economic policies would have to manage the entire EMU-zone, because it is likely that common monetary policies would prove unsuitable to the circumstances of outlying economies, potentially resulting in the reinforcement of both inflationary and depressed zones on the margin of the EMU economy. On the most optimistic scenario, EMU could re-create a golden era similar to the original Gold Standard of the nineteenth century or post-war Bretton Woods, when members shared decades of economic growth and relative price stability.

However, at worst, it would generate the conditions pertaining in the 1930s depression, as adherence to a fixed exchange rate unsuitable to the economic realities of individual countries compounds the misery of mass unemployment.

Conclusion

This chapter has sought to highlight the development of the economic element of the wider debate concerning the future relationship between the UK and the EU. Shifting from a referendum specifically concerning whether the UK should continue as a member of the EU or pursue an independent model of development, the majority of critics of further integration have tended to shift towards opposing piecemeal new initiatives rather than concentrate upon the advocacy of withdrawal. This is not to say that these arguments are not still being made—hopefully this chapter will have highlighted a number of areas where this is still very much the case—but it is certainly true that this signifies a significant shift. Likewise, whilst certain of the issues may remain as relevant today as they did thirty years ago, others have been considerably relegated in importance. Thus, whilst the cost of food and the inflationary impact of the EU were two of the major issues concerning the electorate in 1975, this one-off shift in prices has occurred and, whilst withdrawal from the CAP might precipitate a likewise drop in the price level, due to a shift to lower world food prices, these are treated as mostly peripheral issues to the main debate. In their place, the potential damage caused by participating in one or other of the EU's fixed exchange rate initiatives, whether ERM or EMU, has become one of the main features of the opposition to further integration using economic arguments.

Eight

Political and Sovereignty Issues of Membership

Introduction

The British debate over participation in the process of regional economic and political integration, through membership of the European Union (EU) or one of its former institutional formats[1], has concentrated upon the former—namely the economic case for and against the project. Yet this *practical* analysis has not entirely been mirrored in other EU member states. Political aspirations were foremost amongst those who influenced the fledgling EU institutional pattern and policy programme. Thus, in many European nations, rather than the debate focussing upon the price of a basket of foodstuffs, it encompassed such weighty subjects as definitions of political sovereignty in the post-WWII period. The preamble to the European Coal and Steel Community (ECSC), ratified in 1951, was quite explicit in its anticipated objectives, when it stated that it perceived the organisation as 'the first step to the federation of Europe', whereas the Treaty of Rome, signed six years later, was to replace this clarity with the statement that it promoted 'an ever closer union of the peoples of Europe' (Broad, 2001:25). Thus, the political debate concerning the future of European integration has long been more advanced in other established EU member states than in the UK. Nevertheless, despite this feature of the UK contribution to the wider debate on the future direction of European integration, there have been a number of political issues which have remained signifi-

---

[1] The EU has been formerly known as the Common Market, European Communities (EC) and only latterly, with the ratification of the 1991 *'Maastricht' Treaty of European Union*, been given its current title.

cant throughout the 1975 referendum debate and the subsequent time period. This chapter will seek to focus upon these key questions.

Table 8.1 – Chronology of British Government Policy Towards Membership

Year	Policy of the UK Government
1950	Labour government declined to participate in the Schuman Plan negotiations – this led to the creation of the predecessor to the EU, namely the European Coal and Steel Community (ECSC).
1957	Signing of the Treaty of Rome establishing the European Economic Community and the European Atomic Energy Community – known as the European Communities (EC).
1959	Conservative government helped to create the European Free Trade Association (EFTA).
1961	Conservative government submitted formal application for EU membership.
1963	French President, Charles de Gaulle vetoed the UK application for EU membership.
1971	UK membership of EU ratified.
1975	UK Referendum – to retain EU membership on the revised terms negotiated by the Labour government or withdraw.
1986	SIM agreed.
1991	Maastricht Treaty – proposing the establishment of EMU
1992	SIM established.
1999	EMU initiated between 11 (later 12) EU member states

Britain and the European Union

The European policy of the British State shifted several times over the post-war period. Between 1945 and 1948 it was enthusiastic about European integration. However, between 1949 and 1960 it tried to steer the process towards an intergovernmental direction, in an attempt to contain the supranational ambitions of the Six. Its failure precipitated a process of gradual engagement, including two failed applications to join the EU in August 1961 and May 1967, culminating in Britain's accession in January 1973. Contrary to expectations, the referendum on continued membership in June 1975 did not settle the issue, leading Britain to be dubbed the 'awkward partner' (George, 1990) and Britons, the 'reluctant Europeans' (Worcester, 2000). Post-war British policy towards European political integration should be situated within the wider context of the post-war world order, with particular reference to the 'special relationship' with the US.

A European Third Force (1945–1948)

The primary objective following the Second World War was to preserve Britain's role and status as a 'great power'. Following a number of studies conducted in 1944, the Foreign Office concluded that, to maintain its 'great power' status, Britain should restore its empire after the war. However, Britain's economic weakness in the early post-war period negated such a strategy. The war cost £7.3 billion, which amounted to one quarter of Britain's pre-war wealth, whilst Britain had also accumulated £3.3 billion worth of debt (Her Majesty's Government [HMG], 1945). Hence, the restoration of Empire strategy was abandoned in favour of a European third force policy, pursued by the Foreign Office between 1945 and 1948, which envisaged the creation of some form of European entity led by Britain. Three schemes were devised: Anglo-French economic co-ordination, the 'Euro-Africa' plan based on the common exploitation of Europe's colonies, and a European customs union. However, the policy was abandoned in 1948 in favour of an Anglo-US 'special relationship'.

Although Britain was initially resistant to US designs, exploring the possibilities of a restoration of Empire strategy, plus an imperial third force policy, its dependence on the US precipitated the cultivation of a 'special relationship' as an alternative means of preserving British power. Hence, the primary objective of British foreign policy since 1948 has been to maintain the 'special relationship' which has guided the actions of successive British governments to the present.

In February 1949 Bevin sanctioned the creation of the Permanent Under-Secretary's Committee, equivalent to the US State Department Policy Planning Staff, to consider long-term questions of foreign policy and to make recommendations. One such report, produced in March 1949, identified the centrality of Anglo-American relations to British policy. 'In the face of implacable Soviet hostility and in view of our economic dependence on the United States, the immediate problem is to define the nature of our relationship with the United States' (Foreign Office, 1949a). Another report produced in March 1949 highlighted the 'importance of our maintaining control of the periphery' around the Soviet Union 'which runs round from Oslo to Tokyo'. It recommended that 'this policy should be concerted with the United States' (Foreign Office, 1949b). In January 1960 the Cabinet Office (1960d) noted that 'our partnership with the United States is an existing source of world power and our status in the world will largely depend on their readiness to treat us as their closest ally'. In September 1964 the Foreign Office (1964) conceded that the 'alliance with the United States is the single most important factor in our foreign policy. The possibility of a hostile Unites States reaction is a considerable deterrent to our adopting a given policy as the certainty of United States support is an encouragement.'

Critically, the one-sided nature of the 'special relationship', a situation of British dependence rather than Anglo-US partnership, was acknowledged as early as August 1945. Britain was a 'junior partner in an orbit of power predominantly under American aegis' (Foreign Office, 1945d). Likewise, the Foreign Office's 1947 assessment warned that 'too great independence of the United States would be a dangerous luxury', whilst acknowledging that the US was 'consciously or unconsciously tending to claim global leadership' (Foreign Office, 1947c). The stark reality of the 'special relationship' was exposed during the September 1949 sterling crisis and the November 1956 Suez crisis. However, post-1948, British policy towards European integration was framed within the context of the 'special relationship'.

Limited Liability (1949–1955)

In January 1949 an interdepartmental meeting of Foreign Office, Treasury, and other officials outlined the essential characteristics of the limited liability policy, which operated between 1949 and 1955:

Our policy should be to assist Europe to recover as far as we can. But the concept must be one of limited liability. In no circumstances must we assist them beyond the point at which the assistance leaves us too weak to be a worthwhile ally for the US if Europe collapses, i.e. beyond the point at which our own viability was impaired. Nor can we embark upon measures of 'co-operation' which surrender our sovereignty and which lead us down paths along which there is no return (quoted in Clarke, 1982, p. 209).

The results of this policy include the Labour's rejection of the Schuman Plan and the Conservatives' opposition to the EDC and EPC in favour of the Eden Plan, plus its attempts to wreck the June 1955 Messina Conference. The Eden Plan, published in February 1952, advocated the reform of the Council of Europe to incorporate the Schuman Plan and the EDC. It aimed to provide an alternative to the 'small group of states which are moving towards political federation by the progressive establishment of organisations exercising supranational powers' (Cabinet Office, 1952). Although the plan was rejected, such efforts led Spaak (1971, p. 225) to conclude that 'we must do without Britain's support if we are to make any headway'. Spaak agreed with Monnet that they should 'create a united Europe and Britain will join'.

The post-Messina period was problematic for the British. In November 1955 the Foreign Office (1955) declared that Britain was not against special groupings of OEEC member countries for functional purposes, but remained sceptical and suspicious of the Monnets of the European world who, having failed so far in their political objectives, were using the slogan of 'economic integration' as their stalking horse.

Before Messina, Treasury economists who had been studying the customs union proposal for several years repeated their work, concluding that its benefits would exceed any loss of Commonwealth markets. The Foreign Office disagreed, warning that a common market would be 'a discriminatory bloc most unwelcome to us' (Foreign Office, 1955). However, the Cabinet Mutual Aid Committee assessment in October 1955 ruled it out on the grounds that it would 'increase the relative importance of our trade with Europe and reduce our economic links with the Commonwealth'. This would have 'a profound effect on the readiness of other Commonwealth countries to co-operate with us in the Sterling Area' and would 'damage the Imperial Preference system'. Furthermore, 'once we became members of a common market, we should be subject to strong political pressures to extend the "harmonisation" of our policies with those of other members beyond the field of tariffs into other fields both of internal and external policy' (Cabinet Office, 1955).

Although the Six had invited Britain to join the Spaak Committee without preconditions, in November 1955 the Cabinet decided to withdraw. Nevertheless by April 1956 it was clear that the limited liability policy was redundant. The Foreign Office (1956) declared that 'if a proposal for a common market of the "Six" came into being' it would be so 'dangerous to our economic interests that we should have to make special arrangements with it, even at the expense of our interests elsewhere'.

Partial Engagement (1956-1959)

The 1956 Suez crisis precipitated a shift in policy, to one of partial engagement, as Britain attempted to re-capture the leadership of Europe. One manifestation was the plan for a free trade area in manufactured goods, presented to the Cabinet by Harold Macmillan in September 1956. 'Plan G' was one of the seven options devised by the Treasury in anticipation of Messina. It envisaged the creation of a 17-member Free Trade Area (FTA), in which the Six would constitute the core of a wider membership. In an attempt to reinstate the intergovernmental principle, and thus supplant the Six, the British recommended the integration of the FTA within the OEEC. However, France and the US rejected the FTA proposal. George Ball (1968, p. 79), Under-Secretary of State for Economic Affairs, set out why the US supported British entry: 'If Britain is now prepared to recognise that the Rome Treaty is not a static document but a process that could eventually lead to an evolving European Community, something in the nature of a European federation, and if Britain can make the great national decision to join Europe on these terms, I am confident that my government will regard this as a major contribution to Western solidarity and the stability of the free world.'

Following the rejection of the FTA proposal in November 1956, Britain opted for the smaller EFTA, whilst Macmillan (1959) decided to turn his attention to 'how to live with the Common Market economically, and turn its political effects into harmless channels for us'. However, Sir Roderick Barclay (1960), head of the British delegation to the European Commission, warned that the aim of the EU 'was not merely harmonisation but the unification of policies in every field of the economic union, economic policy, social policy, commercial policy, tariff policy and fiscal policy'.

Near Identification and the First Application (1960–1963)

During the early 1960s a new generation of pro-EU officials joined the civil service, displacing those loyal to the Commonwealth. This precipitated the development of a new pro-entry orthodoxy within the Foreign Office and the Treasury, a process assisted by the transfer of Sir Frank Lee to the Treasury in January 1960. As noted by Bell (1995, p. i), the shift 'amounted to a revolution in political thought; in a short period at the beginning of the sixties entry to the EU was turned from an impossibility into an imperative'. The rationale behind this new orthodoxy was identified by Evans (1975, pp. 81–82): the Foreign Office began to see the EU as 'an empire on our doorstep', whilst the Treasury believed that 'if Britain could acquire an expanded home market, then industrial revival would follow'.

In March 1960 an interdepartmental committee of senior civil servants, chaired by Lee, was established to review Britain's European policy. The Lee memorandum, published in May, argued that negotiating entry would involve 'difficult and unpalatable decisions' including some surrender of sovereignty (Cabinet Office, 1960a). It recommended a policy of near identification, that is, accepting many of its obligations without formal membership. Macmillan subsequently stated that the 'policies of "near identification" and of joining the Common Market were so similar that one might well lead to the other, and if we were prepared to accept near identification, it might be preferable to contemplate full membership' (Cabinet Office, 1960b).

In June 1960 Macmillan circulated a memorandum to officials, asking them to answer 23 questions. The subsequent report, discussed by a Cabinet committee, stated that: 'We cannot join the Common Market on the cheap. First we must accept that there will have to be a political content in our action – we must show ourselves prepared to join with the Six in their institutional arrangements and in any development towards closer political integration. Without this we cannot achieve our foreign policy aims. Secondly, there must be a real intention to have a "common market" in general we must accept the common tariff' (Cabinet Office, 1960c). The memorandum also considered the issue of timing, recommending a delay of between 12 and 18 months, rather than an immediate application.

The Cabinet discussed the Lee memorandum, plus the answers to the 23 questions, in July 1960. However, it was apparent that it was divided on the benefits and costs of entry. Two weeks later,

Macmillan restructured the Cabinet in favour of pro-EU ministers. Looking back on this period, Young (1998, p. 123) noted that no ministerial paper was put to the Cabinet, making this 'an officials' operation. Denman (1996, p. 211) charged that 'it must be the only occasion in British history when a memorandum by an official was largely responsible for a momentous change in British foreign policy'.

In March 1961 George Ball re-emphasised US support for British entry. In a meeting with Heath and Lee, Ball stated that 'the United States deeply regretted that the United Kingdom had not yet felt able to accept the Rome Treaty commitments. British membership of the Community would represent a contribution of great importance to the cohesion of the Free World' (Foreign Office, 1961).

Between April and July 1961 several Cabinet committee meetings discussed the implications of entry with the Cabinet considering several papers that had been produced by a number of officials. The Lord Chancellor assessed the legal implications, warning that:

> (a) Parliament would be required to surrender some of its functions to the organs of the Community. (b) The Crown would be called on to transfer part of its treaty-making power to those organs. (c) Our courts of law would sacrifice some degree of independence by becoming subordinate in certain respects to the European Court of Justice. In the long run, we shall have to decide whether the economic factors require us to make some sacrifices of sovereignty. My concern is to ensure that we should see exactly what it is that we are being called on to sacrifice, and how serious our loss would be (Foreign Office, 1960).

Other officials acknowledged the loss of sovereignty, stating that:

> in the past, the loss of national sovereignty has been the most potent argument against British participation in supranational institutions. It was to a large extent responsible for our decision, in 1950, not to join the ECSC and, in 1955, to withdraw from the discussions which led eventually to the drafting of the Treaty of Rome. Although the Treaty of Rome does not express this explicitly, it has underlying political objectives, which are to be brought about by a gradual surrender of sovereignty (Cabinet Office, 1961).

Officials also conceded the risks involved in qualified majority voting. By signing the Treaty of Rome, Britain 'would be committing itself to a range of indefinite obligations over a wide field of action within the economic and social sphere'. Officials warned that these 'might subsequently be translated into specific obligations by means of a decision, regulation or directive adopted by the Council with which we would not necessarily agree' (Cabinet Office, 1961).

However, these assessments were never placed in the public domain and in June and July of 1961 Macmillan consulted with the Commonwealth about British entry. In July the Cabinet agreed to open negotiations with the Six. Macmillan announced his decision to Parliament on the 31st July, giving an undertaking that he would consult parliament before entering into any agreement. However, he refused to publish a White Paper. Furthermore, as noted by Bell (1995, p. 72), paraphrasing Camps (1964), once the House of Commons

> had approved the government's motion it would be extremely difficult for it to oppose entry unless the terms were clearly unsatisfactory. By the use of the argument that they were seeking approval only for the terms, the government got the House onto the narrow technical ground.

On the 9th August Macmillan formally submitted Britain's first application to join the EU and the negotiations opened in October.

The Second Application (1964–1967)

Following Labour's 1964 General Election victory, Harold Wilson reaffirmed the party's five conditions for entry: safeguarding Britain's trade with the Commonwealth, its freedom to pursue an independent foreign policy, its obligations to the EFTA, its ability to plan the economy and its commitment to British agriculture. However, under the influence of pro-EU civil servants, Wilson began to shift in favour of entry. In April 1965 Michael Palliser announced that Labour was conducting a 'genuine reappraisal' of its European policy and warned that 'any continuing insistence on the five conditions will seriously hamper Labour's efforts in this direction' Foreign Office (1965). Shore (2000, p. 71) charged that Palliser, then Private Secretary to the Prime Minister, 'ensured that no Eurosceptic argument or critique put to Wilson went unchallenged'. Whitehall's campaign to sideline the conditions also included Sir Con O'Neill's paper *How to get into the Common Market* circulated in August 1966.

By the spring of 1967 Wilson was determined to join and, together with Foreign Secretary George Brown, embarked on an official tour of the European capitals to sound out opinion. At the end of April the Cabinet voted 13-8 in favour of reopening negotiations with the Six, with a view to joining the EU. When the decision was put to the House of Commons in May, three-line whips were imposed on both

Conservative and Labour MPs. The decision was carried by 488 votes to 62, with 35 Labour MPs voting against. Britain's second application to join the EU was formally submitted on the 10th May 1967, only to be vetoed by de Gaulle in November. Nevertheless, Shore (1993, 2000) revealed that a Cabinet sub-committee of pro-EU ministers was established in 1969 to prepare positions and papers for a third application. However, the full Cabinet was not informed of this.

Accession (1970-1972)

The primary objective of the Conservatives, following their 1970 General Election victory, was to secure entry. Heath (1998, p. 724) expressed his 'belief in the general benefit for Europe, as well as for Britain, of our being a full, and full-hearted, member'. To achieve this, Heath established the European Secretariat in the Cabinet Office and the third leg of Britain's negotiations began. Heath inherited Labour's negotiating team and proceeded on that basis between July 1970 and January 1972.

O'Neill (2000), who led the negotiations, claimed that there was no discontinuity between the third application and those submitted by previous governments. However, there was one aspect of discontinuity: the direction and responsibility for the negotiations was transferred from the Foreign Office to the Cabinet Office, in order to facilitate direct executive control.

The Conservatives' White Paper, stressing the economic and political benefits of entry, was published on the 7th July 1971. However, it dismissed the notion that entry would undermine national sovereignty. 'What is proposed' it claimed, 'is a sharing and an enlargement of individual national sovereignties in the general interest' (HMG, 1971).

O'Neill (2000, p. 355) declared that Britain's priority was 'to get into the Community, and thereby restore our position at the centre of European affairs which, since 1958, we had lost'. However, he acknowledged that post-war US foreign policy, long supportive of European integration, had shifted to a more sceptical position under President Richard Nixon. The shift was based on the fear that, 'in the long term the EEC may develop into a gigantic trading area which will effectively discriminate against US interests'. O'Neill advised Heath to assuage US concerns by emphasising 'the importance we attach to making progress with the political integration of Europe, including closer defence co-operation alongside the economic development' (O'Neill, 2000 p. 371–372).

Following the successful conclusion of the entry negotiations, and with public opinion moving in the required direction, the Conservatives decided to act. The House of Commons debated a motion in favour of entry in October 1971. As a result of the 69 Labour MPs defying the party whip and voting with the Conservatives, the motion was carried in the final division on the 28th October. In January 1972 the Conservatives signed the Treaty of Accession and published the European Communities Bill. There were 104 votes during the Bill's passage, and although government majorities fell to single figures several times, not one vote was lost. Using the guillotine measure to expedite its passage, the Bill was passed on the 17th October 1972. Britain joined the EU on the 1st January 1973.

1975 and All of That

The circumstances pertaining at the beginning of the referendum debate, in 1975, were that the governing political party, the Labour Party, was split on the issue, with a 'withdrawal' policy passed by the annual conference effectively opposed by the party's leadership, which resorted to the novel device of the referendum as a means to avoid a damaging split. The other mainstream political parties supported continued EU membership. Thus, the debate was held between two broad cross party coalitions—the pro-EU campaign dominated by the Conservative Party together with key figures from the Labour Party (i.e. Jenkins, Williams and Healey), whereas the anti-EU campaign was dominated by individuals from the Labour Party (i.e. Gaitskill, Benn, Castle) and trade unions, together with individuals such as Enoch Powell from the Ulster Unionists. The 'Yes' campaign was therefore associated with centrists from British politics, whereas the 'No' campaign brought together individuals from the Right and Left of the political spectrum. The 'Yes' campaign received substantially greater funding than the 'No' campaign, and enjoyed additional resources such as the informal use of corporate personnel managers to impart influence over their workforces on the basis that withdrawal from the EU might affect future investment and employment levels (Mullen and Burkitt, 2004).

It was, therefore, not surprising that the cohesion of the 'No' campaign was lacking, and it was difficult for all participants to agree on a positive vision of an alternative, independent Britain due to deep differences in objectives. For example, whether withdrawal should shift towards a low tax economy, characterised by neo-liberal economics, or alternatively to avoid constraints the EU might place upon the transition to a British socialist (or social democratic) economy, or, like Crossman, to be used to create 'an offshore, socialist Britain, cutting its overseas commitments and trying to attain an economic position as favourable as Japan's in the Far East' (Broad, 2001:69).

Public opinion polls were still relatively new tools of political analysis, in 1975, and rudimentary in design and methods of evaluation. Nevertheless, the data derived from these polls indicated that British voters were concerned with a range of issues which concerned them about membership, which could broadly be separated into economic and political elements, the former being discussed in Chapter 7. Of those declaring a preference, 58% of those polled claimed that the issue of the cost of living was central to how they would vote, with 37% stating food prices, 15% unemployment, and 9% each to independence and sovereignty (Broad and Geiger, 1996:98).

Overall support for EU membership had peaked at 65% in 1967, when membership was being theoretically debated, to a low of 18% in 1970, when membership became imminent, with 70% declaring their opposition to the proposal (Wistrich, 2001:41; Mullen and Burkitt, 2004:9). When seeking to determine the degree of intensity of belief on the question, Butler and Kitzinger (1999:94-5) claimed that the British electorate was divided into three roughly equal groups; pro-EU, anti-EU and what they termed the 'hesitants'. Thus, the opinion poll evidence did not necessarily signify such a firm position for the 'No' campaign at the start of the referendum process, because this signified the starting point that 'hesitants' preferred remaining non-aligned. However, their ability to be influenced by the arguments delivered during the referendum campaign meant that the superior resources available to the pro-EU forces could be utilised to try to sway this group and thereby create a working majority for continued EU membership.

Issues Dominating the Political Debate—Then and Now

Defence and Foreign Policy

Motivation towards considering EU membership typically involved one or more aspects of international relations, relating chiefly to being the means of preventing war amongst neighbouring European nations. Thus, the devastation of the 1939–45 war led to the search for new political structures to encourage co-operation between France and Germany, and thereby minimise the danger of another European conflict. Secondly, the creation of the EU as a cold war institutional arrangement arose from the fact that no single European nation felt confident about resisting potential Soviet aggression through its own efforts and therefore each sought to combine its military efforts with its neighbours. Although the former argument is still used by advocates of EU integration as proof that the organisation works in practice, both of these points have lost much of their former relevance. The Soviet Union has collapsed and, although new entrant member states to the EU (i.e. Baltic states) may have cause for concern that the Russian Federation may seek to unduly influence political and/or economic events in neighbouring countries, the military threat has faded from that feared throughout the early years of EU establishment.

More recently, one of the arguments relating to maintaining EU membership, and indeed adopting new initiatives designed to deepen political and economic integration, has focused upon the ability of the EU to act as a world power, and therefore that the UK and other member states would gain far greater influence in the development of world affairs by being one voice within the organisation than acting as an independent, moderately sized nation state. It is claimed that, rather than speaking with multiple, diverse voices, a single unified EU position would command greater importance and respect.

Sovereignty

Issues of national sovereignty were at the heart of the political debate over EU membership in 1975 and have continued to feature strongly in more recent years. Sovereignty relates to the pre-eminence of national decision-making and the independence of the nation state to pursue its own distinctive agenda. Sovereignty is related to a nation's supremacy within its own territorial boundaries. In a parliamentary democracy, the supreme power rests in the sovereignty of the people, temporarily ceded to their elected parliamentary representatives and used to create legislation that has pre-eminence over all other rules created by other nations outside this national territory.

Critics of EU membership pointed to the fact that, prior to EU membership, UK citizens were sovereign through parliament, and there was nothing that they were unable to accomplish in UK territory, by law. No other authority inside or outside the UK possessed superior powers within the UK. EU membership meant significant changes in a number of respects, including the fact that EU law took precedence over British law. One powerful example of this concerned the *aquis communitaire*, which refers to the process whereby all new entrants to the EU must accept all existing laws, rules and regulations without having the ability to question or renegotiate anything in the national interest. Moreover, this European Court has ruled that, when the EU has laid down rules for the implementation of a common policy, EU institutions have exclusive competence to enter into agreements with non-member states that affect these rules. Thus, the House of Lords is no longer the supreme court in the land, but must refer questions of EU law to the European Court and be bound by its rulings. It is, moreover, the duty of national governments to implement EU laws within their territory. Hence, EU regulations impose quotas upon UK fishermen exercising their trade in UK territorial waters and a nation would violate Article 5 of the Treaty of Rome if it attempted to enter into any international treaty conflicting with EU law. Furthermore, EU competence even extends to the ability to raise taxation and spend monies within each member state independently of the government's overall macroeconomic policy stance. Certainly, this provoked the then leader of the Labour Party opposition, Harold Wilson, in a speech given to the Parliamentary Press Gallery, on 30 January 1973, to claim that:

> In 93 legislative words, the safeguards gained after centuries of constitutional struggle, and even bloody civil wars, were swept aside by a provision that said simply that hereafter anything enacted by the EEC automatically becomes a British law, annulling any laws which were inconsistent without debate. We have sold, with hardly a murmur from the media, our constitutional birthright for a mess of highly problematical economic pottage. (Burkitt, 1975:8).

An additional element encompassed within the concept of national sovereignty refers to the ability of a nation state to create sufficient political and economic space to be able to create a different type of society than other leading world economies. In this regard, it has been suggested that, by joining together, medium and small European nations can form a sufficiently large economic bloc to be partially independent of the pressure exerted by globalisation to adopt the 'American model' of market-determination and flexible labour markets, in favour of a 'European model' characterised by a social market approach. The creation of a European Social Model, discussed in greater detail in Chapter 5, is one example of this argument.

By contrast, opponents of EU membership argue that the restrictions placed upon UK sovereignty, imposed by EU membership, are of a different scope and nature from the obligations involved in membership of other international organisations (i.e. UN, GATT/WTO, NATO, EFTA) because none of these can make laws which automatically take precedence over UK legislation. In terms of economic policy, the Treaty of Rome removes the retained power, held by the British government, to prevent the take-over of a UK company by foreign capital, whilst statutory bodies are prohibited from discriminating against contractors from other member states, thereby ending the system of crown preference, and enforcing compulsory competitive tendering, across the union. Types of industrial policy are also outlawed, including initiatives intended to provide short-term protection against aggressive take-over by competitors for a fledgling company with excellent competitive future prospects, or subsidising export-led growth development. The UK is prevented from regulating inward and outward flows of capital, thereby weakening democratic control over the economy, and raising the probability of the economy being rocked by speculative short term flows having little or no relation to the underlying economic fundamentals of the economy. Immigration and manpower policy will be affected by the EU rule in favour of unlimited movement of labour across member states. Moreover, the desire to create a common internal market across all EU member states prevents national governments from raising impediments to this free trade, whether intended to protect workers, consumers and/or the environment.

Of course, orthodox political economists would claim that these interventionist policies are not only 'out of date' in contemporary circumstances, but that they represent sub-optimal economic policy options. Nevertheless, the fact remains that EU membership does indeed constrain national governments from pursuing certain types of economic and political policies, and therefore limits national sovereignty. The question rather shifts to whether governments would actually *want* to pursue such policy options rather than less interventionist, neo-liberal alternatives.

In the 1975 referendum, there was considerable discussion of the concept of 'pooled' sovereignty, namely where a number of individual member states might gain greater influence over their own economies by acting in concert, even though they have to surrender their monopoly over decision-making in the process. Thus, small nations may gain greater influence over their external economic and political environment through group action, even where this may result in a form of compromise that does not deliver to each nation everything that it would wish. Critics of this concept argued that it was not convincing because people either have the right to govern themselves subject to constraints outside their control, or this right is transferred, in whole or in part, to supra-national bodies. Hence, there is no intermediate point in between these alternatives. This point at least seems to have been conceded by supporters of continued EU membership, such as former Labour party Deputy Leader, Roy Hattersley, who, writing 25 years after the referendum, questioned whether the pro-EU campaign had been straightforward on the sovereignty issue. For Hattersley: 'Joining the European Community involved loss of significant sovereignty, but by telling the British people that was not involved, I think the ... argument was prejudiced for the next 30 years.' (Cited in Broad, 2001:108).

One early critic of UK membership of the EU, namely Aneurin Bevan, accepted the fact that this argument was superficially persuasive, but that the preservation of national sovereignty was the best means for governments to pursue their objectives. He argued that:

> ... the nation is too small an area in which to hope to bring the struggle [for democratic socialism] to a final conclusion. It is true whether the nation is large or small. Thus the attainment of political power in the modern state still leaves many problems outside its scope. National Sovereignty is a phrase that history is emptying of meaning ... Many seeing this are inclined to turn away from the difficult task of establishing Socialism in their own country. They say, 'What is the use of doing so? We shall find ourselves possessed of only a partial victory. Only world victory will suffice, so let us concentrate on that.' This is an engaging view and many have succumbed to it. If you are going to plan the world you must first of all control the part of it that you want to fit into the whole (Bevan, 1952:170-1).

Indeed, Bevan's contemporary, the then Labour Party leader Gaitskell, famously claimed that EU membership would mean '... the end of Britain as an independent state ... the end of a thousand years of history' (Labour Party Conference Report, 1962:154-165).

Democracy

The UK system of parliamentary democracy rests upon the concept of the sovereignty of the people. Through their exercise of the franchise, they lend their sovereign power to elected representatives to exercise on their behalf for the limited duration of a single parliament. Membership of the EU may, therefore be claimed to threaten the British representative system of democracy by transferring control over a sizeable section of public life to the EU Commission and the Council of Ministers, which were, at that point in time, collectively unable to be collectively elected nor dismissed by the British electorate (Burkitt, 1975:5).

At the time of the 1975 Referendum, the EU Parliament had not been properly established, nor invested with the powers that it exercises three decades later, as it seems to hold the EU Commission and Council of Ministers to account. Thus, the EU's organisational structure exhibited a significant democratic deficit at its heart at the time of the referendum debate, and moreover its an open question whether this basic design flaw remains to this day. The maintenance of individual liberties requires the existence of effective channels of communication between citizens and their government, and the structure of EU institutions frustrates this process, thus making government less responsive to the wishes of the electorate.

British membership of the EU involves a significant transfer of powers from the legislature to the executive, even on those areas where Britain retains a degree of control. The British executive determines the degree of parliamentary scrutiny that takes place relating to EU regulation and legislation, whilst the secrecy surrounding Council of Ministers meetings hampers the accountability of individual ministers for their decisions to parliament and hence the British people. Parliamentary democracy establishes the right for electors to elect and dismiss MPs and, thereby, governments, thereby enshrining accountability. EU institutions are not equally accountable. Indeed, no commissioners, and only one member of the Council of Ministers, can be elected and dismissed by the British people, and then only indirectly.

One important safeguard for the protection of individual liberties arises from the separation of executive, legislative and judicial functions. The EU violates this principle because the EU Commission possesses an element of initiative in each of the three areas. Furthermore, EU membership imposes constraints and duties upon these individuals which do not derive from UK legislation, and thereby in discharging their duties, government ministers and civil servants are not accountable to parliament nor the British people. Members of the British parliament can vote to change any law or tax on a majority vote, yet EU regulations and directives cannot be repealed or altered by the UK parliament. The British law courts are intended to uphold and enforce all legislation passed by parliament, until such a time as parliament repeals or changes it. EU membership, by contrast, requires UK courts to uphold and enforce EU laws that have not been passed nor scrutinised, amended or repealed, by the British parliament. Furthermore, clause 2:4 of the EC Act stipulated that EU regulations and treaty articles prevail over Acts of Parliament — thus giving EU law precedence in the even of any conflict with UK law.

Finally, the enshrinement of the free movement of labour and capital within the Treaty of Rome, effectively prevents British citizens deciding to extend the scope of democratic influence into the economic sphere, and thereby facilitating macroeconomic and industrial relations policy. The creation of a single internal market further erodes the power of a nation state to pursue certain social and economic programmes, even if these had been explicitly endorsed by majority democratic opinion. Thus, EU membership arguably conflicts with democratic policy self-determination.

Identity

The issue of the UK's position in the world is clearly related to the related concepts of democracy and national sovereignty. Nevertheless, cultural perceptions may account for a degree of the continuing Euro-scepticism held by a majority of UK citizens. Distinctive British characteristics have been facilitated by their relative isolation as an island nation, lying at the periphery of the European continent. The resulting Anglo-Saxon culture was reinforced, rather than being undermined, by its differences with continental European Roman, Napoleonic and Christian Democrat influences. Compared to other large powers (i.e. USA, USSR, China), the EU is a collection of nations united neither by political interests nor beliefs and nor a common heritage. Therefore, it is not surprising that cultural differences emerge. Like many forms of nationalism, this element of British cultural perception may tend towards introspection and, occasionally, towards racism. Nevertheless, it may explain reluctance for British cultural perceptions to be subsumed beneath an alien continental European culture.

British identity is additionally influenced by more recent history, both as creating a successful Empire and as victor in the two world wars. Other EU member states suffered the indignities of physical invasion by their European neighbours during the past century, and many endured decades of rule by communist or fascist dictatorships. Consequently, these nations might be more willing to compromise over issues of national sovereignty and be prepared to sacrifice elements of autonomy for international relations intended to maintain peaceful relationships. Thus, whilst the UK took part in the post-WWII reconstruction decision-making, and therefore enjoys contemporary influence in excess of that which present political and/or economic strength would suggest should be forthcoming, other EU member states were not so fortunate. The UK therefore might seek to maintain an independent voice in the world, including seats on the UN Security Council, rather than have this replaced by a joint EU representative.

Federalism

The issue of federalism was not a major issue at the time of the 1975 referendum, yet it has become increasingly significant in more recent years. One reason for this reflects the different position of the UK economy relative to the EU in 1975, when membership itself was the issue at stake and therefore fundamental questions such as the pooling of sovereignty were naturally enough the weighty issues. Given that a large majority of the British political elite currently take EU membership almost for granted, it may be assumed that this debate is of lesser significance even if it is a question not decisively answered by supporters of continued European integration. Thus, if the UK has shifted from debating the merits of membership to debating the kind of 'Europe' that all member states are set to create, it is not surprising that the issue of federalism has grown in importance.

Differences in national preferences towards wider and deeper European political and economic integration, amongst EU member states, remain equally pronounced today as in 1975. However, one element of disagreement relates to the definition of federalism. This is often used in the British debate to refer to the expansion of the EU super-national institutions, and the operation of policies at that level, and their transfer from national self-determination. It is therefore associated with the growth of the number of issues upon which the central EU institutions and political elites dominate policy development. For other Europeans, however, federalism relates to a less centralised form of organisation for the EU. Like other federal nations, such as Switzerland, Germany, Australia, the USA and Canada, federalism may refer to a high degree of flexibility and autonomy held by individual regions constituting the complete country. To this extent, disagreement over the future 'federal' composition of the EU is at least partly concerned with problems of definition rather than a real division over the degree of decentralisation permitted within the EU.

The European Constitution

One feature of more recent debate surrounding the future direction of European political and economic integration, together with the reform of the EU institutional framework to better facilitate the objectives of the 'new Europe', related to a debate concerning the design and implementation of a federal European constitution. Described by its supporters as anything between an exercise in simply consolidating and tidying-up the existing Euro-treaties, or alternatively the opportunity to embrace a radical design for a future European super-state, there has been considerable confusion surrounding the proposal. The draft constitution was both supposed to champion subsidiarity, and yet to strengthen the roles of central EU representatives and their institutional support in the creation of a new 'country called Europe'.

Not surprisingly, this proposal met considerable opposition and currently lies 'frozen', as referendums in France and the Netherlands rejected its implementation in its current form. The UK Labour government promised a referendum on the constitution if it ever came to the position where the UK parliament proposed its ratification, but this looks rather unlikely in the near future. The issue, nevertheless, reflects the need for wider debate, in the UK and throughout Europe, relating to what type of Europe its citizens want to create — a loose federation of nation states, co-operating on those issues they choose (Europe a la carte) or a firmly integrated federal substitute (a country called Europe), complete with parliament, army, flag, national anthem, passport, its own currency and constitutional settlement.

Conclusion

This chapter firstly examined the historical background to the relationship between Britain and the EU and disaggregates this into several discrete stages of shifting ideas and aspirations. This section provides a unique in-depth analysis of various manoeuvring of the British political establishment which wavered from enthusiasm to apathy through the late 1940s and 1950s until the initial membership applications in the 1960s. It then provides an insight into the road to accession in the early 1970s. Secondly, the chapter outlines the principal issues of debate regarding the political aspects of membership: defence and foreign policy, sovereignty, democracy, identity and federalism. In particular it reviews the changing pattern of importance of these factors. Finally, it briefly considers the latest major political development concerning the EU, the signed, but not ratified, Constitutional Treaty.

Nine

Implications of the Referendum for Britain and Europe

Introduction

This chapter examines three principal themes relating to the consequences of the 1975 Referendum, the future conduct of UK referendums and their role in the process of EU integration. The first section argues that the result of the 1975 Referendum only provided a temporary depiction of harmony between Britain and the other member states. Closer inspection indicates that fundamental differences existed prior to membership and that renegotiation of its entry terms was evidently inadequate to resolve these. It then proceeds to review the history of UK referendums, thereby illustrating their paucity, 9 over 31 years, and irregularity in terms of recourse and operation. However, their formalisation has now been enshrined in the Political Parties, Elections and Referendums Act and through the powers of the Electoral Commission which are discussed in detail. The chapter then concludes with an original empirical analysis of EU integration related referendums since their inception in 1972. In particular, these are disaggregated into those concerning accession and ratification referendums to reveal divergent trends in their approval rates over the period 1972-2005. This indicates that whilst accession referendums have maintained a high level of success, the trend for ratification referendums has demonstrated a significant decline to an approval rate of 29% in the current decade.

Consequences of 1975 Referendum

It is conceivable that this section could constitute a book in itself, given the numerous implications that the 1975 Referendum possses for British politics, both intra- and extra-parliamentary, and its economic relationships. Indeed, we have sought to summarise some of these in the proceeding chapters. However, given that the main underlying theme of this book concerns the relationship between the UK and the EU, we narrow this potential Pandora's box to address two key issues. Firstly, whilst the various economic and political issues that triggered the renegotiation of Britain's membership were essentially short-term points of irritation between the UK and its new partners, a series of fundamental issues can be identified to illustrate why Britain has so often appeared to be at odds with its European neighbours (George, 1992, 1998). The 1975 Referendum failed to resolve these issues; indeed it is feasible that its outcome temporarily drew a shroud over these differences that provided an illusion of Britain's position in terms of 'an ever closer union' with its European partners. Secondly, in terms of the adoption of the referendum as a device to resolve either constitutional issues or those of a more intra-party nature, the lessons from 1975 indicate that it has been the former reason that has determined their usage. However, in relation to future EU-related issues, such as EMU membership and a revised Constitutional Treaty, it is debatable which of these two determinants is ascendant. Both major political parties are deeply divided over Britain's future relationship with its European partners, thus the perennial issue of 'Europe' is likely to rekindle memories and comparisons to 1975.

Britain as an Awkward Partner

The prevailing deep-seated problems between Britain and its continental neighbours could not remain submerged for long and although the short-term crisis between Britain and the other member states continued to revolve around the familiar themes of budgetary contributions, reform of the CAP and the degree of pooled sovereignty, it became increasingly apparent that these are surpassed by more overarching debates regarding the current and future direction of European integration. Thus profound differences continue to emerge, for example, concerning the deepening versus widening of integration and the speed of supply-side reforms versus the established European Social Model. Hence to gain an understanding of the relationship between the UK and its European partners, it is essential to review these deep-rooted points of conflict.

The first theme revolves around the notion of an unbroken history. In particular, this relates to the lack of invasion, absence of revolution and being an 'old' state in a 'new' world. Firstly, it is impossible to understand Britain's place in Europe without appreciating the importance of the institutional continuity of British political structures in terms of the absence of invasion and that it has not undergone dramatic revolutionary upheaval. The closest was the Civil War (1642-8) and the Glorious Revolution (1689) that established the principle of parliamentary sovereignty and a constitutional monarchy, but crucially they reformed, not replaced, the institutions of governance. Secondly, Britain is an 'old' state in a 'new' world in comparison to other European states who have gone through upheavals in the 20th century (e.g. Germany, Italy, Spain, Portugal, Greece, Hungary, Poland, the Czech Republic, Latvia, Lithuania and Estonia).

A further unique aspect to Britain relates to the concepts of empire and war. The legacy of empire and the assumption of global influence are explanatory causes of Britain's non-alignment with the rest of Europe. The aftermath of empire resulted in a pattern of international trade and cooperation that looked towards the Commonwealth. Consequently, one of the major considerations when Britain joined the EEC was the treatment of its Commonwealth partners, who found their goods and services outside the Common External Tariff (Burkitt and Baimbridge, 1990). Although Britain can no longer regard itself as a global power it still tends to 'punch above its weight' particularly through its 'special relationship' with the USA, rather than deeper cooperation in Europe.

A third element is the development of a distinctive legal system, whereby Britain operates a very different legal system to the Napoleonic Code. The British system of law differs, for example, in terms of the jury system which is not generally found in Europe, where magistrates and judges tend to bring in a verdict as well as conducting a trial, whilst the adversarial system of justice is also alien to the European inquisitorial tradition. A further aspect concerns the different rights of citizenship, whereby there is a presumption in continental European law that citizens' rights are granted and safeguarded by the state through a written constitution. In contrast, it has been assumed that individuals in Britain have the right to do whatever they choose provided the law does not explicitly prohibit it.

A fourth difference is that Britain possesses a distinctive type of capitalism typified by the City of London, liberalised markets and its welfare state regime. Through the City of London, the size and significance of its financial services market is a unique feature of the British economy. Moreover, underlying differences exist between the British and continental capitalist systems in terms of the degree of liberalised markets. For example, Albert (1993) contrasts many of the features found in 'Rhine' model countries with those characteristic of the more liberal systems (neo-American model) of capitalism and identifies key differences in these alternative capitalism systems. Additionally, welfare state regimes further illustrate the divide between the British and continental European capitalist systems. A key study by Esping-Andersen (1990) identified three distinctive 'welfare regimes' in Europe: liberal regimes (e.g. Britain) where there is an emphasis on social security as a 'safety net' rather than universal provision; corporatist welfare regimes (e.g. Germany) where the emphasis is on socially inclusive forms of insurance, but in accordance to people's position in the labour market; and social-democratic welfare regimes (e.g. Scandinavia) where the emphasis is on equality resulting in benefits being both high and universal.

A final general difference is Britain's distinctively individualistic culture (Hofstede, 1980). Thus, within the Western group of countries the most individualistic countries were the USA, Australia, Britain and Canada whilst most EU member states came considerably further down the scale.

Referendums in Britain

As Table 9.1 illustrates, referendums remain rare in the UK with only nine having been held since the first in 1973, only one being nation-wide (1975) and all regarding constitutional issues.

Following the desired outcome for the Wilson Government from the 1975 Referendum, however, the defeat of the devolution votes in 1979 effectively contributed to the demise of the Labour Government, whereby the consequences of electoral failure via a referendum became all too apparent. Thus although considered by the Thatcher government, they now possessed a tarnished appeal which was further diminished through the effective use of general election mandates both inside and outside the House of Commons. Consequently, the referendum device lay fallow for the 1979–97 period of Conservative administrations until revived again by the 1997 Labour Government as a central aspect of its legislation on constitutional reform regarding devolution in Scotland, Wales and Northern Ireland, a directly elected mayor for London and directly elected assemblies for the English regions. The relative ease of implementation of these proposals was enhanced through both its electoral mandate and the lessons of the failed referendums of the late 1970s (Coxall *et al.*, 2003).

However, for each major referendum in the UK, the Government of the day has created new rules, as no generic legal provisions relating to referendums existed. Therefore, each referendum was conducted using slightly different procedures. Consequently, in its report of October 1998, the Committee on Standards in Public Life chaired by Lord Neill made a series of recommendations designed to provide consistency surrounding the conduct of referendums. In response, the Government introduced legislation to provide a standard framework for the conduct of referendums in Part VII of the Political Parties, Elections and Referendums Act 2000 (see next section for a detailed discussion). Such a development would appear to further entrench the referendum as a substantive device within the British political landscape since it removes the ad hoc nature of their conduct and formalises it for the first time. Thus it is not unreasonable to venture that all parties, particularly as majorities in the House of Commons dwindle further, might seek refuge in the referendum regarding constitutional amendments in terms of the EU (EMU membership, a revised Constitution, or even renegotiation of membership), devolution (new fiscal powers for the Welsh Assembly and enhanced ones for the Scottish Parliament, the revisiting of English assemblies and the status of Northern Ireland), or even a new electoral system (proportional representation). Although as Qvortrup (2002) argues, it is equally possible that referendums will play a lesser role than they have done in the late 1990s given that recent experience has illustrated their double-edged nature both domestically (English regional assemblies) and on the EU stage (Constitutional Treaty).

The Future Conduct of UK Referendums

As previously indicated, for each previous major referendum the Government created new rules, with each referendum conducted using different procedures. However, following its report of October 1998, the Committee on Standards in Public Life made a series of recommendations designed to provide consistency surrounding the conduct of future referendums in the UK, although specific primary legislation is still required to trigger a referendum. In response to these recommendations, the Labour Government introduced legis-

Table 9.1 Major UK Referendums (1973–)

Theme	Date	Question(s)	Outcome	Turn out (%)	Government response
Whether Northern Ireland should remain part of the UK	8 March 1973	1. Do you want NI to remain part of the UK? 2. Do you want NI to be joined with the Republic of Ireland, outside the UK?	Option 1 – 591,820 (98.9%) Option 2 – 6,463 (1.1%)	58.1	No action since results in favour of remaining part of the UK
Whether the UK should remain part of the EC	5 June 1975	Do you think the UK should stay in the European Community (Common Market)?	Yes – 17,378,581 (67.2%) No – 8,470,073 (32.8%)	64.5	Membership retained on basis of renegotiated terms
Whether there should be a Scottish Parliament	1 March 1979	Do you want the provisions of the Scotland Act to be put into effect?	Yes – 1,230,937 (51.6%) No – 1,153,500 (48.4%)	63.8	The Scotland Act 1978 was repealed in March 1979
Whether there should be a Welsh Assembly	1 March 1979	Do you want the provisions of the Wales Act 1978 to be put into effect?	Yes – 243,048 (20.3%) No – 956,330 (79.7%)	58.8	The Wales Act was withdrawn by the government

Topic	Date	Question	Result	% Turnout	Outcome
Whether there should be a Scottish Parliament and if it should have tax-varying powers	11 Sept. 1997	1. I agree that there should be a Scottish Parliament 2. I do not agree that there should be a Scottish Parliament 1. I agree that a Scottish Parliament should have tax-varying powers 2. I do not agree that a Scottish Parliament should have tax-varying powers	Option 1 – 1,775,045 (74.3%) Option 2 – 614,400 (25.7%) Option 1 – 1,512,889 (63.5%) Option 2 – 870,263 (36.5%)	60.4	Government passed the Scotland Act 1998, creating the Scottish Parliament and Scottish Executive
Whether there should be a Welsh Assembly	18 Sept. 1997	1. I agree that there should be a Welsh Assembly 2. I do not agree that there should be a Welsh Assembly?	Option 1 – 559,419 (50.3%) Option 2 – 552,698 (49.7%)	50.1	Government passed the Government of Wales Act 1998, creating the Welsh Assembly
Whether there should be a Mayor of London and Greater London Authority	7 May 1998v	Are you in favour of the Government's proposals for a Greater London authority, made up of an elected mayor and a separately elected assembly?	Yes – 1,230,715 (72.0%) No – 478,413 (28.0%)	34.1	Government passed the Greater London Authority Act 1999, creating the GLA
Acceptance of the Good Friday Agreement	22 May 1998	Do you support the agreement reached at the multi-party talks on Northern Ireland and set out in Command Paper 3883?	Yes – 676,966 (71.1%) No – 274,979 (28.9%)	81.1	Government passed the Northern Ireland Act 1998
Elected regional assemblies for North East England	8 Nov. 2004	Should there be an elected regional assembly for the North East region?	Yes – 197,310 (22.1%) No – 696,519 (77.9%)	47.7	No legislation

lation to provide a standard framework for the conduct of referendums (except local mayoral referendums), specifically, Part VII of the Political Parties, Elections and Referendums Act 2000 (the PPERA). This Act should, theoretically, address many of the accusations of unfairness in terms of funding that were voiced during and after the 1975 Referendum (Butler and Kitzinger, 1976, Williams, 2006). Although on such a hotly debated and contentious issue as 'Europe' with significant moneyed interests on all sides of the campaign and division cutting across political parties, it is perhaps too simplistically optimistic to place unmitigated faith in a single piece of legislation.

However, in an attempt to ensure such a level playing field, a key feature of the PPERA was the establishment of the Electoral Commission, which has responsibility for:

- commenting on the wording of the referendum question,
- registration of permitted participants,
- designating lead campaign organisations,
- monitoring referendum expenditure limits and donations,
- the conduct of the poll,
- the announcement of the result.

Subsequently, the Regional Assemblies (Preparations) Act 2003 gave the Electoral Commission the following additional responsibilities:

- encouraging voting at regional referendums,
- explaining the local government options being presented to those living in two tier areas of a region,
- presenting the yes and no arguments if designation is not possible.

The standard framework provided for by the PPERA stipulates matters regarding the timetable, expenditure, designated organisations, the referendum question, publicity and vote counting.

In relation to the issue of the timetable, then before a referendum is held there is a formal 'referendum period' in which restrictions surrounding campaign expenditure and publicity apply although the exact length of the referendum period would be provided for in the enabling legislation. Figure 9.1 illustrates the order in which events would occur once a referendum period is announced, based on a ten-week example where it is expected that the relevant period for any particular referendum will normally begin on the day the Bill providing for the referendum is introduced in Parliament and end with the date of the poll.

Figure 9.1 – Order of Events for a UK Referendum

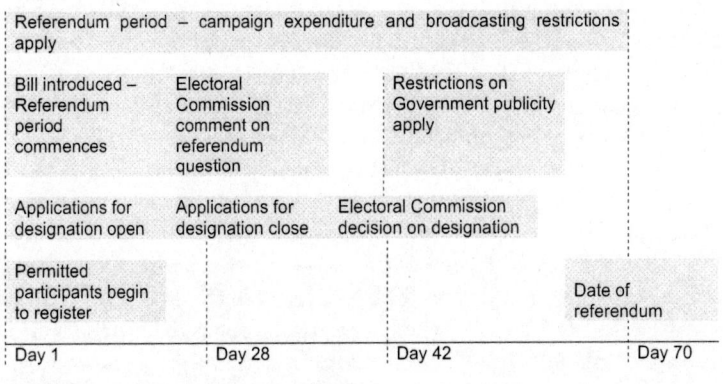

Source: Electoral Commission (2003)

From the first day of the referendum period the Electoral Commission will commence registration of permitted participants in the campaign, and it is from this point that campaign expenditure restrictions will apply. A permitted participant is defined as a political party, other group or individual wanting to campaign in relation to a referendum, and which intends to spend £10,000 or more on their campaign.

Moreover, a permitted participant can also apply to become a designated organisation, which is a permitted participant that the Electoral Commission has chosen to be the lead campaign group for one of the possible outcomes to the referendum. However, after the initial four-week registration period the Electoral Commission will no longer accept applications from those wishing to become designated organisations. During the following two weeks, the Electoral Commission will consider appointing designated organisations, whilst the remaining four weeks will be the main campaigning period assuming a referendum period of ten weeks. Finally, the date of the poll will be the last date of the referendum period.

Secondly, referendum expenditure limits are prescribed by the PPERA for a UK wide referendum, whilst for a national or regional referendum the expenditure limits would be set out in an Order. For a UK wide referendum, such as that envisaged for the issues of EMU membership and/or a revised Constitutional Treaty, the level of expenditure for political parties is based on the proportion of the electorate who voted for the party at the previous general election. If a UK wide referendum were to be held based on the 2005 General Election results, the Labour and Conservative parties would be entitled to spend up to £5 million each and the Liberal Democrats could spend up to £4 million. No other political parties would qualify for additional spending limits and so could each spend up to £500,000, the limit for other permitted participants.

Subsequently, permitted participants and designated organisations would be required to submit expenditure and donation returns to the Electoral Commission within three months of the referendum if total expenditure does not exceed £250,000. Expenses above that sum would be subject to auditing procedures and returns would have to be made to the Electoral Commission within six months.

In terms of the overall funding of a referendum, it is expected that the enabling legislation will make provision for the cost of conducting a referendum to be met from the Consolidated Fund, in regard to which the Electoral Commission will undertake an exercise to provide an estimate of the likely costs.

Thirdly, permitted participants could apply for designated status. However, the Electoral Commission would not be obliged to designate organisations if it did not feel any organisation sufficiently represented the views of the people on whose behalf it claimed to be campaigning. Moreover, as a safeguard to promote a balanced debate, the PPERA prevents the Electoral Commission from designating on only one side of the campaign. However, the benefits for designated organisations are numerous:

- Additional spending limits — a designated organisation will have an expenditure limit of £5 million for UK-wide referendums and so will be able to campaign on the same scale as the large political parties.
- Mail shot — designated organisations are entitled to the free postal distribution of one piece of referendum literature to each household or elector.
- Broadcasting — designated organisations will be the only groups eligible for referendum campaign broadcasts, although

the broadcasters may determine the length and frequency of the broadcasts. However, in determining their policies, the broadcasters will have regard to any views expressed by the Electoral Commission.
- Grants — if the Electoral Commission appoints designated organisations it is required to award equal grants of public money of up to £600,000, to help ensure that there is a minimum level of campaigning on all sides of the argument. However, the Electoral Commission can also attach conditions to the grants, for example, requesting that the designated organisations submit details of their cash flow predictions for the duration of the campaign.Public rooms — designated organisations are entitled to the free use of public rooms for meetings with the exception of Northern Ireland.

Although the Government is responsible for proposing the wording of any referendum question, the Electoral Commission has a duty to consider whether any question (and any preamble) is intelligible. Indeed, its Chairman has stated publicly that in particular it will consider the fairness of any question and in the interests of transparency any views conveyed to the Government will be made public. The Electoral Commission has developed a set of guidelines that are used to help assess a question once it is announced. In particular, in assessing intelligibility, it will have regard to the question's effectiveness in presenting the options clearly, simply and neutrally. Thus, the question assessment guidelines are:

- The question should prompt an immediate response - it should be clear what decision the voter is being asked to make. Hence, voters should not have to work out, or try to interpret the question; the voter's preferred answer should be immediately identifiable. In particular, voters should not have to re-read the question several times to understand its content. Thus, the question should be written in a way that encourages each reader to interpret it in the same way. To achieve this, clear and unambiguous language should be used, such that the response options should be phrased in terms that are consistent with those used in the question. For example, if the question contains the words 'agree' and 'disagree' the possible answers should also be 'agree' and 'disagree'.
- Words and phrases used in the question should not have positive or negative connotations - certain words or phrases may encourage support for one particular outcome. For example, words such as 'new' and 'approve' may in some instances

imply that something is a positive concept. Equally, negative words and phrases should be avoided. For example, 'abolish', 'old' and 'reject' may in some instances imply that something is a negative concept. Attempts should be made to find unbiased descriptive words to replace such terms. Consideration should be given to perceptions that voters may have about the subject matter and potential negative or positive connotations associated with particular words.

- Words and phrases used in the question should not be intentionally leading - the question should not be phrased so as to guide the voter towards one particular outcome.
- Words and phrases used in the question should not be loaded - the question should be balanced and should not contain words or phrases which do prompt one particular answer. Words and phrases that are, or could be perceived as, false or misleading should be avoided.
- The question should not contain 'jargon' — this is defined as words, phrases and acronyms that are only commonly used and understood by specialist groups and should be avoided.
- The language used in the question should be consistent — whereby if certain words or concepts are referred to once in a question or preamble, their use should be consistent throughout the entire text.
- Words and phrases used in the question should reflect the language used and understood by the voter — thus consideration should be given to the language used during any informal campaigning that may have taken place prior to the referendum period commencing, providing this could not be perceived as potentially influencing the outcome.
- The question should not provide more information than is necessary to answer the question meaningfully — hence the question should not contain unnecessary detail about the options or subject matter. The question should focus on the main issue(s), rather than less important consequences or implications. Therefore, policy alternatives that are not directly related to the referendum question should not be mentioned, as they will only make it less clear what the voter is being asked to do.
- The question should not be longer than necessary — in particular, it should be sensitive to the level of public awareness surrounding the referendum issue. If there is limited public awareness of the subject, it may be appropriate to include more detail about the choices. Where the referendum issue is a com-

plex one or unfamiliar one, it may be appropriate to use a preamble to explain the context and/or provide additional information to the voter, rather than have a long question.
- The question should be well structured - the text of any question should be carefully structured and easy for the voter to read. Questions should present the issues and key words in a logical and rational sequence. This may involve the use of several short sentences and/or a preamble. Reverse wording or 'double negatives' should be avoided as they can make it difficult for the voter to understand the question.

A cogent example of this newfound scrutiny was illustrated on 25 January 2005 when the Government introduced the European Union Bill to Parliament providing for a referendum to be held on the European Constitution. The Bill included the following proposed wording to be used in any such referendum: 'Should the United Kingdom approve the Treaty establishing a Constitution for the European Union?'

In relation to its published guidelines, the Electoral Commission welcomed the brevity of the proposed question and was content that the question was structured in such a way that it prompts an immediate response and encourages each voter to interpret it in the same way. Furthermore, it was satisfied that the referendum question makes it immediately clear what decision the voter is being asked to make. Moreover, the level of public awareness surrounding the European Constitution and the referendum process will be sufficiently high to remove any necessity of having a preamble. However, the Electoral Commission believed that it is important to refer to the correct name of the treaty in the referendum question ('A Treaty establishing a Constitution for Europe'), as opposed to a modification of the treaty title, although it believed that this detracts little from the overall intelligibility of the question.

The PPERA also contains provisions relating to publicity concerning a referendum. In particular, the Government and other bodies that are mainly publicly funded are prohibited from issuing any publicity material relating to a referendum in the 28 days immediately prior to the poll. However, this does not relate to material specifically sought by a member of the public, to factual information relating to the conduct of the poll or the issue of press notices. The BBC and S4C are exempt from the restriction, as is the Electoral Commission itself. Indeed, the Electoral Commission would be seeking to raise public awareness of the referendum and the voting arrangements in order to encourage turnout. With respect to any individuals or groups publishing material relating to a referendum, they must include certain information on their material, so that its originator is clearly identifiable and to help enable the Electoral Commission to monitor compliance with the campaign expenditure limits.

Finally, the Chairman of the Electoral Commission, or another person appointed by the Chairman, would be the Chief Counting Officer (CCO) for any referendum held under the PPERA. As such, the CCO is required to certify the number of ballot papers that have been submitted and to announce the final result. To assist in this task counting officers will be appointed at local authority level in Britain, whilst in Northern Ireland the Chief Electoral Officer for Northern Ireland will be the counting officer.

History and Role of Referendums in EU Integration

Finally, in light of analysing the future aspects of EU-related referendums, it is important to consider their true European dimension, since it will not be Britain alone that determines whether a referendum is held, but rather it is the process of creating 'an ever closer union' by all EU member states that will dictate its future path. Indeed, in light of the momentous changes following from the instigation of post-war European economic and political integration, referendums in the initial decades were notable by their absence. As Hug (2002:23) states, the development of European integration 'was to be pursued by elites, fostering common ground, which later, presumably automatically, would be embraced by the common citizens'. Hence, it was not until the first round of enlargement with Denmark, Ireland, Norway and the UK that the notion of referendums entered the (then) European Community psyche. However, by the end of the 20th century 22 national referendums concerning European integration had occurred, with a further 19 in the first five years of the 21st century.

Table 9.2 summarises the history of referendums in chronological order relating to European integration for the period 1972-2005 during which time there have been 41 referendums with 11 (27%) resulting in a 'no' vote and 30 (73%) in a 'yes' vote. However, the average percentage 'yes' vote was 68.2% indicating a far from overwhelming endorsement to those issues placed before national electorates. Indeed, it was not until the series of enlargement referendums in 2003 that affirmation rates above 90% (Slovakia and Lithuania) were attained, whilst the nadir was reached in 2001 with the fourth Swiss membership referendum when only 23.2% were in favour. However, the average 'no' vote is 57.9% indicating that these are frequently more marginal than the attained affirmative endorsements.

Table 9.2 — Referendums on European Integration (1972–)

Country	Date	Theme	Yes vote (%)
France	23 April 1972	Enlargement	68.3
Ireland	10 May 1972	Membership	83.1
Norway	24-25 Sept 1972	Membership	*46.5*
Denmark	2 October 1972	Membership	63.1
Switzerland	3 Dec 1972	EC-EFTA Treaty	72.5
U.K.	5 June 1975	Membership	67.2
Greenland[1]	23 Feb 1982	Membership	*26.1*
Denmark	26 Feb 1986	Single European Act	56.2
Ireland	6 May 1987	Single European Act	69.6
Italy	18 June 1989	Mandate for MEPs	88.1
Denmark	3 June 1992	Treaty on European Union	*49.3*
Ireland	18 June 1992	Treaty on European Union	68.7
France	20 Sept 1992	Treaty on European Union	51.1
Switzerland	6 Dec 1992	EEA Treaty	*49.7*
Liechtenstein	13 Dec 1992	EEA Treaty	55.8
Denmark	18 May 1993	Treaty on European Union	56.8
Austria	12 June 1994	Membership	66.6
Sweden	18 Sept 1994	Membership	52.3
Finland	16 Oct 1994	Membership	56.9
Norway	28 Nov 1994	Membership	*47.8*
Ireland	22 May 1998	Amsterdam Treaty	61.7
Denmark	27 May 1998	Amsterdam Treaty	55.1
Switzerland	21 May 2000	Bilateral agreements with EU	67.2
Denmark	28 Sept 2000	EMU membership	*46.9*
Switzerland	4 May 2001	Membership	*23.2*
Ireland	7 June 2001	Nice Treaty	*46.1*
Malta	8 March 2003	Membership	53.7

[1] The percentage figure represents the 'no' vote in this case since the option was to leave the EC.

Country	Date	Theme	Yes vote (%)
Slovenia	23 March 2003	Membership	89.6
Hungary	12 April 2003	Membership	83.8
Lithuania	11 May 2003	Membership	91.0
Slovakia	17 May 2003	Membership	92.5
Poland	8 June 2003	Membership	77.5
Czech Rep.	14 June 2003	Membership	77.3
Estonia	14 Sept 2003	Membership	66.9
Sweden	14 Sept 2003	EMU membership	**44.1**
Latvia	20 Sept 2003	Membership	67.0
Spain	20 Feb 2005	EU Constitutional Treaty	76.7
France	29 May 2005	EU Constitutional Treaty	**45.2**
Netherlands	1 June 2005	EU Constitutional Treaty	**38.2**
Switzerland	5 June 2005	EU Schengen agreements	54.6
Luxembourg	10 July 2005	EU Constitutional Treaty	56.5

Source: Adapted and up-dated from Hug (2002)

This series of referendums have occurred in a remarkable uniform pattern of alternating between those associated with membership (1972-75, 1994 and 2003) and ratification (1986-1993, 1998-2001 and 2005) issues. The initial six referendums concerned the first wave of EU enlargement that was endorsed by French voters in 1972. Although Norway's rejection of membership in 1972 signalled the first pause in the integration process this was largely overlooked given that Norway was seeking membership in the first instance. However, this was followed by the unique event of a membership referendum where the question posed referred to Greenland leaving the EU, which secured 74.9% of the vote such that Greenland left the EU in January 1985. The next major phase of referendums was associated with ratification of the Single European Act and the Treaty on European Union that fulfilled the EU's long-term objectives of creating a single internal market. However, the result of the 1992 Danish referendum was not only a severe blow to EU integration, but also highlighted the precarious nature of referendums in influencing the speed of achieving an 'ever closer union'. The fourth phase of referendums occurred in 1994 in relation to the proposed Nordic enlargement, with Norway once again rejecting membership, whilst

Sweden's voters signalled their early scepticism, which was later reflected in their 2003 rejection of EMU membership.

The next phase of referendums again followed the established pattern of largely concerning ratification issues (the Treaties of Amsterdam and Nice). However, of the six referendums held during this period only three were successful with electors of Switzerland in 2001 registering the strongest anti-EU sentiment to date regarding their proposed membership. The penultimate series of referendums occurred in 2003 as part of the accession process for nine of the ten proposed 2004 enlargement countries. These resulted in some of the highest approval votes, with all but Malta being in excess of two-thirds in favour of EU membership. However, as previously mentioned, this near perfect sequence was spoilt by the Swedish electorate's rejection of the euro. The final phase to-date of EU referendums occurred in 2005 following the signing of the Constitution Treaty by Heads of Government in Rome on 29 October 2004. However, the precise mode of ratification was entrusted to individual member states, which in turn alternated between parliamentary ratification alone (Austria, Belgium, Cyprus, Estonia, Finland, Germany, Greece, Hungary, Italy, Latvia, Lithuania, Malta, Slovakia, Slovenia and Sweden), a combination of parliament and referendum (Ireland, Luxembourg, the Netherlands, Spain and the UK) and by referendum alone (Denmark, France and Portugal). Hence, only one-third of EU countries sought to use the referendum device as either the sole or partial method of ratifying the European constitution. However, this process was brought to a shuddering halt by the outcomes of the French and Dutch non-ratification in late May and early June 2005.

Table 9.3 – Referendums by Theme of European Integration

Theme	Country	Referendum Year
Accession	Ireland	1972
	Norway	***1972**, **1994***
	Denmark	1972
	Switzerland	1972, ***1992***, 2000, ***2001***, 2005
	UK	1975
	Greenland	***1982***
	Liechtenstein	1992
	Austria	1994
	Sweden	1994
	Finland	1994
	Malta	2003
	Slovenia	2003
	Hungary	2003
	Lithuania	2003
	Slovakia	2003
	Poland	2003
	Czech Republic	2003
	Estonia	2003
	Latvia	2003
Ratification	Denmark	1986, ***1992***, 1993, 1998, ***2000***
	Ireland	1987, ***1992***, 1998, ***2001***
	France	1992, ***2005***
	Sweden	***2003***
	Luxembourg	2005
	Spain	***2005***
	Netherlands	***2005***
Symbolic	France	1972
	Italy	1989

Source: Adapted from Table 9.2
Note: Year in ***bold and italics*** indicates defeated referendum

To enable further analysis of these European referendums, Table 9.3 condenses the information contained within Table 9.2 in relation the referendum's theme: 'accession', 'ratification' and 'symbolic'.

Implications of the Referendum for Britain and Europe 207

Evidently, the majority of referendums, 24 or 59%, have been related to EU membership usually conducted prior to entry following a period of candidature and negotiation, the exceptions being that of the UK in 1975 and Greenland in 1982. Further, the prospect of EU membership has resulted in an average 'yes' vote of 74.2% with only Norway (1972 and 1994) and Switzerland (1992 and 2001) ever having voted against accession whilst Greenland opted to leave in 1982. In contrast, to the established history of accession referendums, those pertaining to ratification, 15 or 37%, are a more recent phenomenon and have only been undertaken by seven member states. These referendums have resulted in both a lower proportion of affirmative votes compared to accession referendums, 53% compared to 79%, and also have a significantly lower average 'yes' vote, 54.8% compared to 63.8%, indicating only marginal approval for those propositions placed before the electorate. They therefore suggest that the political leaders of some EU member states have proceeded at a pace of integration in excess of that palatable to their population as a whole, who are yet to be convinced of the merits of the EU's deepening process exemplified by EMU and more recently the proposed Constitution. Finally, the 'symbolic' classification relates to the two largely internalised referendums undertaken in France and Italy that are atypical and unlikely to be repeated.

To gain a temporal perspective of this pattern of EU-related referendums, Table 9.4 illustrates their trend disaggregated by each decade since their introduction in the 1970s. Firstly, as previously described, the founders of post-war European integration felt it unnecessary to consult their electorates until some 14 years after the commencement of the European project of achieving 'an ever closer union'. Hence the initial cluster of referendums does not occur until the 1970s when six are held. However, the trend declines in the 1980s with only four, before sharply accelerating in the 1990s (12 or 29%) and the first half of the current decade (19 or 46%). Thus from an absence in the 1950s and 1960s, the use of referendums subsequently gathered significant momentum with three-quarters occurring in the final two decades alone. It therefore appears that the adoption of referendums for accession (e.g. Bulgaria, Romania, Turkey and the Balkans) and ratification (e.g. a revised Constitution and EMU membership) will be a commonplace feature of future EU developments that will continue this established pattern.

Table 9.4 – European Integration Referendums by Decade

	1970s	1980s	1990s	2000s
Total referendums	6	4	12	19
Total approval-rate	83.3%	75.0%	75.0%	68.4%
Accession referendums	5	1	6	12
Accession approval-rate	80.0%	0.0%	66.7%	91.7%
Ratification referendums	0	2	6	7
Ratification approval-rate	na	100.0%	83.3%	28.6%

Source: Adapted from Table 9.2

A second aspect to emerge from Table 9.4 is, however, in acute contrast to the positive trend previously outlined. The approval-rate, which illustrates the successful attainment of a 'yes' vote, has diminished over the decades, declining from 83.3% in the 1970s to a plateau of 75% through the 1980s and 1990s, before falling to 68.4% in the 2000s. This suggests that the pace of integration has affected views and/or national electorates have found their voice, and therefore requires more detailed analysis. Thus the data on referendums is also presented in a disaggregated form which illustrates the EU's enlargement pattern reflected in the now routine accession referendums, which had fallen out of favour in 1980s with none held for Greece, Spain or Portugal, only to re-emerge again in the 1990s and latterly for the 2004 entrants. However, it is the growth in ratification referendums that clearly demonstrates an upward trend. These occurred at least as frequently as accession referendums in the 1980s and 1990s and could yet do so in the incomplete current decade given the likelihood of future treaties. However, it is analysis of the success-rate of these two referendum categories that is the most revealing feature of their historical development and future trends.

In relation to accession referendums, the Greenland withdrawal creates a statistical anomaly of 0% success-rate in the 1980s, which is clearly overshadowed by the success-rates of 80% in the 1970s, the 66.7% in the 1990s and the 91.7% in the 2000s. Hence, the significant majority of countries who have sought approval in a referendum have been answered in the affirmative with only the electorates of Switzerland and Norway being recalcitrant on this issue. Indeed, there is no reason to suspect that this trend will not continue with the imminent accession of Bulgaria and Romania. In contrast, a perceptible decline has occurred in the success-rate of ratification referendums. From an initial 100% confirmation in the 1980s, albeit based on merely two such plebiscites this record of achievement fell to 83.3% in the 1990s and then to a lowly 28.6% in the current decade. Thus the issue of ratification now clearly constitutes a significant problem for national Heads of Government and the EU Commission in seeking to pursue 'an ever closer union'. Any governing authority that is reduced to less than one-third of its legislation being accepted by the general populace is evidently out of step with their priorities and aspirations.

Hence, the double-edged nature of referendums has sharply reversed the previous accelerating trend of integration through the ratification of treaties whether economic (Single European Act, Treaty on European Union) or political (Amsterdam Treaty, Nice Treaty, Constitutional Treaty). Consequently, given such a recent record of abject failure in terms of ratification, it would be prudent of the EU to carefully consider future deepening initiatives prior to placing them before national electorates. Alternatively, as was witnessed regarding the proposed Constitution, the majority of member states (Austria, Belgium, Cyprus, Estonia, Finland, Germany, Greece, Hungary, Italy, Latvia, Lithuania, Malta, Slovakia, Slovenia and Sweden) chose to by-pass the referendum option and ratified the Treaty within domestic parliaments alone. However, as many have found, the referendum is a genii that once out of the bottle is hard to again contain.

Conclusion

This chapter sought to conclude this book by examining a number of issues relating to the post-1975 repercussions of Britain's only nationwide referendum. Firstly, we demonstrate that the referendum result did little to change the fundamental differences between the UK and its European partners. Indeed, the issue of 'Europe' has come to be a dominant feature of British politics and to a lesser extent economic policy. Thus the 1975 Referendum failed to decisively settle the question of membership with the current level of interest and debate probably being at its highest since membership was first raised. However, in terms of the conduct of referendums significant progress has been made which alters the balance of power away from the incumbent government who were able to set the referendum's rules. Hence, the Political Parties, Elections and Referendums Act (2000) now formalises the procedures regarding the timescale, expenditure, designated originations, the question, publicity and vote counting. Consequently, it can be expected that the operation of future referendums will be more balanced particularly in terms of the campaign's financing. Finally, the chapter analyses the record of referendums relating to EU integration, in particular concerning accession and ratification of treaties. It indicates that there has been a dramatic decline in the approval rate of the latter. The collapse in successful ratification rates to 29% in the current decade potentially explains why 15 member states ignored the referendum option when seeking to ratify the EU's Constitutional Treaty. However, if public opinion is increasingly opposed to integrationalist trends then merely bypassing direct-democracy through parliamentary affirmation could still fail if electorates subsequently remove pro-integrationalist parties.

Bibliography

Abbott, K. (1997) The European Trade Union Confederation: Its Organisation and Objectives in Transition, *Journal of Common Market Studies*, 35(3), 465–481.

Adams, C. (2005) Strategy to push referendum under way, *Financial Times*, 16 May.

Albert, M. (1993) *Capitalism against capitalism*, Whurr, London.

Arestis, P. and Sawyer, M. (2000) The deflationary consequences of the single currency; in Baimbridge, M., Burkitt, B. and Whyman, P. (eds.) *The impact of the euro: debating Britain's future*, Macmillan: London.

Aspinwall, M. (2003) Britain and Europe: Some Alternative Economic Tests, *Political Quarterly*, 74(2), 146–157.

Baimbridge, M. and Whyman, P. (2003) *Economic and monetary union in Europe*, Edward Elgar, Cheltenham.

Baimbridge, M. and Whyman, P. (2006) *Britain, the euro and beyond*, Ashgate: Aldershot.

Baimbridge, M., Burkitt, B. and Whyman, P. (2000) *The impact of the euro: debating Britain's future*, Macmillan, London.

Baker, D., Gamble, A., Ludlum, S. and Seawright, D. (1996) Labour and Europe: A Survey of MPs and MEPs, *Political Quarterly*, 67(4), 353–371.

Bakhoven, A.F. (1989) *The Completion of the Single Market in 1992: Macroeconomic Consequences for the European Community*, Central Planning Bureau, 56, The Netherlands.

Barnard, C. and Deakin, S. (1997) European Community Social Law and Policy: Evolution or Regression?, *Industrial Relations Journal* (European Annual Review), 131–153.

Barr, N. (1992) Economic Theory and the Welfare State: A Survey and Interpretation, *Journal of Economic Literature*, 30, 741–803.

Benn, T. (1990) *Against the Tide: Diaries 1973–1976*, London: Arrow

Berger, S. and Dore, R. (1996) (eds.) *National Diversity and Global Capitalism*, Cornell University Press, Ithaca.

Bevan, A. (1952) *In Place of Fear*, Heinemann, London.

Biffen, J. (1977) *Political Office or Political Power*, London: Centre for Policy Studies

Blair, A. (1998) Speech at The Hague, 20 January.

Blair, A. (2000) *Managing Change: A National and International Agenda of Reform?*, speech given at the World Economic Forum, Davos, Switzerland, 28 January.

Blair, A. (2000) Prime Minister's speech on the knowledge economy, 11 September.
Blitz, J. and Newman, C. (2005) Secrets of ERM debacle revealed, *Financial Times*, 10 February
Bogdanor, V. (1981) *The people and the party system: the referendum and electoral reform*, Cambridge University Press, Cambridge.
British Management Data Foundation (2000) Document: A Letter to *The Times*, Transcript of BBC Radio 4 programme, broadcast on 3 February, British Management Data Foundation, Stroud.
Broad, R. (2001) *Labour's European Dilemmas: From Bevin to Blair*, Palgrave, Basingstoke.
Broad, R. and Geiger, T. (1996) The 1975 British Referendum on Europe, *Contemporary Record*, 10 (3) pp 82–105.
Burkitt, B. (1975) *Britain and the European Economic Community: A Political Re-Appraisal*, British Business for World Markets, Shipley.
Burkitt, B. and Baimbridge, M. (1990) Britain, the European Economic Community and the single market of 1992: a reappraisal, *Journal of Public Money and Management*, 10(4), 57–61.
Burkitt, B. and Baimbridge, M. (1991) The Cecchini Report and the impact of 1992, *European Research*, 2(5), 16–19.
Burkitt, B., Baimbridge, M. and Reed, S. (1992) *From Rome to Maastricht: a reappraisal of Britain's membership of the European Community*, Anglia Press, Sudbury.
Burkitt, B., Baimbridge, M. and Whyman, P. (1996) *There is an Alternative*, Nelson and Pollard, Oxford.
Burkitt, B., Baimbridge, M. and Whyman, P. (2000) *The impact of the euro: debating Britain's future*, Macmillan, London.
Butler, D. and Kavanagh, D. (1984) *The British General Election of 1983*, Macmillan, London.
Butler, D. and Kitzinger, U. (1976) *The 1975 Referendum*, Macmillan, London.
Butler, D. and Kitzinger, U. (1996) *The 1975 Referendum*, 2nd edition, Macmillan, London.
Butler, D. and Ranney, A. (eds.) (1980) *Referendums: a comparative study of practice and theory*, Cambridge University Press, Cambridge.
Butler, D. and Ranney, A. (eds.) (1994) *Referendums around the world*, Macmillan, London.
Cabinet Office (1952) Memorandum by Sir Anthony Eden, 15 February, London: Public Records Office [PRO], CAB 129/49C (52) 40
Cabinet Office (1955) Minutes of the Cabinet Mutual Aid Committee, 24 October, London: PRO, 134/1030, MAC (55) 200
Cabinet Office (1960a) The Six and the Seven: Long-term Arrangements, 25 May, London: PRO, CAB 134/1852, EQ (60) 27
Cabinet Office (1960b) Minutes of the Cabinet European Economic Association Committee, 27 May, London: PRO, CAB 134/1819
Cabinet Office (1960c) The Six and the Seven: The Long-term Objectives, 6 July, London: PRO, CAB 129/102, pt.1, C (60) 107
Cabinet Office (1962a) Minutes of Cabinet Meeting, 5 July, London: Public Records Office, CAB 128/36, CC (62) 44

Cabinet Office (1962b) Minutes of Cabinet Meeting, 27 September, London: Public Records Office, CAB 128/36, CC (62) 48
Callaghan, J. (1987) *Time and Chance*, Collins, Glasgow.
Callaghan, J. (2000) *The Retreat of Social Democracy*, Manchester University Press, Manchester.
Cambridge Econometrics (1990) *Regional Economic Prospects*, Cambridge Econometrics, Cambridge.
Carey, A. (1995) *Taking the Risk Out of Democracy: Propaganda in the US and Australia*, University of New South Wales Press, Sydney.
Cecchini, P. (1988) *The European Challenge – the benefits of a single market*, Wildwood House, Aldershot.
Cerny, P.G. (1990) *The Changing Architecture of Politics*, Sage, London.
Coates, D. (1999) Models of Capitalism in the New World Order, *Political Studies*, 47, 643–660.
Conservative Party (1970) *General Election Manifesto*, Conservative Party, London.
Coxall, B., Robins, L. and Leach, R. (2003) *Contemporary British politics*, Palgrave, London.
Craig, F. (ed.) (1982) *Conservative and Labour Party Conference Decisions, 1945–1981*, Parliamentary Research Services, Chichester.
Cronin, T.E. (1989) *Direct democracy: the politics of initiative, referendum and recall*, Harvard University Press, Cambridge.
Currie, D. (2000) EMU: threats and opportunities for companies and national economies; in Baimbridge, M., Burkitt, B. and Whyman, P. (eds.) *The impact of the euro: debating Britain's future*, Macmillan: London.
Dalyell, T. (2006) No regrets: then, now or for the future; in Baimbridge, M. (ed.) *The 1975 referendum on Europe: reflections of the participants*, Imprint Academic, Exeter.
Daniels, P. (2003) From Hostility to 'Constructive Engagement: The Europeanisation of the Labour Party; in Chadwick, A. and Heffernan, R. (eds.) *The New Labour Reader*, Polity Press, Cambridge, pp. 223–230.
Denman, R. (1996) *Missed Chances: Britain and Europe in the Twentieth Century*, Indigo, London.
Deva, N. (2002) *Who really governs Britain?*, The June Press, Totnes.
Donoughue, B. (2006) The inside view from No.10; in Baimbridge, M. (ed.) *The 1975 Referendum on Europe: reflections on the participants*, Imprint Academic, Exeter.
Dorril, S. (2000) *MI6: Fifty Years of Special Operations*, London: Fourth Estate
Dyson, K. (2000) *The politics of the euro-zone: stability or breakdown?*, Oxford University Press, Oxford.
Eden, A. (1962a) Memorandum to Lord Chandos, 12 October, London: Public Records Office (PRO), AP 23/17/62A
Eden, A. (1962b) Memorandum to Lord Chandos, 30 October, London: PRO, AP 23/17/63B
Edmonds, J. (2000) The Single Currency and the European Social Model; in Baimbridge, M., Burkitt, B. and Whyman, P. (eds.), *The Impact of the Euro: Debating Britain's Future*, Macmillan, London, pp. 191–9.

Edmonds, J. (2006) Learning to love the 'rich man's club'; in Baimbridge, M. (ed.) *The 1975 Referendum on Europe: reflections on the participants*, Imprint Academic, Exeter.

Eichener, V. (1996) Die Ruckwirkungen der europaischen Integration auf nationale Politikmuster; in Jachtenfuchs, M. and Kohler-Koch, N. (eds.), *Europasiche Integration*, Opladen, Leske & Budrich, pp. 249–280.

El-Agraa, A. (2002) *The euro and Britain*, Financial Times Prentice Hall, London.

Electoral Commission (2003) *Briefing: referendums*, The Electoral Commission, London.

Esping-Andersen, G. (1990) *The Three Worlds of Welfare Capitalism*, Polity Press, Cambridge.

European Commission (1995) *Eurobarometer: Public Opinion in the European Union, Trends 1974–1994*, Table B4 (Attitudes towards the Unification of Western Europe), European Commission, Brussels.

Evans, D. (1975) *While Britain Slept: The Selling of the Common Market*, Gollancz, London.

Feldstein, M.S. (1974) Social Security, Induced Retirement and Aggregate Capital Accumulation, *Journal of Political Economy*, 82, 905–926.

Feldstein, M.S. (1976) Temporary Layoffs in the Theory of Unemployment, *Journal of Political Economy*, 84, 937–957.

Finer, S., Berrington, H. and Bartholomew, D. (1961) *Backbench Opinion in the House of Commons, 1955–1959*, Pergamon Press, Oxford.

Gallagher, M. (1997) the referendum in Europe; in Auer, A. and Flauss, J-F (eds.) *Le referendum europeen*, Bruylant, Brussels.

Gallagher, M. and Uleri, P.V. (1996) *The referendum experience in Europe*, Macmillan, London.

Gallup (1968) Public Opinion and the EEC, *Journal of Common Market Studies*, 6(3), 231–249

Garrett, G. (1995) Capital Mobility, Trade and the Domestic Politics of Economic Policy, *International Organisation*, 49, 657–587.

Garrett, G. (1998) *Partisan Politics in the Global Economy*, Cambridge University Press, Cambridge.

Garrett, G. (2000) Shrinking States? Globalisation and National Autonomy in the OECD; in Higgott, R. and Payne, A. (eds.), *The New Political Economy of Globalisation*, Edward Elgar, Cheltenham.

George, S. (1998) *An awkward partner: Britain in the European Community*, Oxford University Press, Oxford.

George, S. (ed.) (1992) *Britain and the European Community: the politics of semi-detachment*, Clarendon Press, Oxford.

Glasman, M. (1997) The Siege of the German Social Market, *New Left Review*, 225, Sept/Oct, 134–139.

Goodhart, P. (1976) *Full-hearted consent: the story of the referendum campaign and the campaign for the referendum*, Davis Poynter, London.

Grant, W. (2002) *Economic Policy in Britain*, Palgrave, London.

Hall, P.A. (1986) *Governing the Economy: The Politics of State Intervention in Britain and France*, Oxford University Press, Oxford.

Hall, P.A. (1987) The Evolution of Economic Policy under Mitterand; in Ross, G. (ed.) *The Mitterand Experiment*, Polity, Cambridge.

Harding, A. (1999) The Burdened Middle: Income Inequality and Welfare Reform; in Carman, M. and Rogers, I. (eds.) *Out of the Rut: Making Labour a Genuine Alternative*, Allen and Unwin, St Leonards.

Hay, C. (1999) *The Political Economy of New Labour: Labouring Under False Pretences?*, Manchester University Press, Manchester.

Healey, N.H. (2000) The case for European monetary union; in Baimbridge, M., Burkitt, B. and Whyman, P. (eds.) *The impact of the euro: debating Britain's future*, Macmillan: London.

Hill, R. (2001) *The Labour Party and Economic Strategy 1979-1997: The Long Road Back*, Palgrave, London.

Hirst, P. (1999) Has Globalisation Killed Social Democracy?; in Gamble, A and Wright, T. (eds.), *The New Social Democracy*, Blackwell, Oxford, pp 84-97.

Hirst, P. and Thompson, G. (1996) *Globalisation in Question: The International Economy and the Possibilities of Governance*, Polity, Cambridge.

Hirst, P. and Thompson, G. (2000) Globalisation and the Future of the Nation State; in Higgott, R. and Payne, A. (eds.) *The New Political Economy of Globalisation*, Volume One, Edward Elgar, Cheltenham.

Hofstede, G. (1980) *Culture's consequences*, Sage, London.

Holland, S. (1995) Squaring the Circle? The Maastricht Convergence Criteria, Cohesion and Employment; in Coates, K. and Holland, S. (eds.) *Full Employment for Europe*, Spokesman, Nottingham.

Hug, S. (2002) *Voices of Europe: citizens, referendums and European integration*, Rowman & Littlefield, Lanham.

Hutton, W. (1994) *The State We're In*, Cape, London.

Jackman, R., Pissarides, C. and Savouri, S. (1990) Labour Market Policies and Unemployment in the OECD, *Economic Policy*, 5(2): 449-490.

Keller, B. and Sorries, B. (1997) The New Social Dialogue: Procedural Structuring, First Results and Perspectives, *Industrial Relations Journal* (European Annual Review), pp. 77-98.

King, A. (1977) *Britain Says Yes: The 1975 Referendum on the Common Market*, American Enterprise Institute for Policy Research, Washington DC.

King, A. (ed.) (2001) *British Political Opinion, 1937-2000: The Gallup Polls*, Politico's, London.

Kitsch, R. (1964) *The Private Life of Public Relations*, MacGibbon, London.

Knutsen, P. (1997) Corporatist Tendencies in the Euro-Polity: The EU Directive of 22 September 1994 on European Works Councils, *Economic and Industrial Democracy*, 18(2), 289-323.

Kopits, G. (1992) (ed.) *Tax harmonisation in the European Community: Policy Issues and Analysis*, IMF, Washington D.C.

Korpi, W. (1985) Economic growth and the Welfare System: Leaky Bucket or Irrigation System?, *European Sociological Review*, 1, 97-118.

Korpi, W. (1996) Eurosclerosis and the Sclerosis of Objectivity: On the Role of Values among Economic Policy Experts, *Economic Journal*, 106(439), 1727-46.

Labour Party (2004) *Britain in the Global Economy*, Labour Party, London.

Lamont, N. (1995) *Sovereign Britain*, Duckworth, London.

Lash, S. and Urry, J. (1987) The End of Organised Capitalism, Polity Press, Oxford.

Lawrence, R. and Schultz, C. (eds.) (1987) *Barriers to European Growth: A Transatlantic View*, Brookings Institution, Washington D.C.

Layard, R. (2000) Joining Europe's currency; in Baimbridge, M., Burkitt, B. and Whyman, P. (eds.) *The impact of the euro: debating Britain's future*, Macmillan: London.

Leibfried, S. (1994) The Social Dimension Of The European Union: En Route To Positively Joint Sovereignty?, *Journal of European Social Policy*, 4(4), 239-262

Leibfried, S. and Pierson, P. (1995) The dynamics of social policy integration; in Leibfried, S. and Pierson, P. (eds), *Fragmented Social Policy: the European Community's Social Dimension in Comparative Perspective*, Brookings Institution, Washington DC:

Macmillan, H. (1959) Memorandum to Sir Anthony Eden, 22nd October, London: PRO, PREM, 11/2985, 22

Macmillan, H. (1972) *Pointing the Way, 1959-1961*, London: Macmillan

Macmillan, H. (1973) *At the End of the Day, 1961-1963*, London: Macmillan

MacShane, D. (2005) Our last chance to make Europe work, *The Observer*, 15 May

Magleby, D.E. (1984) *Direct legislation: voting on ballot propositions in the United States*, John Hopkins University Press, Baltimore.

Major, R.L. and Hays, S. (1970), Another look at the Common Market, *National Institute Economic Review*, 54, 29-43.

Marginson, P. and Sisson, K. (1996) Multinational companies and the future of collective bargaining: a review of the research issues, *European Journal of Industrial Relations*, 2(2), 173-197.

Marquand, D. (1999) Premature Obsequies: Social Democracy Comes in From the Cold; in Gamble, A. and Wright, T. (eds.) *The New Social Democracy*, Blackwell, Oxford.

Marsden, D. (1992) Incomes Policy for Europe? Or Will Pay Bargaining Destroy the Single European Market?, *British Journal of Industrial Relations*, 30(4), 587-604.

Michie, J. (2000) The economic consequences of EMU; in Baimbridge, M., Burkitt, B. and Whyman, P. (eds.) *The impact of the euro: debating Britain's future*, Macmillan: London.

Milne, I. (2004) *A Cost Too Far? An Analysis of the Net Economic Costs and Benefits for the UK of EU Membership*, Civitas, London.

Minford, P. (1990) Corporatism, the Natural Rate and Productivity, in *Trade Unions and the Economy: Into the 1990s*. Employment Institute, London.

Minford, P. (2000) The single currency – will it work and should we join?; in Baimbridge, M., Burkitt, B. and Whyman, P. (eds.) *The impact of the euro: debating Britain's future*, Macmillan, London.

Minford, P., Mahambare, V. and Nowell, E. (2005) *Should Britain leave the EU? An economic analysis of a troubled relationship*, Edward Elgar, Cheltenham.

Mishra, R. (1999) *Globalisation and the welfare state*, Edward Elgar, Cheltenham.

Monbiot, G. (2000) *The captive state: the corporate takeover of Britain*, Macmillan, London.

Monks, J. (2000) A single currency for Europe – considerations for workers; in Baimbridge, M., Burkitt, B. and Whyman, P. (eds.) *The impact of the euro: debating Britain's future*, Macmillan, London, pp. 185–190.

Mullen, A. (2005) *The British Left's 'Great Debate' on Europe: The Political Economy of the British Left and European Integration, 1945–2004*, unpublished PhD thesis, University of Bradford. (available online at www.andymullen.com)

Mullen, A. (2006) From Imperial third force to the 1975 Referendum; in Baimbridge, M. (ed.) *The 1975 Referendum on Europe: reflections on the participants*, Imprint Academic, Exeter.

Mullen, A. and Burkitt, B. (2003) European integration and the battle for British hearts and minds: New Labour and the Euro, *Political Quarterly*, 74(3), 322–33.

Mullen, A. and Burkitt, B. (2004) *Spinning Europe: pro-European Union propaganda campaigns in Britain*, Democrat Press, Merseyside.

Nairn, T. (1973) *The Left Against Europe?*, Penguin, London

Nevin, E. (1990) *The economics of Europe*, Macmillan, London.

Newman, C. (2005) Blair to appoint senior minister to push for Yes vote on EU, *Financial Times*, 6 May.

O'Hara, K. (2006) *The referendum roundabout*, Imprint Academic, Exeter.

Owen, D. (2006) Manoeuvres towards the Referendum; in Baimbridge, M. (ed.) *The 1975 Referendum on Europe: reflections on the participants*, Imprint Academic, Exeter.

Patel, P. and Pavitt, K. (1991) Large firms in the production of the world's technology: an important case of non-globalisation, *Journal of International Business Studies*, 22(1), 1–21.

Porter, M.E. (1990) *The competitive advantage of nations*, Macmillan, London.

Qvortrup, M. (2002) *A comparative study of referendums: government by the people*, Manchester University Press, Manchester.

Reynolds, D. (1991) *Britannia overruled: British policy and world power in the Twentieth century*, Longman, London.

Rhodes, M. (1992) The Future of the Social Dimension: Labour Market Regulation in Post-1992 Europe, *Journal of Common Market Studies*, 30(1), 23–51.

Rideau, J. (1997) Les referendums nationaux dans le contexte l'intergraion europeene; in Auer, A. and Flauss, J-F (eds.) *Le referendum europeen*, Bruylant, Brussels.

Rodrik, D. (1996) *Has globalization gone too far*, Institute for Research Economics, Washington, DC.

Rourke, J.T., Hiskes, R.P. and Ernesto, C.Z. (1992) *Direct democracy and international politics*, Lynne Riemer, Boulder.

Sassoon, D. (1996) *One hundred years of socialism: the West European left in the Twentieth century*, I. B. Tauris, London.

Sinn, H-W. and Ochel, W. (2003) *The new systems competition*, Center for Economic Studies and Ifo Institute for Economic Research, Working Paper No. 623, Munich.

Sisson, K. and Marginson, P. (1995) Management: systems, structures and strategy; in Edwards, P. (ed.) *Industrial relations: theory and practice in Britain*, Blackwell, Oxford, pp. 89–122.

Sked, A. (2006) Reflections of a Eurosceptic; in Baimbridge, M. (ed.) *The 1975 Referendum on Europe: reflections on the participants*, Imprint Academic, Exeter.

Smith, G. (1976) The functional properties of the referendum, *European Journal of Political Research*, 4(1), 1–23.

Strange, G. (1997) The British Labour Movement and Economic and Monetary Union in Europe, *Capital and Class*, 63, 13–24.

Streeck, W. (1992), Social Institutions and Economic Performance: Studies of Industrial Relations in Advanced Capitalist Economies, Sage, London.

Streeck, W. and Schmitter, P.C. (1991) From National Corporatism to Transnational Pluralism: Organised Interests in the Single European Market, *Politics and Society*, 19(2), 133–64.

Suksi, M. (1993) *Bringing in the people: a comparison of constitutional forms and practices of the referendum*, Martinus Nijhoff, Dordrecht.

Swank, D. (1998) Funding the Welfare State: Global Taxation of Business in Advanced Market Economies, *Political Studies*, 46, 671–692.

Teague, P. (1991) Introduction to the Cross-National Research Seminar on *Workers' Rights in Europe*, London School of Economics and Political Science, 13 April.

Teeple, G. (1995) *Globalization and the Decline of Social Reform*, Humanities Press, Atlantic Highlands, NJ.

Temperton, P. (2001) *The UK and the euro*, Wiley, London.

Thatcher, M. (1988) *Britain and Europe*, Bruges Group, London.

Thatcher, M. (1992) *The Downing Street Years*, HarperCollins, London.

Thirwall, A.P. (1982) The Balance of Payments Constraint, Capital Flows and Growth Rate Differences Between Developing Countries, *Oxford Economic Papers*, 34, 498–510.

UNCTAD (1996) Trade and Development Annual Report, UNCTAD, New York.

Vaughan-Whitehead, D.C. (2003) *EU Enlargement versus Social Europe? The Uncertain Future of the European Social Model*, Edward Elgar, Cheltenham.

Verdun, A. (2000) *European Responses to Globalization and Financial Market Integration: Perceptions of Economic and Monetary Union in Britain, France and Germany*, MacMillan, London.

Wade, R. (1996) Globalization and Its Limits: Reports of the Death of the National Economy Are Greatly Exaggerated; in Berger, S. and Dore, R. (eds.), *National Diversity and Global Capitalism*, Cornell University Press, Ithaca, NY, pp. 60–88.

Walsh, J., Zappala, G. and Brown, W. (1995) European Integration and the Pay Policies of British Multinational, *Industrial Relations Journal*, 26(2), 84–96.

Watson, M. (1999) Rethinking Capital Mobility, Re-Regulating Financial Markets, *New Political Economy*, 4(2), 55–75.

Whyman, P. (2001) Can Opposites Attract? Monetary Union and the Social Market, *Contemporary Politics*, 7(2), 113–128.

Whyman, P. (2006) *Third Way Economics*, Palgrave, London.

Williams, R. (2006) The 1975 Referendum and beyond; in Baimbridge, M. (ed.) *The 1975 Referendum on Europe: reflections on the participants*, Imprint Academic, Exeter.

Wilson, H. (1975) End of 14 years' argument, Mr Wilson says, *The Times*, 7 June.
Windolf, P. (1989) Productivity Coalitions and the Future of European Corporatism, *Industrial Relations*, 2(1), 1–20.
Wistrich, E. (2001) Lessons of the 1975 Referendum; in Beetham, R. (ed.) *The Euro Debate: Persuading the People*, Federal Trust, London.
Worcester, R. (2000) *How to win the euro referendum: lessons from 1975*, Foreign Policy Centre, London.
Young, H. (1998) *This Blessed Plot: Britain and Europe from Churchill to Blair*, Macmillan, London.
Zakheim, D. (1973) Britain and the EEC – Opinion Poll Data, 1970–72, *Journal of Common Market Studies*, 11(2),191–233.
Zysman, J. (2000) The Myth of a 'Global' Economy: Enduring National Foundations and Emerging Regional Realities; in Higgott, R. and Payne, A. (eds.) *The New Political Economy of Globalisation*, Volume One, Edward Elgar, Cheltenham.

Index

Agriculture 15, 24, 104
Agricultural Guidance Guarantee Fund (AGGF) 19, 24
Ancram, Michael 96
Atomic Energy 17
Attlee, Clement 56
Australia 47, 186, 192

Bogdanor, Vernon 10, 34-41, 45, 48
Baimbridge, Mark 10, 112, 149, 158, 160, 191
Baldwin-Beaverbrook 35-6
Barratt, Michael 123, 137
Belgium 18, 57, 205, 209
Benn, Tony 10, 13, 46, 61, 63, 67-8, 132, 177
Bill, The 38, 67, 87
Blair, Tony 14, 70, 71, 116, 138, 141-3, 157
Blitz 92
Body, Richard 11
Bretton Woods 20
Britain 14, 19, 21-2, 24-6, 28, 36-7, 41, 42, 45-7, 56, 58, 60-3, 65, 69, 80, 86, 89, 92-4, 101, 121, 123-6, 128, 132, 134, 150-1, 156, 169, 172, 174, 176-7, 189, 191-2, 202
British 10, 12, 21-2, 31, 36, 41, 44, 46, 58, 67, 70, 72, 82-3, 85-6, 93, 95, 100-1, 105, 110, 114, 121-2, 125, 128, 135, 146, 150-1, 153-4, 158, 162, 169, 170, 174-5, 178, 180, 185, 190, 209
Brittan, Leon 94
Broad 32-3, 147, 153-4, 167, 178, 182
Brown, Gordon 14, 68, 137-8, 141, 158
Brown, George 57-9, 175
Brussels 72, 91, 95, 97
Budget 24, 61, 71, 78, 86, 100, 134-5, 153, 156
Burkitt, Brian 69, 112, 141, 153, 160, 162, 177-8, 183, 191

Butler, Robin 10, 31-4, 42, 47, 84, 132-3, 135, 147, 178
Cabinet 58, 61, 64, 70, 81, 82, 83, 84, 86, 129, 170, 171, 173, 174
    Shadow 9, 61, 95
Callaghan, James 12, 39, 45, 61, 62, 157-8
Cameron, David 13, 97
Canada 186, 192
Caribbean 46
Castle, Barbara 46, 177
Cecchini, Paulo 151-2
China 184
Chirac, Jacques 39
Churchill, Winston 35, 80
Clarke, Kenneth 94-6, 171
Coates, Ken 109, 123, 137
Cockfield, Lord Arthur 90
Cole, G.D.H. 56
Commission 19, 172
Common Agricultural Policy (CAP) 17, 19, 23-4, 53-4, 59-60, 62, 64, 78-9, 89, 92, 96, 100, 134, 153, 166
Common Assembly 18, 21
Commonwealth 21-2, 58, 61, 67, 81-2, 85, 123, 126, 171, 175
Communist 15, 47
Community 18, 23, 25, 41, 45, 63, 174
Conservative 12-13, 21, 23, 26-7, 35, 37, 45-6, 57, 61, 65-6, 68, 75, 84-5, 87, 89-90, 94, 96-8, 101, 110, 126-30, 134, 142, 160, 176-7
Constitution for Europe 11, 32
Cyprus 205, 209
Czech Republic 191, 204, 206

Dalyell, Tam 11, 40
Davis, David 97
Deficit 15, 24, 103
de Gaulle, Charles 18, 60, 86, 126-7, 129, 176

Index

Delors, Jacques 66, 90, 106-8, 135, 137, 157
Democracy 28-9, 31, 33-5, 47, 90, 102, 106, 179, 183
Denmark 14, 19, 22-3, 44-5, 48, 202-3, 205-6
Dicey, A.V. 35-6
Donoughue, Bernard 46
Dominions 21
Dublin 46
Dyson, Kenneth 10

Economic Monetary Union (EMU) 11, 20, 41, 52, 60, 67, 87, 92, 100, 106-7, 111, 137, 160
Eden, Anthony 81, 82, 84
Edmonds John 10, 47, 105, 110
Enlargement 15, 54, 65, 67, 69, 71, 79, 86, 92, 204
Estonia 191, 204-6, 209
Europe 13-22, 62-3, 76, 80, 85-6, 93, 97-8, 106, 116, 131, 147, 162, 166-7, 171, 186, 191-2, 201
European Assembly 16
European Coal and Steel Community 17, 81, 123, 163-7, 174
European Constitution 11, 14, 27, 38-9, 41, 72, 145-6, 186
European Defence Community 17, 81
European Economic Community (EEC) 9-10, 19, 22, 24-5, 33, 176, 180-1, 191
European Economic Cooperation, Organization for, 16, 82, 148
European Free Trade Agreement (EFTA) 50, 57, 85, 152, 172, 175
European Integration 14, 26-7, 29, 31, 48-9, 72-3, 98, 100, 102, 105, 112, 116, 119, 121, 158, 179
European Parliament 13, 21, 56, 63, 69, 89
European Union 9, 10, 16, 25, 75, 147, 166-7, 169, 175, 179, 181, 184, 205
European Exchange Rate 15, 20, 64, 70, 107, 161

Fiscal 19, 61
Foot, Michael 13, 65, 105
France 17-19, 24, 34, 48, 57, 124, 172, 179, 186, 203-5, 207
Free Trade Agreement (FTA) 50, 57, 82, 172

Gaitskell, Hugh 58, 177
Gallagher, Michael 10, 45

General Elections 60, 62, 64-6, 68, 80, 86, 90, 92, 94-5, 97, 127-9, 134, 196
Germany 17-18, 57, 71, 111, 161-4, 179, 186, 191-2, 205, 209
Giscard d'Estaing, Valery 11, 21
Goudenhove-Kalergi, Richard 15
Greece 191, 205, 208-9
Greenland 203-4, 206-8

Hague Summit 9, 15-16, 19-20, 22, 94
Hague, William 94-5, 97
Hain, Peter 143
Hannan, Daniel 97
Heath, Edward 12, 45, 86, 89, 94, 129, 174
Heseltine Michael 94
Holland, Stuart 123, 137
House of Commons 23, 35, 40, 58, 64, 66-7, 84-5, 87-8, 90, 92, 96, 130, 192
House of Lords 35
Howe, Geoffrey 91
Hug, Simon 10, 31-2, 45, 204
Hungary 18, 191, 204-6, 209
Hurd, Douglas 94

Ireland 14, 19, 22-3, 43-5, 48, 202-3, 206
Northern 42-4, 47, 192-5, 199
Italy 16-18, 57, 191, 205-7

Japanese 164
Jay, Douglas 57
Jenkins, Roy 12, 61, 177

Keynes, John Maynard 104-5
King, Anthony 10, 134, 137, 142, 147
Kitzinger, Uwe 10-11, 42, 47, 132-3, 147, 178

Labour Party 12-13, 21, 23, 26-7, 37, 49, 58-9, 63, 65-6, 68-72, 86-7, 92, 97, 104-5, 119, 124, 126, 130, 134, 138, 142, 177, 182, 186, 192-3
Lamont, Norman 93
Latvia 191, 204-6
Lawson, Nigel 91
Lee, Sir Frank 83, 124-6, 173-4
Liberal 12, 89, 93, 126, 198
Lithuania 191, 202, 204-5, 209
Lothian, Sir Philip 56
Luxembourg 17-19, 57, 108, 204, 206
Compromise 19

Macmillan, Harold 82-4, 124-6, 173, 175
Mackay, Richard 56
Major, John 68, 91-5, 148
Malta 143, 203, 205

Marginson 118
Messina 171, 172
Michie, Jonathan 158
Milne, Ian 160, 112
Minford, Patrick 158, 160, 112
Monks, John 99, 108
Monnet, Jean 18
Mullen, Andrew 69, 71, 77, 141, 177-8
Murdoch, Rupert 69-70, 138, 143
Murray, Len 105

Nairn, Patrick 103-4
Netherlands 17, 34, 57, 186, 204-5
New Zealand 25, 46, 150
Nicholson, Emma 93
Nixon, Richard 176
North American Free Trade Area (NAFTA) 95, 140
Norway 17, 19, 22, 44-5, 48, 202-4, 206-8

O'Neill, Con 176-7
Oslo 170
Owen, David 10, 45

Patten, Chris 94
Poland 191, 204
Pompidou, Georges 19, 44, 86
Portillo, Michael 94
Portugal 205, 208
Powell, Enoch 13, 47, 87
Protestant 37

Qvortrup, Mads 10, 193

Ranney, Arthur 10, 31, 32-4
Redwood, John 93
Rippon, Geoffrey 131
Rhodes, Rod 116-18

Scandinavian 111, 192
Scottish 42, 193-4
Shore, Peter, 1, 46, 57, 175-6
Schuman, Robert 17, 57, 100
Six, The 20, 24, 57, 82, 83, 172
Slovakia 202, 205-6, 209
Slovenia 204-5, 209
Smith, Iain Duncan 31, 96
Sovereignty 28, 36, 47, 62, 82, 164, 179, 182
Soviet 18, 170, 179
Spain 191, 204, 206, 208
Sweden 17, 203, 205-6
Swiss 202
Switzerland 116, 186, 203-4, 206

Tawney, R.H. 56
Taylor, Teddy 11

Thatcher, Margaret 46, 65, 87-9, 91, 94, 98, 110, 135
Tebbit, Norman 94
Thorpe, Jeremy 12
Tickell, Crispin 131
Todd, Ron 106
Tokyo 170
Trade 15, 62, 104, 109-10, 118-19, 124
Trade Union Confederation 101, 104-6, 124, 129, 137-8
Treasury 11, 126, 173
Treaty 11, 22, 173, 205
    Accession, 23, 45
    Amsterdam 94, 209
    Brussels 18, 20-1, 83, 101, 174, 181, 184
    Constitutional 28-9, 209
    Maastricht 53, 67-8, 76, 92, 100, 108
    Nice 79, 96, 204
    North Atlantic, Organization (NATO) 23, 159, 181
Tucker, Geoffrey 130, 146
Turkey 71, 207

United Kingdom (UK) 14, 17, 19, 24-5, 28, 37, 39, 42-4, 46, 100-4, 107, 111-12, 119, 147-9, 151-6, 161-2, 164, 166-8, 174, 179-181, 183-5, 191-4, 197-8, 201-3, 205-7
United States of Europe 61, 73, 98
United States of America (USA / US) 15, 47, 56, 71, 80, 95, 124, 159, 164, 169, 172, 174, 176, 184, 186, 192

Value Added Tax (VAT) 19, 61, 154
Verdun, Amy 106, 108

War
    Cold 9, 80
    Post-, era 9
    Post-, II 14, 165, 169
    II World 15, 42
Watson 113
Welsh 42
Western Union 15, 59, 60, 80-1, 117
Whitehall 10
White Paper 60, 64, 86, 88, 176
Whyman, Phil 10, 99, 106, 112, 149, 160
Williams, Shirley 12, 177
Wilson, Harold 9, 12, 14, 39, 47, 56-9, 62-3, 127, 175
Wistrich, Ernest 11, 131, 134
Worcester, Robert 12-13, 169
World Trade Organization (WTO) 159

Young, Hugo 83, 89

also of interest from **imprint-academic.com**

A Throne in Brussels: Britain, the Saxe-Coburgs and the Belgianisation of Europe

Paul Belien

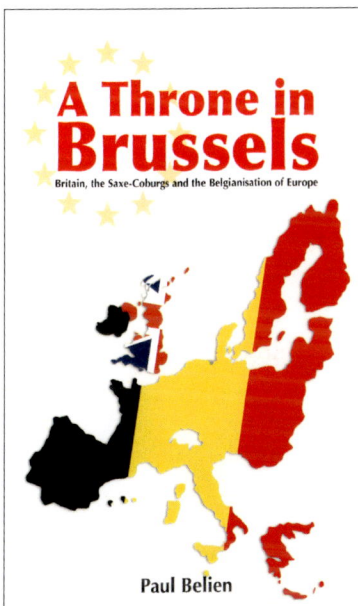

In 1817 Leopold of Saxe-Coburg became king of Belgium — a new, artificial state inhabited by Catholic Dutch in the North, and French-speaking Walloons in the South. Belgium is often compared to multilingual Switzerland, but whereas Switzerland grew organically, Belgium is an artificial state, in which two peoples were forced to live together and where no national consciousness developed. It could fall apart in the next ten years.

Paul Belien argues that the pan-European super-state currently in the making will resemble a 'Greater-Belgium' rather than a 'Greater-Switzerland', as Europe will also be an artificial construct. Belgium has infected EU political attitudes and acts as a model for the EU — an attempt to build a nation out of different peoples with separate languages and traditions. To learn what the EU as a single state might be like, take up this highly readable mix of history, analysis and warning.

'Mr. Belien tells the story of this slimy dynasty with great gusto and lays out this bill of indictment very powerfully.' **John O'Sullivan**, *American Spectator*

'If you plan to read only one book on foreign affairs in the next year, you should read Paul Belien's *A Throne in Brussels*'.
Thomas Fleming, *Chronicles*

'It must never be forgotten that the Belgian royal family are Coburgs, with all the larger-than-life qualities and failings that Coburgs possess. This is a fascinating book after which I cannot but see the Belgian royal family in a completely new light.'
Hugo Vickers

'An unusual blend of history, analysis and warning . . . Belien is to be congratulated not only on his courage and erudition, but also on his writing skills.' *Eurofacts*

'This thoroughly researched book explains how Belgian political attitudes have infected those of the EU.' **Philip Claeys MEP**, *Right Now*

© Corbis

Leopold II, King of the Belgians

'An excellent example of how history should be written.'
Merrie Cave, *Salisbury Review*

'Meticulously researched and delightfully readable.' **Daniel Hannan MEP**

'An important, relevant, well-researched and extremely readable book which should be paid attention to by the citizens of EU member states.' *Free Republic*

350 pp., £14.95 / $29.90, 1845400658 (pbk.); £25 / $49.90, 184540033X (cloth)

also of interest from **imprint-academic.com**

The 1975 Referendum on Europe
Volume 1: Reflections of the Participants

edited by Mark Baimbridge

250 pp., £17.95/$34.90, 1845400348 (pbk.)

Volume 2: Current Analysis and Lessons for the Future

ed. Mark Baimbridge *et al.*

250 pp., £17.95/$34.90, 1845400356 (pbk.)

These books provide an analysis of the past, current and future relationship between the UK and the EU, treating the key overarching issues in the 1975 referendum and looking ahead to the prospect (eventually) of further referendums. Contributors to Volume 1 include David Owen, Tam Dalyell and Teddy Taylor. Mark Baimbridge is senior lecturer in economics at the University of Bradford with research interests focused on European integration.

Alarming Drum: Britain's European Dilemma

Peter Morgan

Alarming Drum is an analysis of the UK's past and present relationship with the European Union, together with a scrutiny of global strategic prospects for the next half century. The thesis is that European countries need trade, defence and security treaties, but the EU treaties actually in force are seriously misconceived. The author lived in Paris for eight years as Marketing Director for IBM Europe and, as DG of the IoD, was involved in the negotiations for the Maastricht Treaty, EMU and the Social Chapter.

'Peter Morgan shines a laser beam into the Euro-fog.' **Peter Jay**

'This book is a mine of facts and data which are likely to be used by everyone writing or speaking about the EU for a long time to come.'
John Mills, *Eurofacts*

'*Alarming Drum* is the product of intensive research and as such is a valuable resource for anyone who needs easy access to the facts.' **Matthew Attwood**, *European Journal*

'An authoritative history and critique . . . with a refreshing lack of hysteria.' *This England*

'A thorough and masterly job.' **Patrick Minford**

'A challenging and important analysis.' **Tim Congdon**

300 pp., £19.95 / $39.90, 1845400151 (cloth)